WINE INSTITUTE LIBRARY

Guide to Fortified Wines

Pauline & Sheldon Wasserman

MARLBOROUGH PRESS
Morganville, N.J.

663.2
W28

Published by Marlborough Press
14 Washington Ave., Morganville, N.J. 07751

Copyright © 1983 Pauline and Sheldon Wasserman

3525

*Additional copies are available from the
publisher for $9.95 plus $1.50 for shipping
and handling.*

Cover design by Pauline Wasserman

*To Carlo Russo,
a good friend
and a fine wine merchant,
in appreciation for
introducing us to
the greatest of all fortified wines—
vintage port—
a wine which has
on numerous occasions
fortified our spirits*

Acknowledgments

In our research for this book there were many people who helped us, generously giving of their time and patiently answering our questions, opening bottles for us to taste, and helping in other important ways. We'd like to thank them all.

First we want to thank Madelyn Larsen, who proposed this project and offered many helpful suggestions.

Bill Kaufman, who suggested us for another project that happily led to this one.

Patrice Gourdin, who provided us with the opportunity to taste many wines — old and new, rare and not so rare, good and not so good.

Robert Gourdin, whose enthusiasm for wine is infectious and who introduced us to Chateâu Chalon.

Philip Smyly of Croft and Henry Cavalier formerly of Frederick Wildman, who helped in ways they don't even realize.

Bernie Fradin, who as always offered encouragement and words of wisdom.

Bernie Weber, who made it easier for us to obtain some of the fortified wines that are in limited supply.

Jeremy Bull of Taylor, Fladgate and Yeatman, who did much to perk up our spirits and fortify our courage when we most needed it; whose appearance at our hotel in Oporto was like a breath of fresh air following the trials and tribulations of research in some of the other regions; and who provided us with the little nuggets of knowledge, such as the response to the inquiry about the Bishop of Chester.

Dott. Giacomo Rallo of Diego Rallo e Figli and Enotecnico Nicolo Fici of Fratelli Fici, who assisted us on marsala. Tom

Abruzzini of TBA Wines and Spirits Ltd., who was cheerfully available to offer significant help.

Rafael Rodriguez Panadero of Alvear, S.A., who was very helpful and gracious, and guided us to some delightful local color.

We also want to acknowledge the assistance of Jim Burke of Sacone and Speed; Huyshe Bower of Fonseca; Rui Lameiras of Taylor, Fladgate and Yeatman; Maria Teresa Braamcamp de Mancellos of Guimaraens (Vinhos) S.A.R.L., Carlos Gois Pinto of Sandeman; Bruno de Sanois, Enologist, at Taylor, Fladgate and Yeatman; Manuel Tavares, Enologist, at Sandeman; A.C. Sarmento de Vasconcellos of the Port Wine Institute; Helder Fernandes, Managing Director of the Madeira Wine Company; Ladislau Tomas de Sousa of the Madeira Wine Company; João José Sales Caldeira Teixeira, Director of Production, the Madeira Wine Company; Avv. Ignazio Alloro, President of the Consorzio Volontario per la Tutela del Vino Marsala; Dott. Marco de Bartoli of Az. Agr. Samperi; Sig. Antonio Galassi of Florio; Mary Mulligan formerly of the Italian Wine Promotion Center; Robbert op de Beek of Alvear, S.A.; Harry Feltenstein of Ronda, Spain; Fernando Garcia-Delgado Bel, Secretary General of the Consejo Regulador de la Denominación de Origen; Fernando Gago of Fernando A de Terry; Gabriel G. González Gilbey of González Byass and Co., Ltd.; Gabriel A. Raya of Antonio Barbadillo, S.A.; José Merello Reynolds of Fernando A de Terry.

Our friend Harry Foulds, who has helped us in so many ways, deserves our special thanks.

As does Michael Smith whose assistance was significant in helping to bring this project to reality.

Table of Contents

Illustrations

Foreword

Pauline and Sheldon's new book is in many ways similar to a great wine, in the sense that behind the delightful prose lies a great deal of dedicated and skilled work. The result is most informative and will be much enjoyed both by the amateur and professional winelover.

The Wasserman's book highlights two important points about wine, the traditional care and enjoyment of fortified wine.

Too much care can never be taken with the storage and serving of wine. Most traditions have grown up around these two points and the majority of them are worth keeping up. It is not necessary to air-condition one's wine cellar; wine improves if there is slow temperature variation. For that matter, smoking or eating food before drinking a wine dulls the taste. It is for this reason that the custom in Oporto is not to smoke before the first glass of port has been served and appreciated at the end of the meal.

Room temperature can be another pitfall. The ideal temperature for port is around 60-degrees Fahrenheit (15-degrees Centigrade). However, in the summer a cool drink is very pleasant, so there is no harm in either cooling the wine in the fridge or even adding an ice cube or two. In winter, just warm it up a little to obtain the best results. It's all a matter of personal taste.

Pauline and Sheldon have given the reader a great many facts about fortified wines, but more importantly, a very enjoyable book.

Try a glass of old tawny port halfway through the chapter on port, as I did, and then both the wine and the printed words will become even more meaningful.

JEREMY E. BULL
Production Director
Taylor, Fladgate & Yeatman, Vinhos SARL

Oporto, August 1982

Foreword

MARSALA WINE is being talked about once more. The old, noble classic Marsala is being discovered once again.

Is this a recurrence of the beautiful old times, of this century's early years when a warm atmosphere was created by sitting around a bottle of good Marsala wine in front of the fireplace?

Not exactly. But, for sure, this phenomenon is a part of the more and more increasing orientation and exigency of the modern man, of today's consumer, to approach those products which represent something more natural, more thought of, something that makes us go back to the roots of a life having a greater dimension of man.

Along Marsala's route we find scholars, specialized journalists, wine lovers who are ever more fond of and vanquished by that wonder of nature.

Along the route of Marsala wine, one Sicilian sunny morning, in October 1978, two young American travellers who had a huge interest in Sicily and its wine paid me a visit. We were in my family's old cellars in Marsala, and the best hospitality I could bestow on them was just a minimum of information, some wine tasting, and a swift visit to the cellars which through their old centenarian casks generally rouse so much curiosity and admiration especially on overseas visitors. But it was not so simple.

The two visitors were Pauline and Sheldon Wasserman, very enthusiastic wine writers, who were looking for any useful information to increase their already remarkable oenological knowledge and who, furthermore, were seriously resolved to write a book on the Mediterranean dessert wines and particularly on "its Majesty the Marsala wine."

In a short time I was overcome by their professional seriousness and the liking I felt for them so that I was ready to answer whatever question they wanted to put to me as a good and modest co-operator.

Therefore unintentionally and discreetly, I was so lucky as to see the birth of the affair between Marsala wine and the

Wassermans. And now, while writing this foreword, I feel almost like a best-man at a wedding.

Still more, I like to recollect that the Wassermans asked me to write this introduction to their research on Marsala wine when I was dining with them at their New Jersey home. At the beginning I was a little puzzled, but I could not offer much resistance, my friends' hospitality was simply . . . so convincing. I was persuaded for this further co-operation by the wines that had been selected by Sheldon. They were divine European and Californian wines which had been chosen by a person of taste, authority and distinction. It could not be differently. It is impossible to write with profound learning about wines without an adequate and direct knowledge and experience.

But, above all, I was convinced by what Pauline and Sheldon wrote about Marsala wine. I was struck by the professional seriousness with which they had gathered the documentary evidences and by the love with which they had dealt with Marsala wine. This wonderful wine has become as something strictly personal for them and deeply cultural. They have gone farther than the simple oenological knowledge because they have had with Marsala wine a real life experience and an intensely human experience. They have had the capacity and sensibility to feel all the nobility, the weakness and strength of this wine in such a way as it is possible to discover them by searching for the roots and the deepest vicissitudes of its history, of the men and generations that belong to it.

Much more than a table wine the Marsala is not an indispensable wine for man and its use finds a justification only in the great pleasure it gives to the person who drinks it. In fact it is an aperitif, a dessert wine and, above all, it must be considered as a wine for meditation.

Of course, Pauline and Sheldon have been able to discover this magic aspect of Marsala wine and have fallen in love with it. They have discovered all about this wine: the very rich nature and the perfecting and somewhat mysterious technique of the "lieviti" of the classic, superior and virgin Marsala wines as well as the particular position of the special Marsalas which are flavoured in various ways and must be kept on a different account, that is, not really as wines but rather as pleasant light liqueurs. They have understood that the most qualified manufacturers direct their efforts and tendencies to restore the value of the classic Marsalas, that is, of those wines of a nobler tradition which are the most immediate and wonderful expression of the Sicilian sun and land.

The new legislative policy is to confine the name of MARSALA only to the classic Marsalas, as the classic Marsalas are authentic wines with a controlled denomination of origin (D.O.C.).

My family has been producing and ageing Marsala wines these last four generations. Wine is our life; it may be that some Marsala wine flows in our veins and that is why I can be positive in affirming that Pauline and Sheldon, by writing about Marsala wine, made a difficult choice but undoubtedly a choice of taste and distinction.

In my opinion the Wassermans' research on Marsala offers excellent and correct information, and it represents a re-discovery and a restoring of the value of this grand wine, and also pleasant and useful reading for people who love wine.

DOTT. GIACOMO RALLO
Director
Diego Rallo & Figli

Marsala, August 1982

Guide to Fortified Wines

Introduction

In a sense, this book is written in two parts. The first is devoted to port wine, and the second to the other fortified wines. We elected to have port appear first because we consider it first in quality. Port is unlike the other great fortified wines. Unlike madeira, marsala, montilla, and sherry, port is generally a red wine; and port retains a truly grapey flavor because the alcohol is added before fermentation is complete, in order to stop the fermentation process. The other wines are generally fortified after fermentation has run its course. Port is the most natural of these wines, the most like a natural table wine in flavor and in treatment; nothing is added but alcohol. In addition, port is the only one of the fortified wines that is not from the temperate Mediterranean climate.

In our opinion, port, especially vintage port, is the greatest of all the fortified wines. No other wine has the high average quality of vintage port. Bad wines come from even the finest regions: Bordeaux, Burgundy, the Rhine, the Mosel, Piemonte, Chianti Classico, the Napa Valley. The best vineyards and producers will in some years turn out bad wines, even those limited like vintage champagne or a special label only used on chosen wine. But even the ports from mediocre shippers are not really bad, only disappointing.

After port, the other wines follow in alphabetical order but also paired according to their country of origin and their similarities. Madeira follows port; both these are from Portugal and make vintage wines.

Marsala follows madeira. Both of these contain (at least in part) wine that has been heated, and both are famous for their use in cooking. They are similar in style and type. Generally you can substitute a marsala for a madeira in all instances before, during, and after the meal. The one exception is a fine old vintage malmsey, which for us has no real equivalent.

Montilla and sherry follow madeira and marsala, which also produce some wines aged in a solera system of fractional blending. Marsala, montilla, and sherry wines are not vintaged. Montilla and sherry are the two most similar fortified wines. Both are Spanish, both get the flor on some of their wines, and both are made in similar ways. Montilla can be substituted for sherry in almost every case.

As the similarities among some of these wines make it possible to replace one for another in certain instances, we have included a table in the appendices on possible substitutions as well as some comparisons.

I

ᵽort

Port is essentially the wine of philosophical contemplation. It demands and produces a mood which glides with ease and a profound satisfaction through those regions of metaphysics where A equals A which tells you nothing and A equals B which is quite impossible, to the ataraxia of the final goal, the cutting of the Gordian problem, by the discovery that whether the external world exists or no, the wine of the Douro is extremely good.

—H. WARNER ALLEN*

The first people to make and to drink wine in Portugal, as far as we know, were the Romans. The Roman army invaded Lusitania, or what is now northern Portugal, in 137 B.C. The Lusitani, a native Celtic tribe, put up heroic resistance for over a decade, but in the end their leader, Viriate, met his death as victim of a Roman plot and Lusitania was conquered.

The Romans settled at the mouth of the Douro River in the towns of Portus, on the right bank, and Cale, opposite, on the left. They built aqueducts, temples, and villas along the Douro, and they planted vineyards. Here they made the first Douro wine. The drink of the Lusitani had been mead, a beverage made from fermented honey.

In 409 Lusitania was invaded by barbarian tribes — Vandals, Alans, and Suebi, or Swabians. While the other tribes continued south, something in the area caused the Swabians to stay behind in northern Portugal. Could it have

*A History of Wine (London: Faber & Faber, 1961).

1

been the wine? We don't know. Perhaps, if they were sensitive to such things, it was the beauty of the region, which is one of the most, indeed, perhaps *the* most beautiful vineyard region in the world. Or it may have been the natural resources; we know that the Romans had mined gold at Jales, above the Douro. In any case, the Swabians probably had little effect on the winemaking of the region, which most likely was done on a small, individual scale.

The next conquerors undoubtedly did have an effect on winemaking in Portugal and in every region they invaded. These were the Moors, who captured the city of Oporto (O Porto, "the port" in Portuguese) in 716. Although they were generally an enlightened people, their religion, Mohammedanism, prohibited the use of alcohol in any form. This strict denial must have discouraged the growth of viticulture in Lusitania.

The Moors' influence in northern Portugal, however, was not strong, or long-lasting. Within the century Pelayo of Asturias (an area of northwestern Spain) led an army of reconquest to win back the Moorish-held lands in the Iberian peninsula. His son-in-law, Alfonso I, extended Pelayo's victories, recapturing the city of Oporto for Christianity. Now all that remains here as a reminder of the Saracen occupation of northern Portugal are the ruins of a few Moorish castles which once commanded the heights of the Numão and Lavandeira peaks above the Douro.

When Dona Teresa, illegitimate daughter of the King of Léon and Castile, was given in marriage to the knight Henry of Burgundy in 1095, this territory, the county of Portugal, was part of her dowry. Henry built his castle at Guimãraes, capital of the *Territorium Portucalense,* and is said to have made an important contribution to viticulture on the Douro by introducing the Pinot Noir grape from his homeland.

Their son, Alfonso Henriques, extended the territory of the county of Portugal, driving the Moors further southward. Following the victory at Lamego, he was hailed as king of Portugal by his troops, a title recognized by the nobles, clergy, and towns of Portugal at the Lamego Cortes (assembly). In the Treaty of Zamora in 1143 Portugal's independence from León and Castile was grudgingly acknowledged by his cousin Alfonso VII.

With an army strengthened by Anglo-Norman, Scottish, Flemish, Rhenish, and Burgundian soldiers of the Second Crusade, Afonso Henriques, now King Afonso I, laid seige to

Saracen-held Lisbon in 1147. The Moors were pushed increasingly southward, and by the middle of the next century Portugal had virtually attained its present borders. The reconquest of Faro on the southern coast brought an end to the Moorish occupation of Portugal in 1249.

Foreign trade, including (though not yet in a major way) trade in Portuguese wine, was an important part of the country's economy. In 1353 a commercial treaty was concluded between the merchants of Oporto and Lisbon and the English king, Edward III. This marked the beginning of an important alliance between England and Portugal which would eventually lead to port wine becoming the "Englishman's wine."

One of the earliest references to the wines of the Douro is found in the journal kept by a Czechoslovakian nobleman, Rozmital, on his travels through Europe in the Middle Ages. Rozmital crossed into the region of the Upper Douro from Spain in 1460. He noted that the area was planted to almond, fig, and strawberry trees, and to vines. He wrote of a wine produced there called Vinho de Grecia (perhaps meaning in the Greek style), which he described as being made from dried overripe grapes.

Rui Fernandes, a Portuguese chronicler writing in the early sixteenth century, mentioned the wine of the Lamego district of the Douro (now in the southern part of the port wine region). He reported that the region had a reputation for wine, producing table wines that were shipped down the Douro to Oporto. There was also a small quantity—about one-tenth the total production—of stronger, "aromatic" wines. These, he noted, were wines that could take three to four years of aging and were the more in demand, fetching four to five times the prices of the regular table wines. They were exported over the difficult mountain trails on muleback to the nobility of Lisbon and Castile.

The treaty of 1654 between Portugal and England was favorable to English commercial interests, a situation that encouraged a number of British merchants to settle in Portugal and establish firms there. The wine trade in northern Portugal at that time was not yet based in the city of Oporto but at Viana do Castelo at the mouth of the Lima, where the light wines of the Minho were brought for export.

Other than the Portuguese themselves, the Dutch were apparently the first to appreciate the Douro wines. In 1675, their trade with Bordeaux cut off by war, Dutch traders traveled to Oporto to buy wine. Again in 1678 Dutch merchants are recorded buying wine from Lamego, Vila Real, and the Upper Douro. But the English were not far behind, and ultimately they became the most important builders of the port trade. Between 1678 and 1685, as a consequence of the war between England and France, the importation of French wines was prohibited in England. At this same time there was a period of poor vintages coming out of Italy. English wine drinkers began to look to Portugal for substitutes.

The wines of the Minho were thin and lacking in the body the English preferred, but the Douro wines were bigger and fuller. Merchants in Oporto began shipping increased amounts of Douro wine, and some of the English community moved their businesses from Viana to Oporto to join the trade in Douro wine.

Peter Bearsley was one of the first Viana merchants to make the move, founding a firm in Oporto in 1692 that is still doing business in port wine today as Taylor, Fladgate and Yeatman. Bearsley was said to be the first Englishman to venture into the wilds of the Upper Douro in search of good wine. He has also been credited with the somewhat dubious honor of being the first man to recognize the possibilities of the elderberry trees that were growing close by the vineyards, noting the dark red color of the elderberry juice. He is supposed to have had the idea of using this to add color to the Douro wine, a practice much lamented in later times, though perhaps mostly because it was abused. There was no denying that the English preferred a dark, rich, red color to their wine.

When Colbert, prime minister to Louis XIV, prohibited the import of British woolen cloth into France, England retaliated with a ban on the import of French wines into Great Britain. According to tradition it was at this time that loyal Englishmen began the practice of drinking the sovereign's health with port in place of the unpatriotic French claret.

The story is told that in 1678, in answer to the demand for Portuguese wines to fill in for the missing French, a Liverpool merchant sent two of his sons to Viana. They traveled up the Douro, stopping overnight at a monastery in Lamego. With their dinner they were served a local wine called *pinhão* which impressed them very much. The abbot explained that several liters of brandy had been added to the must during fermentation, which preserved some of its natural sweetness. The basic idea for this procedure, he said, had come from Spain. The

4

young men bought a supply of the local wine to ship to England, and before it left their hands they fortified each cask with a judicious dose of brandy.

In that same year the first shipment of wine to be recorded as *Vinho do Porto* was shipped from Oporto. The annual total amounted to a mere 408 casks, or pipes, but this rose to an average of about 7,000 pipes a year over the next few years. Some sophisticated imbibers in England found it a poor substitute, to say the least, for their beloved claret, but as claret was not to be found, they obviously—albeit in desperation—drank what was.

When for a short period French wines again were permitted into England, sales naturally exceeded those of Portuguese wines. By 1689, however, war had again broken out between the traditional enemies, England and France, and Portuguese wine began making its first real inroads into the English market. When the war was over and French wines were freely imported once more, the tariff on them was much higher, more than double that on Portuguese wines, a situation which encouraged the English to develop a taste for the wines of Portugal.

While tastes were changing, the wine itself underwent some changes too. In a curious medical book entitled *Compleat English Physician,* published in 1693, Dr. William Salmon gave a description of port, then called "Portoport": "It is a very strong Bodied Wine, and a great Stomatick, but not very Palatable, and therefore not so much drunk as other Wines."

In 1703 the historic Methuen Treaty was signed by England and Portugal. It stated that in exchange for privileges to the British woolen trade, Portuguese wines would never be taxed more than two-thirds the tariff levied on French wines. This treaty gave the port shippers the security to plan far into the future, and it gave an important impetus to the port trade.

The vineyards in the Douro were generally owned and managed by peasant farmers whose winemaking methods were rudimentary. Some of the English shippers advised the farmers on methods to improve their product, thereby influencing the style of the wine which, over the course of time, became perfectly suited to the British taste. The shippers also blended the Douro wines they purchased to make them more appealing to the British market.

The Douro wines were described as big, rough, strong wines with a high natural alcoholic content. Over the years it became customary to increase the wine's natural alcohol by the addition of brandy. When this practice was started is not known. It was a gradual change beginning some time in the eighteenth century with a handful of farmers adding a few gallons of brandy to their wine.

English, Scottish, Dutch, and German merchants founded firms in Oporto, but it was the British who became the dominating force in the trade. Their brethren in England constituted the wine's greatest market. The English preferred wine high in alcohol; and, in fact, merchants often fortified the pipes, or casks, of port when they were received in England (clarets received the same treatment). In the middle of the eighteenth century, port drinkers in England were calling for dark wines high in alcohol, rich, and sweet. Their tastes shaped the course of port's development.

Brandy was added to fortify the wines in Madeira and Spain also at about that time. But stopping the fermentation to retain some of the natural grape sugar is a more complicated procedure.

A handbook on winemaking published in 1720 advised that three gallons of brandy per pipe of wine should be added to the must (grape juice) during fermentation. By 1793, the amount of brandy had increased to an estimated 15 to 20 liters (4 to 5 gallons) per pipe*, which was further increased in the following years. In time, as methods were perfected, the amount stabilized around 100 liters (26 gallons) of brandy per pipe (145 gallons or 550 liters) of wine. By the middle of the nineteenth century fortification during fermentation had become the general practice for port, producing a sweet, rich wine high in alcoholic content.

The early merchants, founders of some of the prosperous port houses of today, underwent considerable hardship to make the journey up the Douro to obtain the best wines from the sometimes all but inaccessible farms in the wild and rugged hills. The trip was made on muleback. At the infrequent inns along the way, they braved suspicious-looking meals followed by restless nights in disreputable beds. One of the early merchants, Thomas Woodmass, described a particularly weary night "sleeping on ye table for reason of ye vermin."

As the popularity of the Douro wines grew in England, the consequent boom in the port trade encouraged the planting of more vineyards in the Upper Douro. Cornfields were ripped

*A pipe (550 liters/145 gals.) would contain 100 liters (26 gals.) of brandy and 450 liters (119 gals.) of wine.

out to make way for the now more profitable vineyards.

The Catholic church became one of the biggest landholders and owned some of the finest vineyards, producing wine that, as John Croft described it in *A Treatise on the Wines of Portugal,* ". . . fetched a higher price, was stouter and stronger than common, and was very fashionable in England where it went by the name of 'Priest Port.' "

Encouraged by the high prices the wine was bringing, the farmers began planting vineyards even on the poorer locations. Men of little integrity entered the trade for fast profits. The reputation of port wine began to suffer from some of the poor wine being shipped — wine that was badly made, stretched with inferior wine from outside the district, strengthened with cheap brandy, sweetened with sugar, and colored with *baga,* the dark red juice of the elderberry.

The bad wine coupled with the general overproduction in response to booming demand brought on the subsequent bust. Prices of Douro wine fell drastically, and the shippers of the British Association threatened to stop buying the wine altogether if the adulteration wasn't stopped.

This drew a strong reaction from the Portuguese government. The prosperous port trade of the British shippers had been the object of resentment and envy in Portugal. In 1756 the Portuguese government chartered the Companhia Geral da Agricultura dos Vinhos do Alto Douro, under the secretary of state, Pombal.

This monopoly company assumed complete control over the port wine trade. The government administrators classified all the wine, dictated the prices, determined how much wine could be shipped, and decided which wine would be granted an export permit. They also controlled the production and sale of the brandy essential for the production of port wine.

This government project ended amid bribery and corruption, but before it was disbanded, it did achieve a few significant accomplishments. The Old Wine Company, as it was known, outlawed the practice of adding *baga* to the wine as well as other flagrant abuses. It delimited the vineyard areas in the Douro where grapes for port could be grown; and the limits of the port wine region were extended to the Cima Corgo, whose vineyards produce some of the best Port wine. In 1780 the Company began the difficult project of clearing gigantic blocks of granite from the gorge at Cachão da Valeira, opening the still dangerous rapids to riverboats that transported the wines of the Upper Douro down to Oporto.

In the 1700s port wine was already on its way to becoming a tradition in England. And port's reputation was spreading worldwide, from South America to Australia to the realm of the Czar of All the Russias. At the Imperial Court sweet white port was the favored drink. This wine was despised by the English, who believed that "the first duty of port is to be red." Not that they objected to a little sweetness in their wines: Dr. Samuel Johnson, a self-acknowledged three-bottle man, was known to have added sugar to his port.

Port became truly the Englishman's wine in this age. King William was a port lover; he provisioned the hampers of his hunting parties with port in quantities exceeding that of any other wine. Port was also the wine used in the communion services at St. James chapel.

Port was drunk at all the better colleges and universities, by dons and undergraduates alike—though not in the same quality to be sure. The undergraduates had a name for the dark, rich port wine poured at their tables; it was familiarly known as "blackstrap." Some of the port drunk in the universities was mulled port (heated, sweetened, and spiced). André Simon, in *Port,* cites this comment from the *The Times* of London, dated 1798, on the place of port in the dining halls of academe.

> "To which University," said a lady, some time since, to the late sagacious Dr. Warren, "shall I send my son?" "Madam," replied he, "they drink, I believe, near the same quantity in each of them."

The port that was being poured on an increasingly regular basis at this time was not served as it is today, after the meal. The custom in England in the late eighteenth century was to serve the port with the dinner—which leads some people to believe that it must have been a drier wine in those days, although the blackstrap designation seems to indicate otherwise. We know that brandy was being added to the wine, sometimes during fermentation in amounts sufficient to stop the process and retain some of the natural grape sugar in the wine.

But tastes were different then. At a dinner given in Hamburg, Germany, in the 1770s, it is recorded that there was a wine to match each dish—in some rather remarkable combinations: "Malaga for fresh beans and fresh herrings, Burgundy with fresh peas, Champagne with oysters, Port or Madeira with costly salted fish." Not quite the choices most diners would make today, with the possible exception of the

Champagne.

In *Notes on a Cellar-Book* by the well-known winelover and authority George Saintsbury, we see again port being served in the middle of the dinner: port, 1858 is listed on the menu opposite the Ecrevisses (crayfish) à la Crème and the Boiled Turkey.*

In 1831, Joseph James Forrester went to Oporto to join his uncle's firm of Offley, Webber & Forrester. This remarkable man was to have a huge impact on the port trade. He came to know and love the Douro region well, expertly mapping the Douro River and the vineyards, and writing scholarly works on winemaking and related subjects that are still read today.

At about this time, certain abuses were again becoming more or less rampant among the less reputable port producers and the farmers who supplied their wine. In 1844 J.J. Forrester wrote a pamphlet drawing attention to these abuses and placing the blame on the port shippers, who he said were encouraging the farmers to artificially color the wines with *baga* and to sweeten them with sugar and *geropiga.*

The latter is very sweet grape must to which brandy has been added early in the fermentation process to retain the high natural sugar content. Apparently there were different recipes and grades of *geropiga,* some of which were pretty outrageous. One, given in Cyrus Redding's *History and Description of Modern Wines* (published in 1833), calls for 56 pounds of elderberries, 60 pounds of coarse brown sugar, 78 gallons of grape juice, and 39 gallons of strong brandy!

Forrester also complained about the practice of adding alcohol to stop the fermentation, which he described as unnatural. This may seem odd to us today, but if the fortification were not done properly, it would result in a bad wine. If the farmers added too little brandy to their wine, as they sometimes did, they were liable to produce wines which, as port shippers earlier had complained, "will not remain quiet, but are continually tending to ferment, and to become ropy and acid."

Some of the merchants in England were putting additions of their own into the pipes of port they received, and the cheap wines sold as port in England were poor imitations indeed of the real thing.

Forrester stirred up a great controversy with his pamphlet, although he personally remained well liked and respected. As a result of his strong stand, some serious abuses were brought

*(New York: Macmillan Co., 1933), p. 169

to a halt, and both the quality and reputation of port wine improved.

By the late Victorian Age, port had evolved into the wine we know today. The only real difference between the port produced at the end of the last century and that made today is the so-called beeswings, tiny, slightly shiny flakes present in the older ports. They had no effect on the taste, but they added to the beauty of the wine when it was held up to the light of a candelabrum or gas lamp. The beeswings were considered a sign of a well-matured and properly handled port, and were found only in the fine old wines.

This curious aspect of the old ports disappeared after the phylloxera blight. The first damage caused by the plant louse *Phylloxera vastatrix* was discovered in the 1870s at Quinta da Azinheira, in the Cima Corgo district of the Douro, where some of the finest port grapes are grown. By 1879 it had spread to the prolific Baixo Corgo district and beyond. The plants attacked by this insect withered and died within three to four years. No antidote was known to reverse or prevent the ruin that the pest was spreading throughout the vineyards of Europe.

Production in the Douro vineyards dropped alarmingly. Figures from one vineyard holding, that of Quinta do Oliveirinho, tell the discouraging tale graphically: 1875 — 38 pipes of wine; 1878 — 8 pipes; 1879 — 0 pipes. It was a desperate period for the Douro farmers. Many left their barren vineyards to emigrate to Brazil in hopes of starting a new life. Among those who stayed, some turned to other crops — citrus fruits, coffee, tea, and tobacco.

There was a panic reaction in the trade. Prices rose sharply for what was presumably the last pipes of port that would ever be produced. The end was predicted for the port wine trade. But in 1882 a way was found to combat the parasite's destruction: grafting the Portuguese vines onto resistent American rootstocks. (It was on these native American vines that the phylloxera louse had lived undetected in the northeastern United States, and on which it had inadvertently been introduced into Europe.) Abandoned terraces were replanted with the American vines onto which the varieties traditional in the Douro were grafted.

The last decades of the nineteenth century was the golden age for port wine. Port was drunk universally in England, by all classes and at all hours of the day, vintage port being the wine most prized by the upper classes. In Russia it was sweet white port; in France, ruby port and the cheaper tawny, drunk as aperitifs. In the United States, port was considered a restorative to be drunk for one's health, while in northern Germany they liked their port flavored with herbs and spices. The port trade prospered handsomely!

At George Saintsbury's dinners of the 1880s, recorded in *Notes on a Cellar-Book*, port was frequently listed as the wine served between the dessert course and the savory at the end of the dinner: Vintage Port, 1872, between the Sardines à la Titania and Ices; Port, Cockburn's 1851, between the Macaroni Pudding and the Shrimp Toast. On another menu, Port 1853 with the Dessert Soufflé, followed by Pedro Ximénès with the Canapés de Crevettes. Port, Warre's 1884, is served between the Beehive Pudding and the Cheese Trifles (now perhaps we're coming closer to the modern port drinker's taste).

In the Edwardian age, port began to replace claret for after-dinner drinking.

The popularity of port continued into the twentieth century, but not to such an enormous extent as previously. The Russian trade was lost in the early part of the century (1907) when the faltering Czarist regime leavied heavy tariffs on this imported luxury. (This no doubt was just before it would have been lost anyway, as one more casualty of the Russian Revolution.)

After World War I, sherry and cocktail parties began to chip away at the port market. Elaborate dinners with many courses finished off with a fine bottle of port were going out of style. Life was faster and the fashions slimmer; diet began to mean not so much what one ate and drank, as what one did not.

The stock market crash of 1929 hurt many of port's best markets, and it was felt with a crunch in Oporto, where some of the port firms went out of business. But port survived this crisis, as it had so many others.

France leads the list in port consumption today, with a healthy 40 percent—more than Portugal itself, which represents only 33 percent of the market. England buys only 20 percent today, down from a substantial 65 percent before the '29 crash; however, 5 percent of this is the finest—vintage port.

In France, where port is mostly drunk as an aperitif, the inexpensive tawny and ruby ports are favored, as well as some white (not much change here). The other big customers are

Holland, Belgium (equally divided between white and red), Luxembourg, West Germany, Scandanavia (drinking mostly tawny, but vintage port also), and Ireland. The U.S. consumes less than 1 percent, but most of this is, admittedly, the higher-quality Port — old tawnies and vintage port.

The port trade seems to be on the upsurge again today after a difficult period; the interest in port among winedrinkers is growing. And it deserves to be; port is an excellent wine, indeed the greatest of all the fortified wines.

THE DOURO VALLEY

The Douro River rises as the Rio Duero in the snowcapped Sierra de Urbión mountains of Old Castile in northern Spain. Flowing west across the Spanish *meseta,* is turns south to form the frontier between Spain and Portugal.

The river enters Portugal at Barca d'Alva where it becomes the Douro. From this point west for nearly a hundred miles, between the villages of Mesão Frio and Barqueiros, 60 miles east of Oporto, the Douro winds through the port wine producing region. This area, covering some 2,600 square kilometers (1,000 square miles), was officially demarcated in 1756 — the first wine region to be so controlled anywhere. The original granite marking stones delimiting the port wine district can still be seen in the Upper Douro.

The Upper Douro is a rugged, mountainous country. The vertically striated granite cliffs, thrust straight up by some ancient volcano, form a gray palisade at the river's edge. Narrow, winding roads lead off to hidden villages. The steeply terraced vineyards climb the mountainsides with row on row of vines following the curve of the slopes in the yellow schistous soil.

Trees dot the landscape — fig and almond trees, groups of orange and lemon, the gray-leafed olive, and the cork tree with its dark red trunk. Vegetables and flowers grow in abundance around the white houses and between the vineyards. In the fall, the landscape is gilded with yellow and red autumn foliage on trees and vines alike.

The Douro is a region of climatic extremes. Though sheltered from northerly winds and frost by the mountains of the Sierra do Marão, winter temperatures in the Douro can plummet to 13-degrees C. (20-degrees F.), while in summer the mercury may soar to 43-degrees C. (110-degrees F.). The year-round temperatures average between 18- and 21-degrees C. (65- and 70-degrees F.).

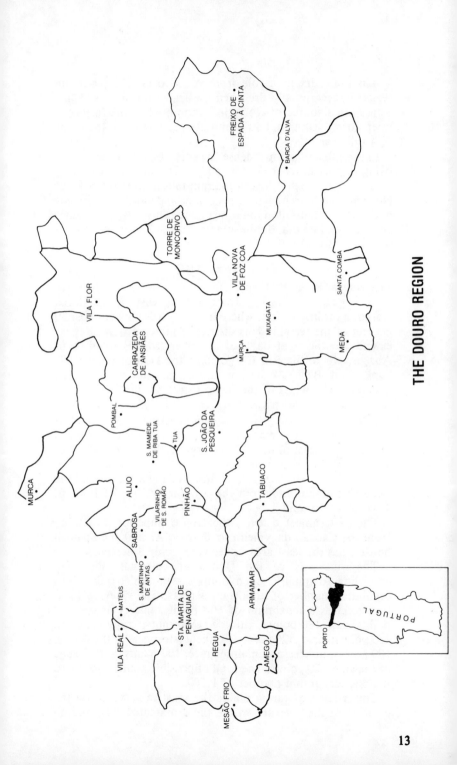

THE DOURO REGION

13

It is quite dry as a rule from April to October, but the region is occasionally drenched by heavy downpours. Hailstones are a source of worry in autumn, when the fury of a brief storm, lasting but a few minutes, can wipe out the labor of a full year.

In the fall and winter, dense fog often fills the river gorge, rising in gray mists from the valley when the sun's warming rays break through. Most of the rain falls in the winter, from November to March, when heavy rains and hailstorms are not uncommon. Rainfall in the wine region is heaviest in the vineyards around Régua, diminishing almost to half in the eastern reaches of the Douro.

THE VINEYARDS

The vineyards of the Upper Douro are separated into three districts. The first, going from west to east, is the Baixo Corgo, a prolific region, where the vineyards cover almost 30 percent of the terrain. This district, centered around Régua, extends on the right bank of the river from Barqueiros to Abaças, where the Rio Corgo joins the Douro; on the left bank, from Barrô to the juncture of the Rio de Temilobos tributary. The wines of the Baixo Corgo are mostly used for ruby and young tawny ports.

The second district, with only about 10 percent of the land under vines, is the Cima or Alto Corgo. This district includes the vineyards east of the Baixo Corgo to the gorge at Cachão da Valeira. The best wines come from the Alto Corgo, especially from the vineyards in the heart of the area, around the town of Pinhão, and from the tributary valleys of Pinhão, Távora, Torto, and Tua.

The easternmost district, the Douro Superior, extending from the Cachão da Valeira to Barca d'Alva at the Spanish border, has the least area under vines, only 3 percent.

The vineyards of the Douro are officially classified according to quality, on a point system which takes into account a number of important aspects. The vineyard location receives a maximum of 600 points; microclimate, 210 points; soil, 180 points; altitude, 150 points; grape varieties, 150 points; yield, 120 points; gradient (steepness of the slope), 100 points; upkeep and maintenance, 100 points; and the age of the vines, 70 points. The total of possible points adds up to the not very round number of 1,680.

This system of rating places the most importance on the location of the vineyard within the demarcated zone and on the microclimate, those two categories accounting for nearly half the number of possible points (810 out of 1,680).

Altitude and gradient (250 points) also contribute to the microclimate since they have a significant effect on the heat, the sunlight, and drainage of the vineyard. These, then, can be considered among the microclimate factors, bringing the total of points to a possible 1,060. The port wine vineyards can be cultivated from a limit of 1,500 feet in elevation down to river level (about 300 feet above sea level). The gradient here is very steep; over 90 percent of the slopes incline more than 30 degrees and the remainder, rarely less than 20. In the Cima Corgo the slopes commonly range from a steep 40 degrees to a precipitous 70 degrees. Only about 10 percent of the district's 605,000 acres are planted to vines. In some places the difficult terrain might be no deterrent to the growth of the vine, but it makes cultivation impossible.

Grape varieties, the age of the vines, and yields account for only 340 points in the classification system. The varieties grown are limited to the accepted types for the region. And in some vineyards yields are limited by natural conditions, which make overcropping there impossible.

The question of soil (180 points) takes into account the nature and composition of the soil in the vineyard. The vineyards of the Douro are composed of shale broken down into a rocky layer of yellow earth on an uneven foundation of granite bedrock. A reserve of moisture from the spring rains is retained deep beneath the soil in the crevices of the rock to nourish the roots of the vines in the hot, dry summer months.

Vines for port can only be planted in this schistous soil; those planted in alluvial soil cannot be used for port.

The rock in many vineyards has been broken down by vineyard workers using the *martelo,* a type of sledgehammer. Nowadays an easier method — dynamite — is often employed to break up the shale and granite of the hillsides for planting.

The soil has very little of the nitrogen or organic content needed to support high yields, but the schistous rock is rich in magnesium and potassium. The vineyards with the greater proportion of schist produce lower yields but higher-quality grapes. The schist also absorbs the heat of the sun, remaining warm after the sun has set.

In the best vineyards it takes 18 vines to yield enough fruit to produce 4.5 liters of wine; in good vineyards 9 vines can yield 4.5 liters of wine; in lesser quality vineyards as few as

4 to 5 vines can yield 4.5 liters of wine; and in the lowest quality vineyards a single vine can produce enough fruit to yield 4.5 liters of wine.

The vineyards, having been given points, are rated from A to F. This grade determines the amount of wine per 1,000 vines that the vineyard is allowed to produce — its authorized yield.

Grade	Points	Yield per 1,000 Vines
A	1,200+	700 liters (185 gallons)
B	1,001	600 liters (159 gallons)
C	801	500 liters (132 gallons)
D	601	400 liters (106 gallons)
E	401	300 liters (79 gallons)
F	201	0 liters (0 gallons)

Production in the Cima Corgo, the best district, is actually already regulated by nature; these vineyards are not capable of producing more than an average of about one pipe (550 liters/145 gallons) per 1,000 vines. In the Baixo Corgo, on the other hand, the vineyards could produce 2,000 liters (530 gallons) or more per 1,000 vines if not judiciously pruned. The lower the yield, though, the higher the quality of the fruit — and therefore of the wine.

Because the vineyards are planted on terraces on the mountainsides, yields are not figured in gallons per acre, or hectoliters her hectare, as is common elsewhere, but in liters per 1,000 vines.

TERRACES

The terraces are built in narrow shelves bearing only a few rows of vines — in the steepest situations only a single row. The terraces are supported by dry walls 10 to 30 feet high made of shale stones taken from the vineyards. Much labor is required to build and repair these walls, and where the cost of maintenance has outweighed the financial rewards, some of the old terraces have been abandoned.

Luiz Vasconcellos Porto, at Quinta do Noval, was the first to experiment with sloping, or inclined, terraces, and now the wider terracing, though still uncommon in the Douro, is being used in some of the new vineyards. These terraces do not retain the winter rainfall as well as the old narrow ones, but they are much less expensive to build and maintain. The vineyard work is also easier, and more machinery can be used.

Much of the work in the vineyards is still done by hand; the main tool of the vineyard workers is the *enchada de bicos compridos*, a forked hoe. Mules are used for the plowing. The narrow terraces don't allow much room for machinery, but small tractors are used where possible.

PRODUCTION

Total production in the port wine region is 200,000 pipes, or 110 million liters (29.06 million gallons).

The 85,000 vineyards of the Douro are divided among 25,000 owners. The average production is small: per farmer, only 8 pipes (4,400 liters/1162 gallons); per vineyard, 2⅓ pipes (1,294 liters/342 gallons). Seventy-four percent of the farmers produce only from 1 to 5 pipes; 12 percent, from 6 to 10 pipes; 9 percent, from 11 to 25 pipes; 3 percent, from 26 to 50 pipes; 1.4 percent from 51 to 100 pipes; and a mere 0.6 percent, 101 pipes or more.

GRAPE VARIETIES

The Douro vineyards are planted to perhaps the greatest number of different grape varieties for one kind of wine than any other wine-producing region. Forty-eight grape varieties, or *castas*, are allowed: 28 red and 20 white.

The Red Varieties

Alvarelhão	Samarrinho
Avesso	Sousão
*Bastardo	Tinta Amarela
Casculho	Tinta Bairrada
Castela	Tinta Barroca
Cornifesto	Tinta Carvalha
Coucieira	Tinta da Barca
Donzelinho Tinto	*Tinta Francisca
Malvasia Preta	*Tinta Roriz
Moreto	*Tinto Cão
*Mourisco	Tinto Martins
*Mourisco de Semente	Touriga Brasileira
Periquita	*Touriga Francesca
Rufete	*Touriga Nacional

17

The White Varieties

Arinto
Branco sem Nome
Boal
Cercial
Codega
*Donzelinho
Esgana-Cão
Fernão Pires
Folgosão
Gouveio or Verdelho
Malvasia Corada

*Malvasia Fina
Malvasia Parda
Malvasia Rei
*Moscatel Galego
Pedernão
Praça
*Rabigato
Touriga Branca
Verdelho or Gouveio
Viosinho

* = Highly regarded varieties.

Of these, the most highly regarded red varieties are Touriga Nacional, Tinto Caõ (red dog), and Tinta Francisca (red French). These three are among the most widely planted red varieties, which also include Mourisco and Tinta Amarela.

Julian Jeffs, in *The Wines of Europe,* writes that the Touriga Nacional is the Cabernet grape of France, but doesn't specify whether he is referring to the Cabernet Sauvignon or the Cabernet Franc. Others also have suggested that this grape may be the Cabernet Franc.

The Tinta Francisca — also called Tinta da Franca, Tinta Francesca, and Pinot Noir — was originally, it is believed, brought to Portugal (Guimarães) by Henry of Burgundy in 1095, and reintroduced to Portugal by Robert Archibald who planted it at his Quinta de Roriz almost 700 years later.

Mourisco, though not rich in color, is said to be of fine quality. Some say the Tinta Roriz produces the highest quality must in the Douro — others say rather that it produces high quantity. Sousão is prolific in the Baixo Corgo but is not grown at all in the Alto Corgo. This grape produces wine deep in color but low in sugar. The port house, carefully blending the wines from the different vineyards where the grapes are grown, can take advantage of a number of qualities — color, acid, sugar, body, and so forth — to produce a fine, balanced wine.

At one time the Moscatel de Hamburgo and Moscatel de Jesus varieties were vinified alone, producing wines that were popular in Brazil and Russia. There was a category of port at one time called muscatel port. Allan Taylor in his book *What Everybody Wants to Know About Wine,* published in 1934, named five types of port: white port, muscatel port, tawny port, vintage port, and ruby port.

There are some fine muscatel wines produced in the Douro today, but they are no longer called port. Moscatel de Favaios is one that we have tasted and found particularly fine — rich in flavor with apricot overtones and a long, complex finish.

The best white ports are produced from the Malvasia Fina and Malvasia Rei varieties. The Gouveio or Verdelho, Boal, and Cercial — all white varieties — are the same grapes that are used in the better madeiras. We've also heard of a white variety grown in the Douro called Estreito which could be the Sercial also, this being the name of an area where some of the best Sercial grapes of Madeira are grown.

THE VINES

Normally the vines are uprooted after thirty to forty years, when they have begun to decline, and are replaced with new vines. The pre-phylloxera native vines, grown on their own roots, are said to have lived much longer.

There has been much debate over whether the grafted vines produce wines as good as those of the old pre-phylloxera vines. The wines today reputedly are not as big and dark as the pre-phylloxera vintages, and not as long-lived. However, this could be the result, not of grafting, but of different vinification techniques and/or the fact that there are no very old vines now, as there used to be in the vineyards before phylloxera. The older vines, it is generally agreed, give smaller yields but of grapes that produce richer and more concentrated wines.

Quinta do Noval has the only vineyard now planted with ungrafted vines in the Douro. These 4,000 *nacional* vines make up a small part of their production. They are sometimes referred to as pre-phylloxera vines, but some — if not all — of the vines have been planted since phylloxera; they are grown in the pre-phylloxera manner — on their own roots. The production from these vines — the Tourigas, Tinta Francisca, and Roriz — is small, only 3 pipes of wine. But it's a wonder that there is any at all.

The wine is reputedly deeper in color, more tannic and harsh in its youth, slower to develop and longer-lived than wine from grafted vines.

THE VINTAGE YEAR

The sap rises in the vines at the first warm weather, and what appeared throughout the snowy winter months to be row upon row of dry sticks reawaken to begin a new year of growth that will culminate in the harvest of the rich, sweet grapes for port. Budbreak comes around the beginning of April, when the buds push through the wood of the vines. The new green shoots sprouting out from the branches of the vine are trained along wires.

By early May flowering has begun. From the miniature grape bunches of hard green beads small greenish flowers emerge. The weather conditions during the cross-fertilization of the grape flowers are critical to the outcome of the year's harvest. Sunny days with gentle breezes are hoped for. Strong winds or heavy rains would sweep away the pollen, drastically reducing the potential size of the year's crop. Toward the latter part of June the vineyards are, as they say, visited by *o Pintor* (the Painter), and the green grape bunches begin to take on color.

As the weather in May, during the flowering, was critical for the quantity of the harvest, conditions in August and September are critical for quality. If it's too cold or wet during these key months, the grapes won't ripen properly; the sugar will be too low and the acid too high to produce a balanced wine. If it is too hot, the grapes may burn or shrivel, throwing the balance off in the other direction. Concern about the weather is not truly over until the grapes have been harvested and are safely in the wineries, or *adegas*.

The *adega,* where the wine is made, is on the vineyard property of the *quinta,* or wine estate. The other buildings on the *quinta* include a *loja,* lodge, where the wine is stored, the owner's house and office, and the facilities for the workmen. The buildings are solidly built to withstand time and the elements, with thick granite walls sometimes decorated with blue glazed pottery tiles.

The microclimates at the different *quintas* vary according to their location. As the mountain range runs north to south, those *quintas* facing west are exposed to the scorching heat of the afternoon sun, while those facing east receive the cooler rays of the morning sun. The vineyards with a southern exposure are in the sun throughout the day. These extra hours of sun and heat shrivel the grapes on the vines, and the quantity of the yield is reduced. But this is believed to result in higher quality, as the juice in the grapes is more concentrated.

THE HARVEST

Normally the *vindima,* or harvest, begins around the third week in September. The actual picking date at the different *quintas* varies depending on the ripeness of the fruit — the level of sugar and acid in the grapes. When to pick is discussed between shipper and farmer, the shipper having the final word. The shippers supervise the vineyards, the harvest, and the making of the wine at the *quintas* under contract to them.

The grapes are picked by a group of harvesters — the *roga,* led by the *rogador* — who come from a neighboring village. The workday starts very early in the morning and continues until sunset. The pickers in the vineyards can be heard talking and singing, and as they work they find a little quiet munching on the sweet ripe grapes too tempting to resist. The harvest is hard work, but it takes on a festival atmosphere when the day's work is done, with singing, dancing, and a general mood of celebration.

The vintage is the high point of the year, and men, women, and children all take part. The women pick the bunches of grapes, cutting the stems with special scissors or knives, and taking out any grapes that are unripe or moldy. The grape bunches are dropped into small baskets picked up by the children, then emptied into a larger basket, the *cesto vindimo,* holding about 100 pounds.

The girls, like the women all over Portugal, easily carry the baskets balanced on their heads; the boys, emulating their fathers, carry the baskets on their shoulders.

The *cesto vindimo* is hoisted to the shoulders of the man who will carry it either up or down the slope to one of the waiting trucks or traditional wooden-wheeled bullock carts. The ancient-looking carts, screeching under their heavy load, are pulled slowly to the *adega* by the plodding beasts.

THE TREADING

Grapes are still crushed in the Douro region by the oldest method known to man — by foot. The Douro is probably the only major wine-producing region in the world where the grapes are still trodden by men with their bare (well scrubbed) feet.

The treading is accompanied by a certain amount of ceremony. In the evening, when the sun has set and the air has cooled, the stone *lagares* — troughs generally made of local granite — are filled with grapes. These large square tanks often hold 10 to 12 pipes of grapes (5,670 to 6,800 liters, or 1,500 to 1,800 gallons); the largest ones may hold up to 30 pipes.

Men wearing shorts await the signal of the foreman to jump into the *lagar.* There may be as many as twenty treaders; the ideal is two men per pipe of grapes, but one man per pipe is far more common. At the start, the men line up on opposite sides of the *lagar,* arm in arm to keep their balance as they make the *corte,* or cut, in the thick, cold mass of grapes.

The foreman calls out the rhythm, *"esquerda, direita"* ("left, right"), as the treading begins. The two lines of treaders march forward, meet, and turn round to tread back again. This steady work goes on for about two hours until the grapes are cut and the cool liquid is rising from the crushed grapes in a purple pool around the thighs of the treaders.

The foreman then gives the signal for the *liberdade* (freedom) and with a shout the men begin to dance in the *lagar,* accompanied by the band of harvest musicians. The man on drums beats out the rhythm as the others — one playing concertina or accordion, another with triangle or guitar — play the traditional *vindima* songs. Outside the *lagar* the women also sing and dance vivaciously, with each other and with the men and boys not occupied with the treading.

After the *liberdade* the men tread at will, according to enthusiasm and stamina, the grape must sucking at each step. The liquid becomes thicker and more deeply colored as the grape pulp and skins are steadily ground against the stone floor of the *lagar.* Energies are recharged with draughts of *bagaceira,* the local marc, and cigarette breaks periodically refresh weary treaders. A loud shout goes up to announce the men cannot take another step until appropriate refreshment is provided.

When the fermentation starts, the men climb out, their legs dripping with the warm purple liquid. Planks are put across the *lagar,* and men with wooden paddles go to work, pushing down and stirring in the *manta,* or blanket, of grape solids and skins that rise to the surface of the must. Fermentation continues for about 48 hours, depending on the temperature; on hot days it goes more quickly; cool weather slows it down. The sugar level in the fermenting must is checked period-ically; when the desired level is reached, the sluice is opened and the must is run off to the vats where it is fortified with *aguardente*—grape brandy—to arrest the fermentation and retain the natural, still unfermented, grape sugars.

CHANGING METHODS

Labor shortages in the early 1960s created changes in the method of crushing. As men for the treading became more difficult to find—being drawn away by easier and higher paying jobs and for military service—boys and even women filled in for them in the *lagares*.

Up until 1960, almost all the grapes for port were trodden by human feet in stone *lagares*. But as the age-old method of treading the grapes by foot became too expensive for any but the finest wines, machines, which had been used in other countries for decades, began to be introduced into the Douro.

Mechanical presses, however, produce a comparatively inferior wine. The larger quantities of grapes handled by the presses and the speed with which they operate make it difficult to control the quality of the grapes going into them—and therefore the quality of the wine coming out. When the grapes are trodden, the quality of the loads can be, and is, checked before they go into the *lagares*. Grapes of varying quality, from different vineyards and different sections, can be kept separate.

Some houses, like Taylor, Calem, and Cockburn, still use treading for all their first-class wines. And we have been told that many other shippers also require the farmers to use treading for their best wines. In the Cima Corgo, where the finest grapes are grown, treading is still used to a large extent. Some *quintas* have gone back to the old way, completely or in part, for at least some of the wines. In the Baixo Corgo district, however, mechanical presses are in general use.

THE MODERN METHOD

In the normal procedure, the grapes are put through a crusher-stemmer, which separates the stems and crushes the grapes. The wood of the stems contains a lot of tannic acid, which will allow the wine to age. In hot, dry years when the grapes are high in sugar, a significant proportion of stems is added to the crush for balance. In cooler years, when the grapes are lower in sugar, extra tannin would dry out the wine, so very few of the stems are left in.

The crushed grapes and fresh *mosto* (must) are pumped into large fermenting vats, *cubas de fermentação,* holding 25 to 30 pipes. The must begins to ferment, activated by the natural yeast on the grape skins. During the fermentation of the red grapes, the must is continually being pumped over the *manta* (the solids that float to the surface of the boiling must), picking up color and tannin to enrich the wine. For white port, the skins are separated from the juice soon after the crushing so that not too much color — which would give the wine a brownish cast — is picked up.

The fermentation continues for about two or three days, depending on the sugar content of the grapes and the residual sugar desired by the shipper for his style of wine — generally 6 to 8 percent. When this point is reached — the must is drawn off into large wooden casks, *toneis,* or more commonly today, into large cement vats, and the brandy is added. Normally 98 liters (26 gallons) of brandy are added per 452 liters (119 gallons) of wine, one pipe holding 550 liters (145 gallons). This brings up the degree of alcohol to a level too high for the yeast to continue its activity, arresting the fermentation and preserving the remaining grape sugar in the wine.

THE FORTIFYING SPIRIT

The *aguardente,* literally "burning water," is distilled from wines grown in Portugal — in the Douro or to the south. This grape brandy, 77 percent alcohol by volume, is supplied by the Junta Nacional de Aguardente. The port producers can buy the *aguardente* only from this government agency, which through the Casa do Douro controls its production, distribution, and price.

In the early seventies this government agency supplied alcohol later discovered not to be distilled from grapes at all. But the port shippers say it did not detract from the port wine fortified with it since it was actually purer than the grape brandy normally used. The law, however, states that the fortifying spirit must be from grapes, which benefits the Douro farmers.

This was not the first time the spirit for fortifying port had come from an unusual source. Apparently, in 1904, due to a shortage of Portuguese brandy, some shippers augmented supplies with alcohol from Germany distilled from potatoes or grain (vodka?), and still produced some fine bottles of port.

Still earlier, in 1897, the port shippers faced a similar problem. The famous Royal Diamond Jubilee Vintage Port, which Master of Wine, Michael Broadbent, describes in Sarah Bradford's *Story of Port* as "still magnificent when drunk in 1976," was said to have been fortified with the best substitute the shippers could obtain — Scotch whisky.

DESPEDIDA

The harvest in the Douro generally lasts about three weeks. At the end of the harvest, before the *roga* of pickers leave for home, there is the farewell — the *despedida.* In the morning of the last day, the *roga* goes in procession — the men leading, followed by the women and children — to the house of the *patrões,* the owners, accompanied by the music of the *vindima* band.

It is time for the presentation of the *rama,* or bouquet, a branch of cane decorated by the harvesters with a bunch of grapes and embellished with colored paper streamers and the like. The young girl chosen for this honor shyly advances and offers the *rama* to the lady of the house who graciously accepts. There is a chorus of *"viva"*'s from the *roga* and more music. After a little celebrating, with wine passed around, the *roga* is off, trooping home to their village amid the fading music of the little band, until the next year when the same *roga* will return to the same *quinta* to harvest the grapes again. Old traditions are still respected in the Douro.

THE PODADORES

In November the *podadores,* or pruners, cut back the vines, leaving only two branches on each vine to concentrate the vine's energy in the following year on fewer grape bunches of richer fruit.

These men make an odd picture, wearing capes made of straw for protection against autumn rains; from the back they look like so many haystacks moving through the vineyards. The *podadores* are known not only for their pruning skill. They have achieved a certain renown, it seems, for their drinking capacity as well, going through some 5 liters (1.3 gallons) of wine in the normal course of a day's work in the damp and chilly vineyards. If pruning as late as December, when temperatures in the Douro can drop to the freezing point, their daily wine consumption is augmented with drinks of the fiery *bagaceira.*

25

Bagaceira is a type of marc made from *bagaço,* the residue left from the pressed grapes. This powerful, unaged white spirit is served to the vineyard workers before breakfast in the early morning "to kill the bug," and is familiarly known as *mata-bixo* (bug killer).

THE NEW WINE

At the end of the year, the sediment in the wine settles to the bottom of the casks, and the wine is said to have "fallen bright." It is then racked off its sediment into clean casks. A sample is taken from each pipe to be analyzed, and the alcohol is tested. Port wine under 16 percent alcohol runs the risk of refermenting, since it contains residual (unfermented) sugar. If necessary, then, additional *aguardente* is added. As a rule, the port is fortified to a level of 19 percent alcohol or higher.

The new port is allowed to absorb the alcohol and rest until the spring. During this period the red port appears to lose color temporarily, but by the spring when the wine has come together, it has regained its previous dark purplish red.

DOWN THE DOURO

In the spring or early summer the new wine is transported to Vila Nova de Gaia, opposite Oporto, on the left bank of the Douro where the port lodges—about 55 in number—are located. Lodge in the context of port has nothing to do with lodgings; the name comes from the Portuguese *loja,* meaning a warehouse. The port lodges at Vila Nova de Gaia are the buildings where the pipes of port (not the port shippers) are lodged.

Formerly the wine was shipped down river in the picturesque *barcos rabelos,* the Douro riverboats; nowadays it goes by rail or in tank trucks which carry it along the river road with its hairpin turns and beautiful vistas.

In the days of the *barcos rabelos,* the wine wasn't shipped until after March 31. This was the time of the spring thaw, when the Douro was swollen with melting snow from the mountains and heavy spring rains. The boats sailed upriver from Oporto, their huge square sails catching the prevailing westerly winds. On the return voyage, each laden with up to 60 pipes of new port wine, they rode the current rushing to the sea, shooting the treacherous rapids under the expert navigation of a helmsman on the boat's high stern.

The river could be very dangerous and was sometimes more than a match even for a helmsman and a crew seasoned by years of experience. The rapids, whipped into crashing foam and sucking whirlpools, threatened tragedy to all who dared ride them out. It was at the rapids of the Cachão de Valeira that the popular and controversial Baron J.J. Forrester was drowned in the Douro. In the spring of 1862, Baron Forrester was traveling by riverboat from the *quinta* in the Upper Douro where he had been staying. The river was high and the current swift. As the boat swept into the rapids of Cachão, it was smashed against the rocks and sank. Forrester was thrown into the current, and according to some accounts, was struck on the head by the mast as the boat pitched over. Pulled down by the weight of the gold-laden moneybelt he was wearing, he was unable to reach the shore. His body was never found.

The *barcos rabelos* of the Douro are said to be smaller descendants of the Viking ships that brought Danish and Norwegian raiders to Portuguese shores in the ninth century. The Douro craft lacked the dragonhead prows of the Viking boats; they were long (the larger ones measuring up to 15 meters /49 feet), broad-beamed, and flat-bottomed, for slipping over the shallows and treacherous rocks hidden just below the water's surface. At certain difficult points in the river, though, oxen had to be harnessed to haul the boats, following a towpath at the river's edge.

Today the last three of these graceful old *barcos rabelos* are moored at the quayside of Vila Nova de Gaia, reminders of the colorful past of the port trade on the Douro.

ON PIPES AND OTHER MEASURES

Port wine is shipped to the lodges of Vila Nova de Gaia in barrels called pipes. A Douro pipe is a cask of 600 liters (159 gallons). The Gaia or lodge pipe holds 550 liters (145 gallons). This difference in capacity is due to evaporation, loss of sediment during racking, and sampling of the wine from the time it leaves the *quinta* in the Douro until it is stored in the lodges of Gaia. (In the days of the Douro boatmen, they say the pipes shipped down river on the *barcos rabelos* got more than the usual depletion for samples. Those hardy men fighting the winds and the currents apparently felt at times the need for a bit of a nip. Whether to steady the nerves, or celebrate the execution of a difficult maneuver, or whatever reason, they were notorious for dipping into the pipes, which they were known at times to conscientiously top up with river water. One firm used to have on display a fish caught in one of the Douro pipes!) For a number of reasons, then, the lodge pipe was of smaller proportions. For shipping, port is transferred to a standard export, or shipping, pipe of 534 liters (141 gallons).

The word *pipe*, meaning a cask or barrel of wine, may strike some ears as odd (though not nearly so odd as *hogshead*), but it is an old name, used for centuries. There is a reference from 1504 that mentions Osey wine from Portugal being sold in casks called pipes.

Besides the pipe, some of the other measures used in the port lodges are *almudes* and *canadas*. There are 22 *almudes* in a pipe*, and 12 *canadas* in one *almude*. These two are Arab measures, borrowed from the Moors—not that they were necessarily used by the Moors for measuring wine (Allah forbid!); they were adopted because, like the pipe, they were found to be practical units of measure. A pipe is the size of cask that can be transported conveniently on a bullock cart. An *almude* was the capacity of the jar that one man could carry on his head and manage to pour into a vat or cask. (In the old days it was believed that the wine benefited from being carried on a lodgeman's head up and down the rows for aeration.) A *canada* is about 2 liters (½ gallon), and they say in Gaia that this is the limit of port that anyone should drink in a twenty-four-hour period unless he wants to wake up with a "bloody awful hangover."

COOPERAGE

In the lodges at Vila Nova de Gaia some of the port is matured in wooden casks of Rumanian or Portuguese oak, and the rest in larger vats built of Macacauba wood, Brazilian mahogany.

Although the lodges generally keep two-thirds of their stock in wood, the growing scarcity and increasing cost of wood has necessitated the use of more and more cement vats, *cubas de cimento*. The cement is sometimes lined with glass, but more often the inside of the tank is painted with a special neutral paint. Cement vats are generally used only for blending and for short-term storage. They do not provide an atmosphere where the wine can actually age as it does in wood.

*A shipping pipe contains 21.5 *almudes*.

Not all the shippers use cement vats. Taylor's, for example, uses wood only—with the exception of a single glass-lined tank. The casks at Taylor's are quite old—some ranging up to 170 to 200 years. These casks, though, have had to be repaired over the years; most have had their end pieces replaced more than once.

It's not unusual to see ruby port stored in large chestnut vats, some of which are more than 100 pipes in volume, although small casks also are used. The chestnut vats, especially the larger ones, give less air contact to the young, deep red wine, which helps to preserve its ruby color. Tawny ports generally are kept in oak casks of 600-litre (159-gallon) capacity for a minimum of two and a half years.

Since all the barrels must be kept full to prevent oxidation in the wine (which would rob it of its freshness and spoil its flavor), they have to be topped up periodically with more wine to make up for the natural loss from evaporation through the pores of the wood. The rate of ullage, or loss of liquid, during storage is estimated to be over 2 percent per year, an amount that includes samples drawn for tasting as well as evaporation.

Because port throws a heavy sediment in cask, the pipes are stored with the front tipped slightly downward. In this position, the wine being drawn off will flow from the back of the barrel to the front, along the surface of the liquid, causing the least possible disturbance to the sediment settled on the bottom of the barrel.

GUARANTEE OF AUTHENTICITY

Port wine is regulated by three agencies: the Instituto do Vinho do Porto, the Casa do Douro, and the Associação dos Esportadores do Vinho do Porto.

The Instituto do Vinho do Porto (I.V.P.), or Port Wine Institute, was set up in June 1933 to "define and defend what nature has created." This government body, with headquarters in Oporto, controls the port wine trade from production to export. The two other agencies are responsible to the I.V.P. No wine is allowed to enter or leave Vila Nova de Gaia without their knowledge, nor is any wine allowed to be stored in the lodges without their being informed of it. To be shipped, all port must by law carry a Certificate of Origin issued by the I.V.P. And the I.V.P. issues the seal of guarantee, *Selo de Garantia,* that is required on the neck of every port sold in bottle.

The Associação dos Esportadores do Vinho do Porto, represents the shippers exporting port wine. The Associação recommends minimum export prices to the I.V.P. It is responsible to the I.V.P. for the wine in the lodges of the members and for carrying out the regulations on maturing, blending, and shipping the wines.

No shipper is allowed to ship more than one-third of his stock in a single year. This means that for every pipe shipped, the firm must have two others in the lodges. This reserve of old wines requires large amounts of capital to be tied up, which naturally adds to the cost of port wine — though also to the quality of the blended ports. A firm is not allowed to ship at all if their stock falls below 300 pipes, the absolute minimum set by law.

This legal requirement of two-thirds stock in the lodges is actually much less than what the port shippers must stock for their own purposes. In order to keep up production and shipments of their forty-year old tawny, for example, a firm must have in reserve 40 pipes of wine for blending into that tawny for every pipe they ship.

The Casa do Douro, located in Régua, the capital of the port region, is a federation of growers that oversees the production of wine in the Douro region. It classifies and regulates the vineyards. All planting and replanting in the Douro vineyards must be authorized by the Casa do Douro. This agency is also in charge of the distribution and use of the brandy added for fortification.

The I.V.P., along with the Casa, determines the maximum amount of port that can be produced each year, issuing a bulletin which states the authorized quantity as well as the minimum prices to be paid for must and brandy. Production is allocated by percentage among the growers on the point system referred to earlier (page 14-16). Any excess production over the maximum limit cannot be used for port; it is declassified to table wine, or is distilled into brandy by the Casa do Douro.

The factors determining how much port can be produced in a particular year are: (1) the quality of the vintage, (2) the amount of port in the shippers' lodges at Vila Nova de Gaia, and (3) demand and projections of future demand.

A regulation on shipment states that all wine exported as port must be shipped over the sandbar at the mouth of the Douro. The wine can't be shipped unless its authenticity has been guaranteed by the I.V.P., Port Wine Institute, which samples every wine to be shipped. If it doesn't meet the minimum standards for its type, no certificate is issued. This is the extent of the I.V.P.'s power. "All else is up to the shippers; the I.V.P. doesn't interfere, they can't interfere, they have no right to interfere," states Sr. A.C. Sarmento de Vasconcellos of the I.V.P.

TYPES OF PORT

Port wine can be classified into two basic categories or styles, depending on how it is aged: bottle ports and wood ports. Essentially, the wood ports are aged in wood (casks) and are not bottled until they are ready to be drunk. These ports don't require further aging, although some wood ports will improve to a certain extent with a few years of aging in bottle. Wood ports are made in three types, named for their color: white port, ruby port, and tawny port.

White port ranges from very dry to medium sweet. For the most part, these ports have little to recommend them. They often have a slightly oxidized quality. It has been said that the first duty of port is to be red, and we couldn't agree more. The best white port we've tasted is Taylor's Chip Dry. It is quite full-bodied, dryish, and smooth in texture.

Ruby port is simply a young wood port that still retains its ruby color. These ports range in color from light to deep ruby, depending on the average age of the wine (the older the wine, the lighter the color). Fonseca's Bin 27, our favorite ruby port, is almost tawny in color. Full-bodied ruby port is generally made up of three to four different vintages, the oldest about seven years old and the youngest three. Ruby ports tend to be sweet and grapey, and sometimes a bit harsh. A few years in bottle, though, can rough them out, smoothing out the roughness.

Tawny port is a wood port that is tawny in color. There are two types of tawny port. The inexpensive tawnies are made by blending 6 to 8 *almudes* of white port with one pipe of four- to six-year-old ruby port. Sir Paul Methuen (son of John Methuen, signer of the Methuen Treaty) is credited with being the first man to make tawny port by mixing the red and white wine together. These tawnies are similar to the ruby ports but somewhat lighter.

Tawny port that has become tawny in color from barrel age is another type of tawny, far superior and more expensive. Ruby port — all red port begins life with a ruby color — takes at least eight years in cask to lose its youthful color and

31

become tawny; to become a really good tawny port it needs at least another twelve. Tawny port does not improve in bottle; it has matured in the wood and is ready to drink when bottled.

Tawny port often has a nutty aroma and flavor, reminiscent of walnuts. The old tawnies tend to be smooth in texture. The best have nuances of bouquet and flavor that challenge the vintage ports. They are sweet, but less so than the ruby ports or the inexpensive tawnies made from a blend of ruby and white port.

The best tawnies are twenty to thirty years old. We find the ten-year-olds still somewhat rough and the forty-year-olds so concentrated as to be almost a liqueur. The average age of a tawny port may be specified on the label. The allowable age statements are ten, twenty, thirty, and over forty years old. This type of port is officially referred to as *Port with an Indication of Age.*

The Bureau of Alcohol, Tobacco, and Firearms (BATF), which controls wine imports and labels in the U.S.A., doesn't allow wines to be labeled with an age specified in years. To get around this quirk, Taylor's (or as it must appear on U.S. labels, Taylor Fladgate) labels its twenty-year-old tawny #20, its thirty-year-old #30, and so on. To the bureaucrats at the BATF this represents truth in labeling.

Port with an indication of age is required to carry the seal of guarantee, *Selo de Garantia,* on the bottle. The label must show: (1) the indication of age, (2) that it was aged in wood, and (3) the year of bottling (on either the front or the back label).

Port with the Date of Harvest is also a wood port, but one from a single year. The word "vintage" is not allowed on the label, however. These ports are aged for a minimum of seven years before bottling. The bottle must carry the *Selo de Garantia,* and the label must indicate: (1) the date of harvest —"Port of 1944," for example, or "1944 Port"; (2) a statement that the wine was aged in wood; and (3) the year of bottling (which may appear on front or back label). This type of port is also known as *Colheita.* The label may also say *Reserva* (Reserve), or some similar description.

Garrafeira port is a dated port that is bottled long before it is sold. These ports are similar to the ports with the date of harvest.

The other style of port, bottle port, takes in the ports that improve in bottle and are meant to be aged in bottle. These ports throw a thick crust of sediment in the bottle (rather than in cask) as they mature.

Vintage port, the greatest of all port (and of all fortified wine) is the epitome of a bottle port. Young vintage port has a dark purplish color which lightens first to ruby, then with sufficient time in bottle, to a tawny hue. These wines are rich and concentrated. When young they often have an intense flavor of ripe grapes, sometimes also hints of other kinds of fruit. This grapey quality becomes less pronounced as the wine matures. Young vintage port can be harsh on the palate from its youthful tannin; the alcohol which hasn't yet married with the wine also gives it a certain roughness.

As the wine matures it smooths out, becoming mellow and harmonious. At its peak, which it will maintain for a few years, it is pure nectar. Then it slowly declines, the alcohol becoming more noticeable, especially on the nose and finish.

Vintage port is the port of a single vintage that has been declared as a vintage by the shipper between January 1 and September 30 of its second year, and bottled between July 1 of the second year and June 30 of the third year after the harvest. The label must specify the year of the harvest and carry the word "vintage." The only other type of port which is allowed to carry the word "vintage" with the date of the harvest on the bottle is late-bottled vintage port (see below).

Since November 1973, all vintage port has had to be bottled in Oporto. Traditionally, up until World War II, vintage port was shipped to England in pipes and bottled there. It was not unusual for the English merchant who bottled the port to put his name on the label, along with that of the shipper (as in the case of bottles of Taylor Dolamore). It was believed that conditions for bottling were better in England, and not much thought was given to the idea of bottling the wine in Oporto. But during the war years, from 1942 to 1945, vintage port was bottled in Oporto, and the practice grew.

Late-bottled vintage port, or L.B.V. port, is a port of a single vintage that has been declared between March 1 and September 30 in the fourth year after the harvest, and bottled between July 1 of that year and December 31 in the sixth year after the harvest (more than three years later than the vintage port may be bottled).

Bottles of L.B.V. port must bear the *Selo de Garantia,* and specify on the label: (1) the year of the harvest, (2) the year when the wine was bottled, and (3) the designation Late-Bottled Vintage, or L.B.V., on one line, in one color, and in the same print.

L.B.V. port is in one sense like a ruby port, ready to be drunk when sold, having been aged in wood for about the same time. But it is richer and more intense. In another sense it is like a vintage port — made from high quality wine of a single vintage and displaying complexity and distinction. It might be considered a type in between the two styles.

Late-bottled vintage port, though ready for drinking when sold, is capable of improving to a certain extent with bottle age; how much depends on the particular wine. These ports are not from the best vintages, which are reserved for the true vintage ports, and their longer wood aging matures them faster than bottle aging would. There are many fine late-bottled vintage ports produced — Taylor Fladgate L.B.V. and the L.B.V. of Warre's come readily to mind.

Crusted port is a bottle port generally made from a blend of two or three vintages of first-class wine. Crusted port is aged for three to four years in cask. It is not recognized as an official type. The name "crusted port" is descriptive; the wine throws a crust in the bottle and, therefore, like vintage port, it requires decanting. Crusted port has been replaced as a type today by late-bottled vintage port, though it is actually more like a vintage-character port in style.

Vintage-character, tipo vintage, or vintage-style port is blended port. The word "vintage" is allowed on the label, but not a year. Vintage-character port is similar in character and style to a late-bottled vintage port, but is not from a single harvest; it is a blend of vintages from the better years. We have tasted some fine vintage-character ports from Warre's.

AGING PORT

In the days of the Roman Empire connoisseurs appreciated their better wines in the fine old vintages. But the practice of aging wine for maturation and improvement was lost after the fall of Rome. It is said that the first wine of the modern era to be given age was port. It was the first wine to be regularly matured in bottle; claret was the second. The practice developed gradually, and didn't become general until the nineteenth century.

Port had been sold as a young wine in the early days of its history. But when fortification became common, it was found that the wine needed some time to marry with the added alcohol before it was at its best for export. The shippers began storing the pipes of port in their lodges at Vila Nova de Gaia for a period of perhaps a year before shipping it. This time gradually increased to three years or more.

In the late eighteenth century there was still a lot of young port, only one year old, being drunk in England, but as the older wines became available they fetched higher prices. The English developed a taste for aged wines, and to this day they consider wine generally at its peak for drinking at an older age than is preferred in most other countries. This preference for old wines led to the practice of laying wine down in bottle to age.

The bottles of the early eighteenth century, though, were heavy, wide-bottomed, long-necked, jug-like affairs designed to remain solidly upright and not tip over and spill or break; they were too bulky to be laid on their sides. Their purpose was to hold wine fresh from cask for short periods. Two changes had to take place before the bottle could be used for aging wine: the neck of the bottle had to be stoppered with a tight-fitting cork, and its shape had to be modified so that it could be laid on its side to keep the cork from drying out.

Bark from the cork oak was known and used by Greeks and Romans as a stopper in bottles and casks and as a plug in sealed amphorae. In Europe, before corks were found to be the ideal stoppers for wine bottles, the bottles were stoppered with wads of paper or cloth, or with plugs of wood wrapped with tow soaked in oil. Cork stoppers were being used in bottles in Europe by the sixteenth century, but they weren't common until the eighteenth.

The shape of the wine bottle evolved over a period of about a century from the squat, fat-bottomed bottles of the early 1700s to the narrow, straight-sided bottles of today. The potbellied design grew slimmer and less bulbous over the decades. By midcentury the shoulder height had almost doubled and the girth had reduced proportionately, and the sides of the bottle became more evenly flat. By about 1793, the wine bottle had virtually attained its present cylindrical shape, well designed to lie on its side to remain undisturbed for many years as the wine aged.

It has been said that the improvement in port which had been matured in bottle led to the belief that not only should port wine be aged, but all wine. Bordeaux first, then other wines were laid down to age. Even champagne, delicate hocks, and moselle wines were bottle-aged for many years — and, strange to say, were considered the better for it.

THE VINTAGING OF PORT

Vintage port as we know it is an eighteenth-century development. The first acknowledged vintage port was the 1775. This wine ushered in the modern age of vintage wines. The practice of declaring a vintage developed a little later. Previously vintages were not declared, but there was a certain amount of first-class wine from each year that was sold unblended, as a vintage wine. The earliest known printed label for a bottle of wine was for a bottle of port; it read "1756 Companhia Geral do Alto Douro."

Even today, nearly every harvest produces at least a small amount of vintage-quality wine; '56, '59, and '73 are some recent years that were the exceptions.

In making the decision whether or not to declare a vintage, the shipper must take into account factors besides the vintage itself. Economic conditions are a major consideration. Any shipper who ties up stocks for fifteen to twenty-five years while the vintage port is maturing must have a healthy reserve of capital. This is becoming less of a factor, though, since today's consumers are willing to buy the wine younger (when it is also less expensive) and lay it down to age in their own cellars until it is ready to drink.

If a shipper bottles too much of his wine as vintage port, his wood ports, especially his old tawnies, will suffer. An old tawny requires first-class wine in its blend to be of high quality.

Before declaring a vintage the shipper must also project ahead for the future of the wine itself, considering how the wine will show in fifteen to twenty years.

In the years when port was shipped in barrel and bottled by wine merchants in England, it became customary for port houses to announce, or declare, to the trade that from a certain harvest they would release a vintage port. This declaration of a vintage in advance allowed time for the wine trade to send their orders, to arrange for delivery of the wine, and then to bottle it within the required time.

Sometimes, if there was not a lot of port vintaged, the shipper didn't bother to make a formal declaration; the wine was not required to be declared to be considered a true vintage port. Some of the vintages listed below are among these; although they are sometimes referred to as "undeclared vintages," they are true vintage ports.

Now that all port is bottled in Portugal, it is no longer

necessary to make the advance declaration to the trade. However, when a port shipper decides to bottle a vintage port he must send samples to the I.V.P. in advance for approval. In doing so, he in effect declares that vintage, though he may or may not make an announcement to the trade. In either case, the wine is a vintage port if it meets all the criteria of the Port Wine Institute.

The greatest share of the praise and fame of port wines goes to vintage port, but vintage port makes up only a small, very small, proportion of the production — somewhere between 2 and 7 percent. This small production is in increasingly strong demand from countries throughout the world. Traditionally the greatest share has been, and still is, shipped to England. But today the United States is becoming an important market also; though consumption is minuscule for the population as a whole, for wine drinkers it is rather respectable.

THE VINTAGES*

Early vintages considered classic: 1811, 1820, 1847, 1851, 1853, 1863, and 1868.

1870—One of the best vintages of the century. Declared by 19 houses.

1872—14 houses declared a vintage.

1873—17 houses declared.

1874—Martinez, Offley, and Tuke shipped.

1875—Very fine though early maturing wines. Declared by 18 houses.

1877—Only Ferreira shipped.

1878—Rivalled the 1870 vintage; it was the last pre-phylloxera vintage. 20 houses declared.

1880—5 houses shipped.

1881—21 shippers declared.

1884—A classic vintage. Declared by 22 houses.

1885—5 houses shipped.

1886—Martinez was the only house to ship.

1887—Declared by 23 houses. Recovery from phylloxera began.

1888—Offley was the only house to ship a vintage port.

1890—Declared by 22 houses.

1892—11 houses shipped.

1894—14 shippers declared.

1896—Some rate this vintage as a classic; others say it was only very fine, not quite first flight. In either case, it was a long-lived vintage. 24 houses declared.

*See appendix D for a list of shippers by vintage.

1897—A good year, but one when there was apparently a shortage of brandy. According to Michael Broadbent, Sandeman fortified with scotch whisky. Besides Sandeman, 8 other houses shipped.

1899—Dow and Warre shipped.

1900—Very fine quality though light and short-lived. 23 houses declared.

1901—Graham shipped.

1902—Offley shipped.

1904—Light wines; while good, not as highly regarded as '00. 25 houses declared a vintage.

1906—Tuke and Taylor shipped.

1908—A classic vintage. Some say it was the best of the century; others hold that '12 was better. 25 shippers declared.

1910—Only Offley shipped.

1911—Martinez, Rebello, and Sandeman shipped.

1912—A classic year. It is still debated whether '08 or '12 was better, though more authorities favor the '12. The wines were dark in color and rich in extract, with enormous concentration. 27 shippers declared a vintage.

1914—Borges alone shipped.

1917—A light year. Declared by 17 houses.

1919—7 houses shipped.

1920—A good though short-lived vintage. Declared by 22 houses.

1921—Offley and Rebello shipped.

1922—Declared by 20 houses.

1923—Hooper, Offley, and Noval shipped.

1924—Some say this was the best year since '12; others feel '20 was better. There were 22 declarations.

1925—Offley shipped.

1926—Kopke, Taylor's Quinta de Vargellas and Graham's Quinta Malvedos were shipped.

1927—A classic vintage. Some find it the equal of '08 and '12. Declared by 32 shippers.

1929—Offley shipped.

1930—Taylor shipped a small amount of Quinta de Vargellas.

1931—An outstanding vintage, but shipped by only 10 houses; because of the depression and the credit squeeze, large stocks of '27 remained still unsold. The Quinta do Noval Nacional is legendary. Besides Noval —Burmester, Dow, Hooper, Martinez, Niepoort,

Offley, Rebello, Sandeman's Quinta do Bragão and Warre were shipped.

1933—Only Noval shipped.

1934—Some favor this vintage over '35; for the most part the wines should be drunk up now. 14 houses declared.

1935—Some port drinkers prefer these wines over the '34s. The wines still retain their sweetness, but the alcohol is beginning to show. 23 houses declared.

1937—Shipped by Burmester, Ferreira, and Niepoort.

1938—Niepoort, Noval, and Taylor (Vargellas) shipped.

1939—Hooper was the only house to ship.

1940—Shipped by Burmester, Graham and Sandeman. The 1940 Sandeman we tasted in December 1980 was still good, though showing alcohol.

1941—Noval, Sociedade Constantino and Taylor shipped.

1942—Owing to war conditions, this vintage was the first to be bottled in Oporto. 14 houses shipped.

1943—Shipped by 6 houses.

1944—Delaforce, Dow, Feuerheerd and Sandeman shipped this vintage, which is considered the best since '35. Generally conceded to be excellent, it was overshadowed by '45.

1945—An exceptional and long-lived vintage, bottled in Oporto. For some it rivals '08 and '12. The wines are still drinking very well. 29 houses declared.

1946—Sandeman and Warre shipped.

1947—Surprisingly, these wines were lighter and shorter-lived than the '48s which followed. They should be drunk up now. The vintage was bottled in London and Oporto. 19 houses declared.

1948—A very fine year. The wines were deep in color, full rich, sweet and powerful. They are quite ready now; Fonseca is outstanding. 14 other houses also declared.

1950—Light, delicate wines that should be drunk now. There were 19 declarations.

1951—Only Feuerheerd shipped.

1952—7 houses shipped.

1953—Sandeman alone shipped.

1954—Shipped by 7 houses.

1955—Full-bodied, rich, well-balanced wines that should live long, but are enjoyable right now; easily the best vintage of the decade. Taylor's is first rate, as is Sandeman's. 31 declarations.

1957—Light wines, ready early. Shipped by 9 houses.

1958—Similar to '57, but fuller; they are very ready. 20 shippers declared.

1960—Light wines, many of which are ready now; they won't live as long as the '55s. 34 shippers declared.

1961—Graham's Quinta Malvedos, Guimaraens, and Taylor's Quinta de Vargellas were shipped.

1962—Shipped by 7 houses.

1963—A classic year: deeply colored, full-bodied, rich wines that won't be ready until 1988, at least. Unquestionably the best vintage since '45. Fonseca is, for us, the best of the vintage. Croft, Taylor and Warre are also splendid. 33 declarations.

1964—Guimaraens shipped; Graham and Taylor shipped their single *quinta* wines.

1965—Kopke shipped; Graham and Taylor again shipped their single *quinta* wines.

1966—Good though fast-maturing wines that will be ready before the '63s. 23 declarations.

1967—Similar though lighter than '66. Croft shipped their Quinta da Roêda for the first time in a hundred years. 11 other houses also shipped.

1968—Taylor shipped Quinta de Vargellas.

1969—Again, Taylor shipped their Quinta de Vargellas.

1970—Very fine, dark-colored, rich wines, though generally not as good as the '63s; Taylor was an exception, producing better wines in 1970. 42 shippers declared a vintage.

1972—Very light, fast-maturing wines that are ready now, or nearly so. Dow, Offley, and Noval shipped; Delaforce shipped their Quinta da Corte; Taylor, their Quinta de Vargellas. We've been enjoying our bottles of the Offley for the past few years; the wine, though, still has room for further improvement.

1974—Kopke, Pintos dos Santos, Delaforce's Quinta da Corte and Taylor's Quinta de Vargellas were shipped.

1975—Uneven wines that will mature sooner than the '70s. 29 houses declared a vintage.

1976—Taylor shipped a small amount of Quinta de Vargellas.

1977—Considered by some on the same level as '63; these wines are certainly the best since. More than 20 houses shipped. (We suspect our list is incomplete in this vintage.)

1978—Quinta do Noval, Delaforce's Quinta da Corte,

Cockburn's Quinta da Eira Velha, Croft's Quinta da Roêda, and Taylor's Quinta de Vargellas were shipped. The Vargellas is of very fine quality.

1979—Delaforce shipped some Quinta da Corte.

1980—It looks like a very good year. Thus far we know of 18 houses that have declared; indications point to a general declaration.

Average Number of Firms Exporting Port

Years	Number of Firms	Year	Number of Firms
1935—1939	104	1966	63
1940—1945	84	1967	64
1946—1950	82	1968	63
1951—1955	81	1969	63
1956—1960	78	1970	62
1961—1965	70	1971	60
		1972	58

THE SHIPPERS

We have tried to provide as complete a list as possible of the shippers and the vintages declared, or shipped. It is, however, a formidable task since no official list exists. Our list was compiled from a number of sources (all believed to be reliable) including various wine and auction lists in Oporto, New York, London, San Francisco, Los Angeles, Chicago, and Washington, D.C. We have attempted to find a second source to verify the vintages and shippers whenever possible.

We have given an assessment of the style of the vintage ports of those shippers whose wines we felt familiar enough with to go out on such a limb.

ADAMS
Vintages: 1935 1945 1947 1948 1950 1955 1960
1963 1966

BARROS ALMEIDA & CO.
Owns Quinta de S. Luiz (150 pipes).
Vintages: 1943 1945 1970 1975
They own Douro Wine Shippers, Feuerheerd and Kopke.

BORGES (Sociedade dos Vinhos Borges & Irmão)
Overall, we have found their wines disappointing and generally lacking in character.
Vintages: 1914 1922 1924 1963 1970

BURMESTER (J.W. Burmester)
Established 1730.
Generally unexciting though reliable wines.

41

Vintages: 1900   1904   1908   1912   1920   1922   1924
             1927   1931   1935   1937   1940   1943   1945
             1948   1954   1955   1958   1960   1963   1970
             1980

BUTLER NEPHEW
Established 1730.
Vintages: 1922   1924   1927   1934   1942   1945   1947
             1948   1955   1957   1958   1960   1970   1975
They are owned by González Byass.

CALEM (A.A. Calem & Filho Lda.)
Owns Quinta da Foz (130 pipes). They still use traditional
methods to produce their deeply colored, full-bodied, slow-
maturing, and long-lasting vintage ports.
Vintages: 1935   1947   1948   1955   1958   1960   1963
             1970   1975   1977   1980

COCKBURN Smithes & Ca. Lda.
Established 1815.
Owns Quinta do Tua. They are the second largest port
shipper; only Sandeman is larger. Their wines are quite
reliable. Cockburn Special Reserve and Directors Reserve
Tawny are good wines. Their vintage ports, which are light-
bodied, though firm, mature early and keep well.
Vintages: 1900   1904   1908   1912   1924   1927   1935
             1947   1950   1955   1960   1963   1967   1970
             1975   1978
They own Martinez, and they are owned by Harveys.

CROFT
Established in 1678 as Phayre & Bradley; they became Tilden,
Thompson and Croft in 1736.
Owns Quinta da Roêda (200 pipes); vintaged in 1868, 1967,
and 1978. Old Particular is a very fine tawny. Their vintage
wines tend to be full-bodied, slow-maturing, and long-lived.
They are among our favorite shippers.
Vintages: 1900   1904   1908   1912   1917   1920   1922
             1924   1927   1935   1942   1945   1950   1955
             1960   1963   1966   1967   1970   1975   1977
             1978   1980
They own Morgan Bros.; they are owned by International
Distillers & Vintners.

DALVA
Vintages: 1970   1977

They are owned by C. da Silva.

DELAFORCE Sons & Co.
Established 1868.
Light-bodied, fast-maturing vintage ports. In some years they ship their single vineyard Quinta da Corte (100-150 pipes). His Eminence's Choice Tawny is well regarded.

Vintages:
1900	1904	1908	1912	1917	1919	1920
1927	1935	1944	1945	1947	1950	1952
1955	1958	1960	1963	1966	1970	1972
1974	1975	1977	1978	1979	1980	

They are owned by International Distillers & Vintners.

DIEZ HERMANOS Lda.
Vintages: 1970 1975

DOURO WINE SHIPPERS & GROWERS ASSOCIATION, Lda.
Their vintage brand is Rocheda.
They are owned by Barros Almeida.

DOW
This is the brand name used by Silva & Cossens.
They produce a lighter-style vintage port—firm, dry, and long-lived; good quality. Boardroom Finest Old Tawny is also good.

Vintages:
1904	1908	1912	1917	1919	1920	1924
1927	1931	1934	1935	1944	1945	1947
1948	1950	1952	1954	1955	1957	1958
1960	1963	1966	1970	1972	1975	1977
1980						

They are part of the Symington group.

FEIST (H. & C.J. Feist)
Vintages: 1922 1970

FERREIRA (, A.A.)
Established 1761.
Owns Quinta do Valado (450-500 pipes) and Quinta do Vesúvio. Their 10-year-old Quinta do Porto and 20-year-old Duque de Brangança are highly regarded tawny ports. Their vintage ports are in the sweeter style.

Vintages:
1900	1904	1908	1912	1917	1920	1924
1927	1934	1935	1937	1945	1955	1960
1963	1966	1970	1975	1977	1980	

They own MacKenzie & Ca. and Tuke, Holdsworth, Hunt, Roope & Co.

FEUERHEERD Bros. & Ca. Lda.
Established 1815.
Vintages: 1900 1904 1908 1912 1917 1920 1924
1927 1942 1943 1944 1945 1951 1955
1957 1958 1960 1963 1966 1970
They are owned by Barros Almeida.

FONSECA
Established 1822.
Owns Quinta de Cruzeiro. They produce what we consider the best ruby port: Bin 27. Their vintage ports are full-bodied, slow-maturing, and long-lived. In our opinion they are only exceeded in quality by Taylor. In lesser years they ship their vintage wines as Guimaraens. Their 20-year-old Rich Tawny is quite good.
Vintages: 1900 1904 1908 1912 1920 1922 1924
1927 1934 1935 1945 1948 1955 1957
1960 1963 1966 1970 1975 1977 1980
They are part of the Guimaraens group.

GONZÁLEZ BYASS & CO.
Owns Quinta da Sabordella (85-90 pipes).
Vintages: 1900 1904 1908 1912 1917 1920 1942
1945 1955 1960 1963 1967 1970 1975
They own Butler Nephew.

GOULD CAMPBELL
Vintages: 1900 1904 1908 1912 1917 1920 1922
1924 1927 1934 1942 1955 1960 1963
1966 1970 1975 1977 1980
They are owned by Silva & Cossens who in turn are part of the Symington group.

GRAHAM (W. & J. Graham & Co.)
Established 1820.
Owns Quinta de Malvedos which they ship as a vintage wine in lesser years.
Their vintage ports are full-bodied, sweet, and rich; they keep well; good quality. Emperor, their 20-year-old tawny, is excellent. They are among our favorite shippers.
Vintages: 1900 1901 1904 1908 1912 1917 1920
1924 1926 1927 1935 1940 1942 1945
1948 1950 1954 1955 1960 1961 1962
1963 1964 1965 1966 1970 1975 1977
1980
They are part of the Symington group.

GREENS
Vintages: 1975

GUIMARAENS
Established 1822.
Label used for the lesser vintages of Fonseca, i.e., those vintages not generally declared. The wines, though lighter than Fonseca, can be quite good; they're just not up to the Fonseca standard.
Vintages: 1958 1961 1962 1964 1965 1968
Taylor, Fladgate & Yeatman and Fonseca are part of the Guimaraens group.

HOOPER (Companhia Geral da Agricultura das Vinhas do Alto Douro)
Uneven vintage wines. Generally of mediocre quality; light-bodied and fast-maturing. Among the lesser quality port shippers, in our opinion.
Vintages: 1923 1931 1935 1939 1943 1954 1958
1960 1962 1963 1967

HUNT, ROOPE & Ca.
Their vintage brand is Tuke, Holdsworth.

HUTCHESON & Ca. Lda.
Vintages: 1970

KINGSTON
Vintages: 1922 1924 1927

KOPKE (C.N. Kopke & Ca. Lda.)
Established 1638.
Reputedly the oldest port shipper. They sometimes bottle a single vineyard wine—Quinta de St. Luis.
Vintages: 1900 1904 1908 1912 1917 1919 1920
1922 1926 1927 1935 1945 1948 1950
1952 1955 1958 1960 1963 1965 1966
1970 1974 1975 1977
Owned by Barros Almeida.

MACKENZIE & Ca. Lda.
Vintages: 1900 1904 1908 1912 1919 1920 1922
1927 1935 1945 1947 1948 1950 1952
1954 1955 1957 1958 1960 1963 1966
1970
Owned by Ferreira.

Manoel D. Porças Junior Lda.
They make a fine 20-year-old tawny.
Vintages: 1960   1963   1967   1970   1975   1977

Martinez Gassiot & Co. Ltd.
Established 1790.
Light-bodied, fast-maturing vintage wines.
Vintages: 1900   1904   1908   1911   1912   1919   1922
 1927   1931   1934   1935   1945   1955   1958.
 1960   1963   1967   1970   1975
Owned by Cockburn, which is owned by Harveys.

Messias (Sociedade Agricola & Comercial Dos Vinhos Messias)
Owns Quinta do Cachão.
Vintages: 1970   1975   1977

Millipo
Vintages: 1970

Morgan Bros. Lda.
Established 1715.
Vintages: 1900   1904   1908   1912   1920   1922   1924
 1927   1942   1948   1950   1955   1960   1963
 1966   1970
Owned by Croft, which is owned by International Distillers & Vintners.

Niepoort & Ca. Lda.
Sweeter style vintage wines, sometimes undistinguished. Their old tawnies are highly regarded. They produce some fine *colheitas* and single vintage old tawnies (port of a vintage).
Vintages: 1912   1927   1931   1937   1938   1942   1945
 1955   1960   1963   1970   1975   1977   1980

Offley Boa Vista (Offley Forrester)
Established 1729.
Owns Quinta Boa Vista. Their vintage ports are of a sweeter style than most; they mature relatively soon. Their Baron de Forrester Very Old Tawny is a fine 20-year-old port.
Vintages: 1900   1902   1904   1908   1910   1912   1919
 1920   1921   1922   1923   1924   1925   1927
 1929   1931   1935   1942   1950   1954   1955
 1958   1960   1962   1963   1966   1967   1970
 1972   1975   1977   1980
They are part of the Seagrams-owned Sandeman group.

Osborne & Ca. Lda.
Vintages: 1970

PINTO DOS SANTOS (A.P. Santos & Ca. Ltd.)
Vintages: 1955 1957 1958 1960 1963 1966 1970
1974 1975

QUARLES HARRIS
Established 1680.
Vintages: 1927 1934 1945 1947 1950 1955 1958
1960 1963 1966 1970 1975 1977 1980

QUINTA DA CORTE
Owned by Delaforce.
Vintages: 1970 1972 1974 1975 1978 1979 1980

QUINTA DE MALVEDOS
Owned by Graham.
Vintages: 1926 1961 1962 1964 1965

QUINTA DO NOVAL
Elegant wines noted for balance and delicacy; though ready
early, they keep well. Their Nacional from ungrafted vines is,
reputedly, deeply colored, slow-maturing, and long-lived.
Their 20-year-old tawnies are very good, as are their L.B.V.s.
Vintages: 1900 1904 1908 1912 1917 1919 1920
1923 1927 1931 1933 1934 1938 1941
1942 1945 1947 1948 1950 1955 1958
1960 1962 1963 1966 1970 1972 1975
1978
Owned by Van Zeller.

QUINTA DA ROÊDA
Owned by Croft.
Rarely vintaged: 1868 1967 1978

QUINTA DE VARGELLAS
Owned by Taylor. Vintaged in lesser years, years not fine
enough to bear the Taylor flag. The wines, though, are still
quite good; they tend to be lighter than the Taylor port.
Vintages: 1917 1926 1930 1938 1947 1957 1958
1961 1964 1965 1967 1968 1969 1972
1974 1976 1978

RAMOS-PINTO (Adriano Ramos-Pinto)
Owns Quinta do Bom Retiro.
Vintages: 1924 1927 1945 1952 1955 1970 1977

REAL VINICOLA (Real Companhia Vinicola do Norte de
Portugal)
Owns Quinta do Sibio and Quinta das Carvalhas (650-670

pipes).
Vintages: 1945 1947 1950 1955 1960 1970

REBELLO VALENTE
The brand name used by Robertson Bros.
Light-bodied, sweeter-style, fast-maturing vintage ports.
They can be quite good.

Vintages:	1900	1904	1908	1911	1912	1917	1920
	1921	1922	1924	1927	1931	1934	1935
	1942	1945	1947	1955	1960	1963	1966
	1967	1970	1975	1977	1980		

They are part of the Sandeman group, which is owned by Seagrams.

ROBERTSON BROS.
Light-bodied vintage wines, usually sold as Rebello Valente.
They are part of the Seagrams-owned Sandeman group.

ROCHEDA
The vintage brand of the Douro Wine Shippers & Growers Associations, Lda.
Vintage: 1970
Owned by Barros Almeida.

ROYAL OPORTO Wine Co.

Vintages:	1934	1945	1958	1960	1962	1963	1967
	1970	1975	1977	1980			

ROZES
They are owned jointly by Moët-Hennesey and the Guimaraens group. They produce standard quality ruby and tawny ports.

SANDEMAN & Ca. Lda.
Established 1790.
The largest firm. Their ruby and tawny ports tend toward the sweeter style. As for their older tawnies, although they are somewhat too sweet for our taste, they can be quite good; their 20-year-old Imperial Tawny and 30-year-old Ambrosette are very good. They vintage often, consequently their vintage ports are uneven, but never bad. The best can be quite good indeed — light, elegant, and sweet. They mature relatively early, but will last.

Vintages:	1900	1904	1908	1911	1912	1917	1920
	1924	1927	1931	1934	1935	1940	1942
	1943	1944	1945	1946	1947	1948	1950
	1953	1954	1955	1957	1958	1960	1962
	1963	1966	1967	1970	1975	1977	1980

They are owned by Seagrams. Robertson Bros. and Offley Forrester are also part of this group.

SILVA & COSSENS
Established 1862.
Their vintage brand is Dow.
They are part of the Symington group.

SMITH WOODHOUSE & Ca. Lda.
Established 1784.
They make some fine tawnies: Old Lodge Finest Rare Tawny and His Majesty's Choice.

Vintages:						
1900	1904	1908	1912	1917	1920	1924
1927	1935	1945	1947	1948	1950	1955
1960	1963	1966	1970	1975	1977	1980

They are part of the Symington group.

SOCIEDADE CONSTANTINO (Sociedade dos Vinhos do Porto Constantino Lda.)

Vintages:						
1912	1927	1935	1941	1945	1947	1950
1958	1963	1966				

SOUSA (Vieira de Sousa & Ca.)
Vintages: 1970

SOUTHARD
Vintages: 1922   1927

STORMOUTH TAIT
Vintages: 1900   1904   1908   1912   1920   1922   1927

TAYLOR, Fladgate & Yeatman
Established 1692.
Originally known as Job Bearsley. In 1816 the name became Taylor; in 1837 Fladgate was added, and in 1844, with the addition of Yeatman, the firm arrived at its present name. It is known as Taylor Fladgate in the U.S., so as not to cause confusion with the Taylor Wine Co. of New York state, a producer of mediocre wines.

Taylor—of Oporto—produces first-rate old tawny ports; the best are the 20- and 30-year-old tawnies, labeled #20, and #30 in the U.S. to satisfy BATF regulations (#10 indicates a 10-year-old tawny). The Late-Bottled Vintage Reserve, their largest selling wine, is first-rate, and usually good value. Taylor owns Quinta de Vargellas, which they vintage in lesser, generally nondeclared, years when the wines, though good, are not up to the high standards necessary to wear the Taylor label.

Taylor's ports are the fullest-bodied and longest-lived of all vintage ports. They are made in the traditional manner. This results in rich and concentrated, first-rate wines. In our opinion, Taylor produces the greatest of all the vintage ports.

Vintages:	1900	1904	1906	1908	1912	1917	1920
	1922	1924	1926	1927	1930	1935	1938
	1941	1942	1945	1947	1948	1955	1957
	1958	1960	1961	1963	1964	1965	1966
	1967	1968	1969	1970	1972	1974	1975
	1976	1977	1978	1980			

They are part of the Guimaraens group.

TUKE, HOLDSWORTH, Hunt, Roope & Co.
Established 1735.
Light, fast-maturing vintage wines.

Vintages:	1900	1904	1906	1908	1912	1917	1920
	1922	1924	1927	1934	1935	1943	1945
	1947	1950	1955	1960	1963	1966	

Owned by Ferreira.

VAN ZELLER
The current owner of Quinta do Noval (220 pipes).

Vintages:	1904	1908	1912	1917	1922	1924	1927
	1935						

They own A.J. Da Silva & Co.

WARRE & Ca. Lda.
Established 1670.
Owns Quinta do Bonfim (85-90 pipes). Their Nimrod is a good tawny. Their late-bottled vintage and vintage-character wines are quite good. Their vintage ports, slow-maturing, full-bodied, long-lived wines, are among our favorites.

Vintages:	1900	1904	1908	1912	1917	1920	1922
	1924	1927	1931	1934	1945	1946	1947
	1948	1950	1952	1955	1958	1960	1963
	1966	1970	1975	1977	1980		

WIESE & KROHN Sucrs, Lda.
Governador Special is a good tawny.

Vintages:	1927	1934	1935	1947	1950	1952	1957
	1960	1967	1970				

CELLARING

The ideal temperature for the port cellar is 15-degrees C.

(60-degrees F.), but temperatures within a range of 4-degrees to 21-degrees C. (40-degrees to 70-degrees F.) are acceptable — even perhaps a bit higher if only for a short period. Change should be gradual. Drafts of air in the cellar are not good for maturing port; vibrations are also bad.

Port should be kept out of the light, which is why it is bottled in those very dark bottles — so dark, in fact, that it is difficult, sometimes downright impossible, to see through them when endeavoring to decant (as decant you must) the old bottles of port. They say in Oporto that the brown bottles, being darker, are better than the green ones. But from the point of view of the one doing the decanting, whoever came up with the idea of using those cursed *black* bottles should be sentenced to an eternity in the infernal regions decanting old bottles of crusty port with the aid of a weak and flickering candle!

Vintage port should be stored lying on its side with the white splash of paint (if present) on the top. This mark, which was dabbed on the upper end of the bottle when it was laid down by the shipper, indicates that the crust is settled on the opposite side. The white splash is seen less often on port bottles today; if it is lacking, the bottle should be laid down with the label up to keep the crust from shifting.

It is important for the best maturation of the wine that the crust not be disturbed. Many believe that a bottle of port should not be moved during its first seven years, while the crust is forming.

Ideally, once purchased and brought home, a vintage port should not be moved until it is time to take it from its bin for drinking. As English wine expert Harry Waugh explains the situation, "Vintage port dislikes being moved around and having its crust disturbed . . . . After frequent moves, it tends to lose some of its colour and certainly some of its grip."*

A light vintage, such as 1960, 1966, or 1975, needs about fifteen years of age to be at its peak. A first-rate year, like 1955, needs twenty; and a superb vintage like 1963 needs twenty-five or more to show at its best. Vintage port improves slowly for the first fifteen to twenty-five years, depending on the vintage; after thirty years of age, it slowly declines. However, it maintains its peak — actually more of a plateau — for some time. Some exceptionally fine vintages may still be superb drinking after a full sixty years.

Winetaster's Choice (New York: Quadrangle/The New York Times Book Co., 1973).

DECANTING VINTAGE PORT

Because of the heavy crust it throws in the bottle as it matures, vintage port must be decanted. At least one day before decanting, the bottle should be gently taken from its bin and stood upright. An older port, say twenty to twenty-five years old, would be better stood up for three days to give the heavy crust on the side of the bottle time to sink slowly to the bottom. This is assuming that the bottle has been lying on its side for at least six months. If the port is very old, say over twenty-five or thirty years old, it needs still longer to settle.

When you stand the bottle up, this is the time to chip off the sealing wax from around the lip of the bottle so that when you are ready to decant, the sediment won't be disturbed by any movement caused by the tapping.

Before attempting the delicate operation of opening and decanting the bottle, you must have your instruments at hand: a corkscrew, a cork extractor, a candle or flashlight, a funnel and a filter, a decanter, and a wine glass.

The corkscrew should be the type with a long thin spiral screw (this type, looked at from the point end, has a space in the center of the coil). The type with a solid screw (which is actually a gimlet) will bore a hole into an old cork, which may then crumble and fall in miserable bits into the wine.

The cork extractor may not be needed, but in case the cork or a large part of it falls in, you can draw it out with this clever little device.

Some say a candle is the best source of light for decanting port, but a bright flashlight, or torch, is quite reliable; it is not so traditional, but efficiency here is perhaps more important than atmosphere.

Next are your funnel and filter. A paper coffee filter will not do — it filters out too much, including some of the flavor of the port, and tends to give a taste of paper to the wine — a poor exchange indeed.

Some suggest that a sterile gauze pad makes a decent filter, but we find that the pad tends to float up in the funnel, allowing flakes of crust into the decanter. A muslin filter in a silver port funnel (the type with a strainer in it) is excellent. A regular funnel can be substituted, but it requires more care in the pouring.

A nylon stocking also makes a fine filter. It shouldn't be scented; the wife needn't be required to peel off the one she's wearing — assuming here that a man is doing the decanting.

Buy a new pair, or ask your mate to do it if you don't relish the prospect of the raised eyebrows and inquiries as to your size, preference in color, sheerness, and so forth. Before use, your port stockings, should be washed out with plain clear water, never with soap.

Instruments at hand, you may begin the operation. First, gently twist in the corkscrew. The cork must be pulled out slowly and carefully. If it falls in, or if a large piece of it does, your cork extractor comes into play. Be careful not to insert the extractor too far into the bottle, as this will stir up the heavy sediment.

Pour the port slowly and steadily into the funnel in the decanter. The slower the better — more wine will come out clear.

The candle flame or beam of the flashlight should be lined up just below the shoulder of the bottle. If you're able to see light through the bottle, pour until you see the sediment moving into the light. If you're decanting one of those black bottles, position the light to catch the wine just as it comes out, and pour until you see the first wisps of sediment. At that point, shift to the wine glass, and continue pouring carefully with the light sediment. You will probably be able to decant another drinkable ounce or two into the glass. The dregs can be used for cooking, in one of the less delicate dishes.

PORT TONGS

There is another method of opening an old bottle of port — simpler and quicker, neater too. It calls for an item not often seen anymore but still available at some shops selling wine accouterments. This is a pair of port tongs, a tool that looks quite similar to the lowly pair of pliers. Port tongs are a bit difficult to come by these days, but if you frequently indulge in vintage port, they are worth the search. They will enable you to open a bottle of vintage port, no matter how old, without breaking a not-too-solid cork. You don't even need to remove the sealing wax. In this method, you simply heat the pincers of the tongs on the stove while having a piece of cloth or a feather standing by in very cold water. Wipe off the neck of the bottle. When the tongs have become red hot, clamp them around the neck of the bottle just below the cork. Grip the bottle neck with the tongs for about half a minute, turning them *(without moving the bottle)* back and forth slowly for about a quarter turn. Then put aside the tongs and run the wet feather (or cloth) along the line marked by the tongs. The bottle top will break off cleanly with the old cork in it. Now simply proceed to decant the port as you would ordinarily.

The next question is: When to decant? The answer: The older the wine, the closer to serving. In Oporto, they recommend decanting a wine less than twenty years old at least five or six hours before dinner, or perhaps even a day ahead. If the wine is twenty-five or thirty years old, a few hours in the decanter won't hurt it. But the older the wine, the less time it should have in the decanter. For a really old port, decant just before serving. The air space in the decanter is much more than it was in the bottle, especially if there was a lot of sediment.

ON PASSING THE PORT

With the sun passing over the vineyards of the Douro on its evening descent, the port decanter is passed sympathetically in an arc from one diner to the diner on his left around the table in Oporto — and elsewhere in the (very) civilized world. Samuel Eliot Morison describes the solemn scene:

> In the old graces and ritual of the table such as observed in the common-rooms of Oxford and the combination-rooms of Cambridge, Port bears an important role. After dinner is concluded with a savoury, the table is cleared, the cloth is deftly removed, dishes of fruit, biscuits and nuts are laid out on the bare table where each one can help himself, and each diner is furnished with a Port glass, a Sherry glass, and a fruit plate, fork, and silver knife. A decanter of Port and one of Madeira or Sherry are placed by the Senior Fellow at the head of the table, and the servant retires, only to reappear if fresh supplies of wine are required. The Senior Fellow first fills the glass of the gentleman at his right hand, next serves himself, and then the gentleman at his left. The decanters are then slid around the polished table on padded coasters, clockwise or "with the sun," because Port will take offense at being circulated "against the sun," and go sour on you. When the head of the table judges that it is time, he starts the decanters around a second time, and sometimes there is a third round of a light sherry for "mouth-wash" after an unusually rich and fruity Vintage Port . . . . When everyone who wants it has had a second glass, the head of the table rings for coffee and cigarettes. Up to that point smoking is absolutely prohibited; and when I first knew Oxford, smoking was never allowed at

any time in the same room where Port was drunk. One had to adjourn to another room after dinner if one wished to smoke.*

Passing the port developed into a ritual fraught with tradition and rule. And one of the most inviolable rules is that the port must go round the table in a clockwise direction.

Some have explained this custom of always passing to the right hand of one's neighbor as being in the direction of the "lucky turn." The Romans and the Celts considered the turn with the right hand as the center of the pivot to be fortuitous, and their ceremonies reflected this belief. The ceremony of passing the port, has been traced back to this ancient belief.

Another explanation put forth, and perhaps a more reasonable though less engaging one, is that most people are right-handed, so if the decanter arrives from the right, it is easier to pick it up and pour a glass without spilling any.

However the tradition developed, it is still followed, and with a fine old wine like vintage port, which is no frivolous drink, but one that must be taken seriously to be truly appreciated, it seems fitting that the old traditions like the old vintage itself be respected.

THE FACTORY HOUSE

Other traditions are also followed in Oporto. The member firms of the British Association (founded in 1727) meet weekly for the Wednesday lunch. The members are Cockburn Smithes, Croft, Delaforce, Gonzalez Byass**, Graham, Guimaraens Vinhos SARL, Martinez Gassiot, Offley Forrester, Robertson Brothers, Sandeman, Silva and Cossens, Taylor Fladgate and Yeatman, and Warre and Co.

The lunch is at the Factory House. This solid old granite building was built in the 1780s (1786 to 1790, to be exact), to provide a suitable meeting place for the English Factory, as the association of English merchants, or factors, was called.

The members and their guests—men only, ladies are not invited to Wednesday lunch—may discuss business, and attempt to name the producer and the vintage of the port that is served. After two o'clock those who smoke may light up; no smoking is allowed earlier.

At formal dinners, the twin dining rooms are both used— one for the dinner, and one for the port. The port is not served in the dining room, where the aromas of the meal

*A Visit to the Port Wine Country, from "The International Wine & Food Society Journal," London, 1938, Issue #19.
**Gonzalez Byass has since resigned their membership.

linger; instead, after the meal, the members and guests adjourn to the second room to be seated around another long mahogany table with the same seating arrangement as was observed at dinner. Here they resume with the port.

ON NOT PASSING THE PORT

If the port decanter gets held up by conversation or inattention on its way round to your position, what can you do to restart it on its route? There are a few phrases you can make use of, designed for just such a crisis. You may, for example, suggest to the delayer, "Your passport is out of order. Please pass the port." Or, to get his attention, "Do you know the Bishop of Chester?" If "No," then "Well, neither do I! Please pass the port." To an affirmative response, "Well, now I'm in trouble—please pass the port."

THE "UNLUCKY TURN"

If you have ever committed the *gaffe* of passing the port decanter in the wrong direction, blush not but take heart at the following story (quite true, we've been assured).

When he was a young man in the Royal West African Frontier Force, Bruce Guimaraens of Fonseca one evening had the honor of being seated at the senior officers' table. He was the most junior officer present.

After the dinner, when the port decanter was being passed, something about it didn't look quite right to him—it seemed that the port was being passed around the wrong way.

At first he said nothing, but on the second turn around, he felt he'd better do something to set the matter right. Armed with the courage of youth and the credentials of his port family background, he respectfully suggested to the senior officer at the head of the table that it appeared to him the port was being passed in the wrong direction.

The officer was a bit taken aback at this bold statement and wanted to know who this very junior officer was to suggest that they were making such a *faux pas*.

"I'm from Oporto, sir. My family are in the business. Port shippers, sir, for some generations."

These seemed good enough qualifications to him; he thereupon ordered that the turn be reversed and the port be sent around the other way.

Guimaraens sat back down and relaxed. But then, watching the port as it was passed from man to man, the horrible thought struck him that he had erred. They were passing the port counterclockwise!

He didn't have the nerve to stand up and change the order again, so he merely sat silently and busied himself concentrating on the quality, rather than the direction, of the port being poured.

Some years later, Guimaraens ran into an old friend from his army days at the airport in Lisbon. In the exchange of pleasantries, he chanced to inquire how things were in Africa.

"Well," the friend replied, "you know, it's the oddest thing—at the officers' mess there they have the strangest practice. They pass the port counterclockwise! That must be the only place in the world where they pass the port decanter round backwards!"

When you come right down to it, it's not so much *how* you pass the decanter as *that* you pass it that counts.

SERVING PORT

Now that you've filled your glass and passed the decanter, in you know which direction, with what do you accompany the port?

Some drink port—white, ruby, or young tawny—as an aperitif. It's done, but not by us. We find port too high in alcohol and too sweet to make a good aperitif.

Ruby port and the young tawnies can be enjoyed by themselves after a meal or with fruit, cheese, or nuts. Melon, fruit salad, and dried fruits, especially dried figs and apricots, go well with young tawny or ruby port. Late-bottled vintage port also can be served with any of these.

The old tawny ports are often served lightly chilled; the port shippers drink them cool. In fact, we were offered ice for our old tawny at the Taylor lodge in Pinhão, and told that one of the directors puts ice in his tawny in the summer. The shippers like to accompany their old tawnies with nuts, especially new walnuts or almonds, and we wholeheartedly agree. These Ports are excellent with a dish of almonds—particularly the marvelous big butter-baked almonds of the Upper Douro as served at Quinta de Vargellas.

Old tawny port also goes well with blue cheese, especially Stilton, and with the cheddar-type cheeses. Port and Cheshire after dinner is a nineteenth-century classic.

Vintage port is a lovely way to finish a meal. For us the

only real substitute for a fine old vintage port after dinner is a fine old vintage malmsey. But we'd more often choose the port.

NEW-WORLD PORTS — AMERICAN

There are some good port-style wines produced in the U.S.A. Generally these wines contain 18-20 percent alcohol and 5-10 percent residual sugar. Even the best of them lack the intensity of flavor and the character of true — Portuguese — port (now called Porto in the U.S.A., to distinguish it from its American imitators).

The best American port-style wine that we've tasted is the vintage port produced by **J.W. Morris** in California. They first produced this wine in 1975, from a blend of 3 grape varieties, in about equal proportions: Zinfandel, Petite Sirah and Ruby Cabernet, grown in Sonoma County.

Their 1976 and 1977 vintage ports were produced from about the same combination of Sonoma-grown grapes. In 1978 they used only grapes grown on the Black Mountain Ranch in the Alexander Valley region of Sonoma.

In that vintage, 1978, they also produced an Early Bottled Vintage Port. This wine, which was given less barrel age, was also made from a slightly different blend of grapes — Zinfandel, Ruby Cabernet, Carignane, and Pinot Noir.

It is interesting to note that the port shippers that we spoke to who had tasted the J.W. Morris Vintage Port were also impressed with its quality (though less so, one must admit, with its name).

J.W. Morris also produces a Founders' Ruby Port from a blend of Sonoma-grown Carignane and Zinfandel with a small amount of Barbera and Pinot Noir. This wine, unlike a true ruby port, is quite rough and tannic when released; for our taste, it needs a few years in bottle to smooth out and knit together. "Crusted Port" would be a more descriptive name; and it does, indeed, with a few years in bottle, form a crust.

Quady, of Madera, California, also produces a good port-style wine. Their first vintage port was produced, as at J.W. Morris, in 1975. This wine and their 1976 Vintage were made from 100 percent Amador County grown Zinfandel grapes.

In 1977 they made 2 vintage ports, both from Zinfandel grapes, but from different locations — one from Rancho Tierra Rejada in the Paso Robles area of California's central coast, the second from the Shenandoah Valley of Amador.

There were 2 different lots of the 1978 Quady Vintage Port,

58

both from Amador-grown Zinfandel grapes.

Quady's 1979 Vintage Port, made from Zinfandel grapes from the School Road Vineyard in the Shenandoah Valley, is their best effort to date. It has a deep purplish color and a rich blackberry-like aroma; while less intense than a true port, it is nevertheless quite a rich wine.

Unlike the port shippers, who age their vintage ports from a minimum of nearly two years to a maximum of almost three years in cask, Quady barrel-ages their vintage port for twelve to fifteen months, in small (60-gallon) barrels.

In 1980 Quady had a vineyard planted in Amador county with a selection of grape varieties which are grown in the Douro: Alvarelhão, Bastardo, Mourisco, Tinta Amarela, Tinto Cão, and Touriga. It will be interesting to see the results when they produce their first wine from these varieties in 1983.

The first producer to make a serious attempt to produce a quality port-style wine in California, and probably in the whole country, was **Ficklin Vineyards.** In the 1940's they planted the Portuguese varieties Alvarelhão, Tinta Cão, Tinta Madeira, and Touriga in their Madera County vineyards, and bottled their first Ficklin Port in 1948.

Ficklin's Tinta Port, in the ruby port style, is made from a blend of vintages. It can be agreeable, rarely more, but it is one of the better wines of its type produced in the U.S.A. From time to time they also produce a vintage port, which we have not as yet tasted, so can offer no evaluation.

The **Woodbury Winery** of San Rafael has been producing California vintage port since 1975. (It was apparently a charmed year for California port producers; quite a few of them having offered their first vintage port from that year. It wasn't, though, a special vintage for the wines — a good year, but nothing exceptional.)

Their vintage port is made from a blend of north coast county grapes. The vintage ports from 1975 through 1978 were from a blend — about one-third each — of Zinfandel, which they chose for its fruit and tannin; Petite Sirah, for color; and Cabernet Sauvignon, for tannin and elegance. The 1979 Alexander Valley Vintage Port "Old Vines" was produced from 40 percent Petite Sirah, 30 percent Cabernet Sauvignon, 20 percent Zinfandel, and 10 percent Petite Sirah.

From 1975 to 1978 Woodbury was using a mixture of low and high proof alcohol and a blend of pot and column still brandies for fortification. In the 1979 vintage they used only pot distilled brandy, usually finer than the brandy obtained from a column still; it should have produced a smoother wine. We find their wines to be, on the whole, hot and alcoholic.

The vintage port is aged for about twenty-two months in small American oak barrels. It is bottled at 19 percent alcohol and 9 percent residual sugar.

They also make a Partners' Reserve Ruby. The few that we've tasted have been rough and unbalanced.

The Christian Brothers offers 2 California vintage ports: a 1969 Tinta Cream Port and a 1973 Vintage Port. The Tinta Cream, made from Tinta Madeira grapes, is—though interesting on its own right—not very port-like. The 1973 Vintage Port is a pleasant dessert wine with an aroma and flavor of vanilla, cream, and raisins.

Berkeley Wine Cellars (formerly Wine & the People) have produced, since 1975, a Zinfandel Port. The 1978 was from grapes from Kelley Creek in the Dry Creek Valley of Sonoma County. It had 18 percent alcohol, and was light in body for a port-type wine.

Shenandoah Vineyards produces a Zinfandel Port from Amador County grapes. It has 18 percent alcohol and is agreeable, though not very port-like.

Paul Masson produces an agreeable Rare Souzão Port (in an unusual brown heart-shaped bottle) at a reasonable price. As pleasant as this can be, it is rather unlike a true port.

As far as most other American ports go, we'd just as soon they went, quietly. None that we know of quite makes it by the standards of true port (and since they use the name, they must inevitably be judged accordingly).

Of the so-called ports produced from native American grapes by the Taylor Wine Co., Great Western, and the other eastern wineries, it must be said that it is a rather misguided attempt. We find them as objectionable as their so-called sherries, tasting more like fortified grape juice than anything else. Even their prices are no virtue.

AUSTRALIAN PORT-STYLE WINES

Port-style wines are also produced in South Africa, Cyprus, New Zealand, and Australia. Overall, the ones from Australia are the best of these.

Most Australian wineries that produce fortified wines produce port. They make the traditional styles—white, ruby, tawny, and vintage port—as well as some of their own styles, including para port, solera port, and liqueur port. Australian ports are made from a wide range of grapes. Shiraz is perhaps the most commonly used. Some producers use Cabernet Sauvignon.

Australian ruby port, often bottled after one to two years in wood, sometimes requires further bottle age to be really ready to drink, unlike the ruby ports of Portugal. Some Australian tawny ports are aged in wood for up to forty years or more. These are the liqueur tawnies. Seppelt's Para Liqueur Port is the most highly regarded of this type. It is also the most sought-after and expensive Australian port, a wine highly regarded for its richness and concentration. It is the product of a single year. Orlando's also produces a tawny port that is a single-vintage wine.

Other highly regarded Australian tawnies include:
All Saints' 1938 Tawny Port (we've heard that it is still in cask!)
Basedow's Very Old Tawny Port
Bleasdale Pioneer Port
Hamilton's V.O. Invalid Port (For medicinal purposes?
 Or, not valid?)
Hardy's Coronet Port
Hardy's Show Port
Hoffman's North Para, Very Old Liqueur Tawny Port
 (aged for over forty years in small oak barrels)
Houghton Centenary Port
Houghton Liqueur Port
Lindeman's Macquarie Port
Lindeman's Reserve Tawny Port
Mildara Reserve Bin Port
Orlando's Five-Generations Tawny Port
Penfold's Grandfather Port
Seppelt's Para Port (not to be confused with their
 Para Liqueur Port)
Yalumba Galway Pipe Port

Over two dozen producers make Australian vintage port, nearly the same number as make true vintage port in Portugal. Few of these are comparable to true vintage port, but the best can be quite good.

Among the well thought of Australian vintage ports:

All Saints'	*Gracerray	Renmano
Angove	Grassi	Reynella
Basedow's	Hamilton	Saltram
*Berri	Johnston's Pirramimma	*Seppelt's

Buring's	Karrawirra	Sevenhill Cellars
Campbell's	*Lindeman's	Stanley Leasingham
Chambers	*Lubiana	Stonyfell Metala
Conteville	*Morris	Waikerie Cooperative
D'Arenberg	Olive Farm	Waldeck
*Genders	Quelltaler	Westfield

* = more highly regarded by Australian wine authorities

NO SUBSTITUTE

As good as some of the port-style wines can be, there is no substitute for a true vintage port, especially one from Taylor, Fonseca, Warre, Croft, Graham, or Dow (to name just a few favorites). These fine old vintage ports are the greatest of all ports, with the possible exception of some superb old tawnies. And port in general is the greatest and most reliable of all the fortified wines.

PORT GLOSSARY

Colheita (cohl-HEH-tah). Another name for "port of (year)".

Crusted Port. A port blended from two or three different years that is bottled before it loses all its sediment — and color — in cask. Consequently, it throws a crust in the bottle. No longer produced.

Garrafeira (gah-rah-FEH-rah). A dated port of a single year that has been aged long enough in wood to become tawny in color, and is then aged further in bottle.

L.B.V. An abbreviation for late-bottled vintage port.

Late-Bottled Vintage. Port of a single vintage that is aged from four to six years in cask. It is ruby in color and ready to drink when sold.

Port of (year). A wood port of a single vintage; this is a tawny port, aged in wood, not in bottle.

Port of Vintage (year). Similar to "port of (year)," but not necessarily all from the single vintage stated; it is sometimes refreshed with younger wines. This type is no longer allowed.

Port with an Indication of Age. A tawny port with an average age (specified on the label) of ten, twenty, thirty, or more than forty years.

Quinta (KEEN-tah). Wine estate.

Reserve. Often used to indicate a special wine of a particular shipper; the term has no official meaning.

Ruby Port. A young wood port that is ruby in color.

Tawny Port. There are two types of tawny port. Both are wood ports, tawny in color. One type is aged in wood long enough to become tawny. The other — cheaper — type is a blend of ruby and white port.

Tipo Vintage (TEE-poh). Same as vintage-character port.

Vintage Character. Port from a blend of two or three years, similar in character to late-bottled vintage port.

Vintage Port. The port of a single vintage, declared by a shipper within two years of the harvest and bottled shortly afterward. Vintage port requires fifteen to twenty-five years of bottle age to be truly ready for drinking and meditation.

Vintage Style. Same as vintage-character port.

White Port. A full-bodied port, ranging from dry to medium sweet, made from white grapes.

II

Madeira

The Madeira archipelago, about 560 kilometers (350 miles) off the coast of Morocco, is a group of islands created in the distant past by volcanic eruption. Madeira is the main island (730 square kilometers/281 square miles); Porto Santo, the second (41 square kilometers/16 square miles). They are joined by two groups of much smaller, uninhabited islands: the Ilhas Desertas (Empty Isles) a few miles to the south, and the Selvagens (Wild Isles) near the Canary Islands.

Madeira has been called "The Pearl of the Atlantic." Lying in the Gulf Stream of the Atlantic, Madeira enjoys a mild climate year round. The mean temperature, winter to summer, is in the 15- to 21-degree C. (60- to 70-degree F.) range. These islands are believed to be the Enchanted Isles of the ancients. Some think they are the Fortunate Islands referred to by Pliny. There is even speculation that Madeira, like many other places, may have inspired the legend of Atlantis.

The beautiful island of Madeira is a garden of subtropical vegetation. Cacti and a profusion of green plants seem to spill over the hills and down into the gorges. Outside of the space taken up by houses and roads, there hardly seems to be a square foot of flat land; the sides of the often very steep hills ripple with terraces. And there is barely a parcel of land left uncultivated on the island. Even the white and pastel painted houses themselves often have plants and flowers on the roofs — those that are flat — and even vines.

The center ridge of the island is a chain of mountains nearly 1,220 meters (4,000 feet) in altitude — the highest point, Pico Ruivo, rising above 1,830 meters (6,000 feet) — which extends from Ponta de S. Lourenço in the east to Ponta do Tristão (Tristan Point) in the northwest.

The terrain on Madeira shifts dramatically from high peaks to deep gorges; red stone precipices drop off abruptly to the turquoise sea below. In the estuaries are picturesque fishing villages with fleets of gaily painted fishing boats pulled up on the rocky beaches. The roads, which twist and wind over the hills and valleys of the island, here and there pass colorfully painted (blue, purple, red) thatched-roof houses where bunches of bananas hang over the doorways. The narrow streets in the towns pass through walls of black volcanic rock, and now and then a door, to a cave or garage perhaps, is seen in the rock.

The island has three zones of vegetation. From sea level to 305 meters (1,000 feet), sugarcane and banana plants are widely cultivated. Here also are vegetables and barbary figs. Higher up, to 760 meters (2,500 feet), are the vineyards, as well as cereal crops (maize, wheat, and oats) and fruit including oranges, pears, plums, apples, mangos, avocados, passion fruit, and custard apples. Above these are evergreen trees, heather, mimosa, acacias, and some pasture land.

Madeira wasn't always so lush in subtropical vegetation and crops. The first explorers, who discovered the island in 1419, gave it the name *Ilha da Madeira,* Wooded Island, since at that time it was covered with a dense forest.

According to legend, in 1344 an English ship went down in a storm at the opening of a bay on the eastern tip of the island. On board the ship were a young couple, Robert Machim and Ana d'Arfet, running away to be married against their parents' wishes. The lovers survived the shipwreck but died a few days later and were buried on the island. Survivors of the wreck captured by Moroccan pirates from a makeshift raft, told their story, which came to the ears of the Portuguese king who sent out an expedition to chart the islands.

According to history, João Gonçalves Zarco ("the Crosseyed"), and Tristão Vaz Teixeira, leaders of an expedition dispatched by the Infante Dom Henriques — called Prince

Henry the Navigator—in 1419, landed first on the island of Porto Santo, then sailed on to Madeira, pulling into the bay now called Machico on its eastern tip. There they are supposed to have found the lovers' grave, beneath a cedar tree; it is said that Machico Bay was named for Robert Machim. Upon returning to Portugal, they reported their discovery to the prince, who charged them with returning the following year to colonize the island.

To open up the dense forest for building and cultivation of crops, a rather drastic method was employed. The primeval forest was set ablaze with a fire said to have raged for seven years. Some have suggested that this fire was perhaps not so intentional as accidental. In any case, it destroyed virtually all of the trees on the island. In a few remote areas spared from the fire's destruction, there are trees 1,000 years old and older still standing—sesame, vinhâtico, tree laurels, cedars, and a few others.

The volcanic soil on Madeira was fertile and rich, and the thick layer of wood ash over the humus of leaves and mosses added to its richness. Following the great fire, the island was planted with agricultural crops and every imaginable type of exotic plant. Madeira today is abloom with hydrangea, geranium, hibiscus, bird of paradise, orchid, bougainvillaea, fuschia, euphorbia, and flowering trees including mimosa, magnolia, red and pink sumaumâ, and purple jacaranda. Grapes are the major crop, the vineyards covering 1,820 hectares (4,500 acres). Next is sugar cane, at 1,215 hectares (3,000 acres); then bananas, nearly 607 hectares (1,500 acres).

The pioneers painstakingly built, without the aid of draft animals, thousands upon thousands of terraces, or *poios,* into the steep hillsides to plant their crops. Even today the only work animals the visitor will see on Madeira are the half dozen or so white and spotted oxen which, led by men in white pajamas and straw hats, pull the traditional canopied sledges over the black lava cobblestones of Funchal on greased runners, slowing down traffic in the busy capital city in a most picturesque and—for the passengers—charmingly nostalgic way. These patient beasts occasionally make a startling picture lying spreadeagled on the Avenida do Mar promenade taking a siesta in the heat of the noonday sun.

Prince Henry the Navigator is credited with introducing the vine to Madeira early in the fifteenth century. This was the Malvasia variety which produced the famous malmsey wine of the island of Crete. The first vines were planted on Madeira's southern coast. Later other grape varieties were introduced. By 1455 the vineyards on Madeira were flourishing; wine is known to have been exported by 1460. For centuries Madeira itself was the world's largest vineyard.

The story is told that at the wedding of Christopher Columbus to Isabela Moniz, daughter of the administrator of Porto Santo, madeira was the wine poured at the nuptial banquet. Decanters of madeira wine have graced the tables of kings and queens; madeira is said to have been a favorite wine at the sophisticated court of François I of France.

Lesser personages have also enjoyed madeira. In Shakespeare's *Henry IV,* Sir John Falstaff is accused by Poins of having displayed an unconscionable weakness for it.

> . . . What says Sir John Sack and Sugar? Jack! how agrees the devil and thee about thy soul, that thou soldest him on Good-Friday last for a cup of Madeira and a cold capon's leg?

According to not particularly reliable sources, during the second half of the fifteenth century, George, Duke of Clarence, in the Tower of London on a charge of treason against his brother King Edward IV, was given a choice of methods for his own despatch and chose to die as he had lived—drowned in a butt of malmsey.

From 1580 to 1640, while Madeira, as part of Portugal, was under Spanish domination, trade in madeira wines suffered a setback. Spain had its own wines and was not eager for the competition madeira might offer. A bit later, however, things turned around. The treaty between England and Portugal signed in 1654 was advantageous for the wine trade on Madeira, encouraging by low tariffs the import of Portuguese wine into England.

The marriage of Catherine of Bragança to Charles II of England brought Madeira, as part of her dowry, under British control. This situation encouraged English merchants to establish firms on Madeira. In the decades that followed, British firms became the largest shippers of madeira on the island.

In 1665, Charles II prohibited the shipping of goods or commodities produced in Europe to British possessions abroad unless they were sent via British ports and in British ships. But it wasn't long before some enterprising fellow found a loophole in the law. As Madeira and the Azores are located some distance from the continent of Europe—

indeed, not far off the coast of Africa—products from these islands were therefore not covered under the decree and could be shipped directly.

Wine from Madeira began to be shipped directly to the colonies, and America became an important market. The colonists not only enjoyed the wine for its own virtues, but also because it represented a form of defiance toward the Crown. Trade in madeira wine was prospering, and English shippers on Madeira encouraged the peasants to plant vines in place of sugarcane.

Madeira became the "Wine of the New World," more in demand in that hemisphere than in its own. Shipping firms in Boston, New York, Philadelphia, Baltimore, Savannah, Charleston, and New Orleans were in hot competition in the trade in madeira wine.

During the late eighteenth and early nineteenth centuries madeira wines often were labeled with the vintage and the name of the shipping family or the ship that had carried the pipes of wine to port. The "Rapid 1817" and the "All Saints 1791" are two mentioned by Rupert Croft-Cooke in his book, *Madeira.*

The popularity of madeira wines reached its height in the eighteenth and nineteenth centuries. The sweet and velvety malmsey was especially appreciated. But it was also in small supply; in 1794 only 100 pipes of malmsey were produced which were in great demand.

It has been said that at the signing of the American Declaration of Independence, the deed was sealed with a glass of madeira. Perhaps so—madeira was reputedly a favorite of George Washington.

Following the American Revolution, British soldiers returning home from the war brought the taste for madeira with them. Some of the loyal British subjects who returned before the war's conclusion no doubt shared this appreciation. Drinking habits in England felt the change, as madeira's popularity in that country rose. This growing interest in madeira undoubtedly received a nice boost when it became known that the trend setting Prince Regent enjoyed the wine of Madeira, preferring it for a time above all others.

Madeira was not a particularly popular wine in France, a country that tends to favor its own wines, but the fashion of taking a glass of madeira with the soup course was said to have been introduced there in the late eighteenth century by Prince Tallyrand. It did become an important part of the

French *haute cuisine,* as the most important ingredient in the famous *Sauce Madère.*

During the Napoleonic Wars, shipments to England of French wine were cut off; exports from Spain and Portugal were also interrupted. In 1801 British troops were stationed on Madeira. In that same year exports of madeira wine to England doubled. Shipments continued to increase for some years, then maintained a plateau. Madeira was second only to port as the most popular wine among the upper classes in the early Victorian age. This was the golden age for madeira wine.

In 1827 Madeira's wine trade with England began a gradual but steady decline. During the 1830's the reputation of madeira wine was hurt by cheap imitations coming out of the Midi in southern France. Wine masquerading as madeira also was being manufactured in Spain. Blandy's won a judgment in a French court in 1898 for the seizure of 500 pipes of fraudulent Spanish madeira.

Still worse things were in store for madeira wine. In 1852 a vine disease—*Oïdium* spread through many European vineyards. On Madeira this fungus was particularly destructive, spreading powdery mildew over the leaves and shriveling the berries throughout the island's vineyards. The harvest was ruined, and for the next eight years there was no madeira wine exported from the island.

Firms went out of business, lacking wine to ship. Thomas Leacock, of the firm that still bears his name, was in the forefront of the fight against the disease. Leacock was one of the early madeira shippers, having arrived in 1741; by 1760 he had established his own trading firm.

In the end it was found that the only cure was to spray the vines with sulphur, a practice that is still being carried out, as a prevention, in the vineyards to this day. By 1873 production of madeira had recovered to about one-third its former output. In that year the worst disaster ever to strike the vineyards of Europe, in fact, of the world—*Phylloxera vastatrix*—was discovered on Madeira.

Phylloxera vastatrix (leaf waster) is an insect that first attacks the leaves, then eats away at the roots of the European *(Vitis vinifera)* vine. This vine louse is native to the eastern vineyards of North America and was inadvertently brought to Europe on cuttings of American vines. It spread rapidly from vineyard to vineyard, leaving growers and shippers alike in despair.

Phylloxera hit hard on Madeira. Leacock again worked desperately to find a means to revive the failing vineyards, but he died in 1883 before a solution was found. The insect could not be controlled. The only way that has ever been found to circumvent its destruction is to graft the vines onto the resistant rootstock of Native American vines.

The American vines will produce grapes that can be made into wine, and this is done — chiefly in New York State — but the wine is of inferior quality. Some wine was made in Madeira from the American vines before grafting was found to be the only solution to phylloxera, but the wine was so poor that production was stopped after the initial experiments. The old vineyards were all laboriously replanted with grafted madeira vines.

Many more madeira firms went out of business during the phylloxera plague. Finally, only three English firms (from a high of seventy-one at the turn of the century) remained — Leacock, Blandy's, and Cossart Gordon.

Charles Blandy first came to Madeira in 1807 as quartermaster in the British garrison stationed on the island during the Napoleonic Wars. He established Blandy's Madeira Ltd. in 1811. The firm of Cossart, Gordon and Co. was established in 1745.

1786-1790 — 65 English firms
1801-1804 — 71 English firms
1805-1809 — 70 English firms
1810-1811 — 57 shippers, including 2 Portuguese firms
1842   — 45 shippers, including 3 Portuguese firms

The bankrupt shippers dumped their stocks of old madeira onto the market. Fortunately much of this supply of irreplaceable old wines was bought up by Blandy who put it away in his cellars. Some of the new wines being produced were improved by additions of the fine old pre-phylloxera vintages. It was at this time that the *solera* system of fractional blending was started on Madeira, by Charles Blandy, using the pre-phylloxera wines. Before this time madeira had been a vintage wine.

Madeira never regained its former glory. By the time it had recovered from the double blights of *Oïdium* and phylloxera fashions in winedrinking had changed. The newer generations forgot what madeira was like or had never tasted it. Other fortified wines, such as port and sherry, had taken its place.

Madeira had been a popular wine at the British officers' messes in India. And the sweeter types were much appreciated in Imperial Russia. With the loss of the Indian and Russian markets, some of the madeira vineyards were replanted with other crops, particularly bananas and sugarcane.

England and the United States are no longer madeira's best markets. Today France is the main importer of madeira, generally in cask and not the finer wines; this madeira is used mostly in cooking. Germany is second in consumption. It wasn't until World War I that madeira wine regained some of its former popularity in Great Britain. In the U.S.A. it has never really done so.

The very name madeira brings to mind, for many who've never drunk it (or have only nipped at the cooking madeira), a picture of little old ladies sipping sweet madeira from cut-crystal glasses and the phrase, "Have some madeira, m'dear." This distinctive wine, though, is certainly no "ladies' wine" — a term off-putting enough to make women turn thumbs down on any wine so described.

THE GRAPES

Four grape varieties on Madeira are considered noble varieties, capable of producing the finest wines. They are, in ascending order of sweetness: Sercial, Verdelho, Boal or Bual, and Malmsey.

Malmsey, which is the earliest known variety planted on Madeira, was brought from the island of Crete where it is called Malvasia. Boal (in Portuguese) or Bual (in English) is thought to have been originally brought to Madeira from Burgundy, Verdelho may be the Verdia of Italy or perhaps the Pedro Ximénez of Spain. Some have suggested that Sercial is the Riesling grape of Germany.

Following the ravages of *Oïdium* and phylloxera, some of the old grape varieties were not replanted. Terrantez was one of these. This once highly esteemed variety was almost totally wiped out by phylloxera; only a few vines survived. It was apparently one of the noble varieties, according to the descriptions by those who tasted it. Raymond Postgate writes in *Portuguese Wine:* "One disappearance was a real loss; it was that of the Terrantez grape. Those who had tasted some of the ancient Terrantez bottles will remember its curious steely taste with great affection." H. Warner Allen, in *A History of Wine,* describes an old Terrantez as having "an ozone-like finish so clean and dry as to be almost bitter, the perfect almond taste."

Terrantez is a red variety, as are Bastardo and Tinta. There are still supposed to be a few bottles of madeira left, very rare and old, made from these varieties. The Listrão and Maroto are two other red grapes which were not replanted.

Very little Moscatel and Babosa are now left. They are white grapes, as are the present four noble varieties: Sercial, Verdelho, Bual, and Malmsey.

In fact, there are far fewer vines of the four noble varieties than there used to be. These grapes are suffering from a viral disease which has caused a serious decrease in production. The vines live for only five to ten years — which means at most only five years of grape production — before the disease kills them.

The problem was first discovered twenty to thirty years ago, and is under study. Scientists have reportedly found ways to improve the vines to make them more resistant and better-yielding. Sercial is the most resistant. Plantings of Malmsey and Boal are also now increasing.

But for some years these four have had to be replaced in the nonvintage wines by a large proportion of lesser varieties. The vintage wines are still made with the noble varieties, but in the other wines, at least 90 percent is from lesser grapes, usually the Tinta Negra Mole, and no more than 10 percent is from the noble variety named on the label.

Some journalists have suggested that there are many plantings of inferior native American varieties and French-American hybrids on Madeira. We have not been able to ascertain whether or not this is true; and, if so, if the grapes are used in madeira.

Nowadays the name Sercial on other than a vintage wine means it is in the Sercial style; in other words, dry. Verdelho means in the style of that grape, semi-sweet; Bual, sweet; and Malmsey, richly sweet.

Tinta Negra Mole or Negra Mole, a high-yielding variety, is the most widely planted grape. It is related to the wine that produced the Tinta Madeira. Some have suggested that it is the Pinot Noir, but in Madeira they say it is a native Portuguese grape. The Complexa and Triunfo varieties are also used to fill in for the scarce noble varieties. Plantings of these two are on the increase.

THE VINEYARDS

The vines for madeira wine are trained on sloping *latadas* (pergolas) 3 to 6 feet high on the terraces and steep sides of the hills. In some places these pergolas are so high — up to 10 feet — that the workers must stand on step-ladders to prune and harvest the vines.

In the fertile soil beneath the vines vegetables are planted. The soil in the vineyards is made up of three basic types: *marsapes* soil, of a clayey consistency; *saibro* soil, broken down from red volcanic rock; and *pedra molle,* from yellow volcanic rock. Situated as they are, on steep slopes and narrow terraced shelves, the vineyards cannot be worked with a plow. The men here must use hand tools, working the land with the *enchada,* a type of hoe.

The climate is quite dry, especially on the southern side of the island, and water is brought to the vineyards by a system of aqueducts, or *levadas.* These narrow stone and cement channels carry water down from the mountains, across bridges spanning deep gorges, and through tunnels in the rock to irrigate the island's crops.

The best vineyards are on the southern side of the island, where most of the noble grape varieties are planted. This side has the best climate for the vine, being sunny and dry and sheltered by the mountains from the cold northerly and northeasterly winds. The vineyards on the colder northern coast are swept by the humid, salty winds from the sea. The southern vineyards also get less rain. The rains fall intermittently from November to February, sometimes into March, and occasionally as late as May. The rest of the year is sunny; the summer is very dry. The yearly rainfall in the capital of Funchal on the southern coast is only 12 to 16 inches, while the rest of the island averages 42 to 45 inches.

Regional names appear infrequently on madeira labels, but you might see a bottle labeled for the region where the grapes were grown. Two areas on the southern coast — Câmara de Lobos, or Cama de Lobos, and Campanário — are considered among the best vineyard areas on Madeira. It's said that there are still some old bottles of malmsey bearing these names. At one time the Jesuits owned the finest vineyard on the island for Malmsey; it was at Câmara de Lobos. Up the mountain, above Câmara de Lobos, at an elevation of about 328 meters (1,000 feet) is the village of Estreito de Câmara de Lobos. The vineyards there reputedly produce the finest Sercial grapes on

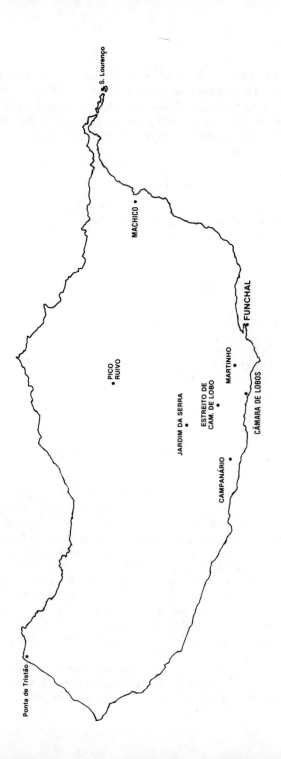

MADEIRA

the island. The Campanário, district was replanted in the 1940's, mostly with the Bual and Verdelho varieties. The vineyards of Jardim da Serra, on the south side of the island, which are at 492 meters (1500 feet) — the highest elevation where the vine will grow — are said to produce some especially fine Sercial grapes.

THE HARVEST

The harvest in Madeira must be one of the longest for any winegrowing region. The picking begins in the vineyards at lower altitudes on the southern coast on about August 25 and continues until about mid-September. The harvesting then moves to the vineyards on the northern side of the island where it continues until the final Sercial grapes on the upper slopes have been gathered, late in October.

The grapes are carried in the typical Madeira baskets woven in the shape of a huge straw hat with the brim turned up on one side (for the baskets, in the opposite position, it's turned down). Men wearing hoods which extend part way down their backs carry these baskets on their shoulders, holding onto them firmly by the wide brims.

Nowadays the freshly picked grapes are crushed by machines. But in the past they were trodden in long troughs by barefoot men singing and keeping time to the music with their rhythmic treading.

The fresh *mosto*, or must, is transported by truck to the lodges in Funchal where it is fermented. In the days when roads on Madeira were stony paths and travel very slow indeed, the vineyards on the northern side of the island made wine from the fresh must and shipped it around the island to Funchal in barrels loaded onto small boats. Men from closer vineyards brought the unfermented must on foot to Funchal where the wine was made. These were the *borracheiros,* who each carried 34 to 45 liters (about 9 to 12 gallons) of must in goatskin *borrachos* on their shoulders. These were the whole skins of goats turned inside out, sewed on the underside and tied tightly at the neck and legs. A strap attached to the ends of the legs was held across the *borracheiro's* forehead to steady the heavy load, which weighed about 68 kilograms (150 pounds).

The must for madeira is no longer transported in this picturesque and slow-moving manner, but you can still sometimes see men in the mountains of the interior, as we did, carrying *borrachos* of local wine along the roads in this fashion.

THE WINE

The *mosto* ferments in wooden casks or vats in the shippers' lodges for about eight days. At this stage the madeira wine is a highly acidic, dry wine—simple *vinho claro*. It must go through a series of steps to become the fortified madeira we pour from the bottle.

The next step is a very important one in the making of madeira. This is the heating.

HEATING

For most wines, heating would be ruinous. But for madeira it is beneficial and even necessary. The first wines of Madeira to receive such a treatment were the pipes of wines sent as ballast in the steaming holds of sailing ships crossing the southern seas.

Pliny noted that wine transported on ships matured sooner: ". . . with wines shipped over sea, . . . it is observed that the effect of the motion on vintages that can stand it is merely to double their previous maturity."

The madeira wine was specially sent in the holds of ships destined for tropical ports, which not only gave it the benefit of the pitching and rolling motion of the ship—thought to be the best way to blend the alcohol into the wine—but also for the heat of the voyage, which produced the characteristic flavor in the wine.

Portugal had a monopoly on trade with India from the beginning of the sixteenth century, and many pipes of wine were shipped from Madeira to the East Indies and back. Ships going in the opposite direction, to the West Indies, also carried pipes of madeira. These voyages were found to mellow and improve the wine.

Madeira that had been shipped around the world was called *vinho do roda* (wine of the circle) and was much prized. This double crossing of the equator was considered very fine for maturing the wine. Some madeira is said to have been given the benefit of four crossings on a journey of six months.

As early as the 1730s less expensive and time-consuming methods were being tried to imitate this effect on the wine without actually shipping it on board. The wine was put in special rooms with glass ceilings where it was baked in the heat of the sun. This wine was called *vinho do sol* (wine of the sun).

During the Napoleonic Wars, when shipping was risky business, stone lodges with hot rooms, *estufas,* were built especially for heating the wines. Leacock's built their first *estufa* in 1800; a few years later most of the other Madeira shippers had done the same.

The practice of heating wine is a very old one which may have been reinvented by the producers of madeira, but it could have been discovered in ancient texts; it was known to the Romans. Roman wines were sometimes cured in a hot attic room, the *fumarium,* into which the heat and smoke from the fires that heated the building rose. The Romans apparently felt, though, that it was the smoke more than the heat that improved the wines. Falernian was one of the wines they subjected to this treatment. This wine has some other interesting parallels with madeira; it also was grown on volcanic soil, and the vines were trained on trellises.

Madeira wine today is heated by one of two methods. The barrels of vintage wine are stacked on a scantle in a *canteiro,* a storeroom heated by the sun beating down on the zinc roof. This wine, *vinho canteiro,* is mostly vintage wine, but some nonvintage wine may also be heated this way. The wines stay in the *canteiro* for a year, sometimes longer, in the natural heat, then are moved to an aging cellar where they are left to mature for twenty years or more.

The casks are topped up periodically as the wine slowly evaporates through the pores in the wood. The rate of evaporation, or ullage, is about 2 percent per year. The barrels of wine shipped on sailing vessels were said to lose 4 percent on a voyage to India.

For the lesser wines there is another, less expensive, method of heating. This is to put the wine into the *estufa* (literally, stove). In the *estufa* room are large cement tanks with coils of stainless steel piping inside. The pipes are filled with steam which gradually heats the wine to temperatures of from 43-degrees C. (110-degrees F.) to not more than 51-degrees C. (125-degrees F.), depending on how long the wine will be in the *estufa.* The period of heating lasts for from three to five months, then the wine slowly, over a month's time, returns to normal. The cooking gives these wines a touch of caramel flavor.

There are government seals on the temperature gauges on the equipment to insure that the maximum highs or lows of temperature are not exceeded or achieved too rapidly (which would cause the seal to break). Some of the vintage wine (from noble grapes) may be heated in an attic room above the *estufa*. The heat in this room reaches a maximum of about 32 degrees C. (90 degrees F.). In the summer it is normally between 23 degrees and 29 degrees C. (75 degrees and 85 degrees F.).

After the heating (*estufagem)* the wine is filtered through charcoal to remove and bad odors caused by the cooking. The wine from the *estufas, vinho estufado,* then goes through *estágio,* a period of rest. This lasts about eighteen months and gives the wine time to recover. Then it is racked off its lees, or sediment, becoming *vinho transfugado,* and is fortified.

FORTIFICATION

Another important aspect of madeira is that it is fortified. This wasn't always so. In the early days, madeira was a table wine. The exact date of the change is not recorded. Sir John Falstaff's cup of madeira, though, would surely have been unfortified.

Brandy is known to have been distilled on Madeira as early as 1704, but we have no sure evidence of its being used to fortify the wine until 1753 when Francis Newton of Cossart, Gordon complained in a letter, of competitors who were putting a "bucket or two of Brandy in each pipe" of their madeira. This stronger wine apparently had more appeal, no doubt particularly to the Englishman who had always preferred a strong wine, one that brought warmth to the spirit as well as to the drinker himself (on all sides, not just the one facing the fireplace). Only two decades after Mr. Newton's letter, virtually all of the successful madeira firms had adopted the practice of fortifying their wines.

Again, there are two methods for fortifying the wine. One is to add the spirits (96 proof brandy used in amounts from 10 percent to a bit over 11 percent) at the point in the fermentation when the desired sugar level has been achieved. This is the more difficult method and is only used for the better wines. The alcohol arrests the fermentation process, keeping the fruit sugar that remains in the must from being converted into alcohol. The level of sugar in the wine depends on the type of madeira: For sercial, which is fermented dry, 1°

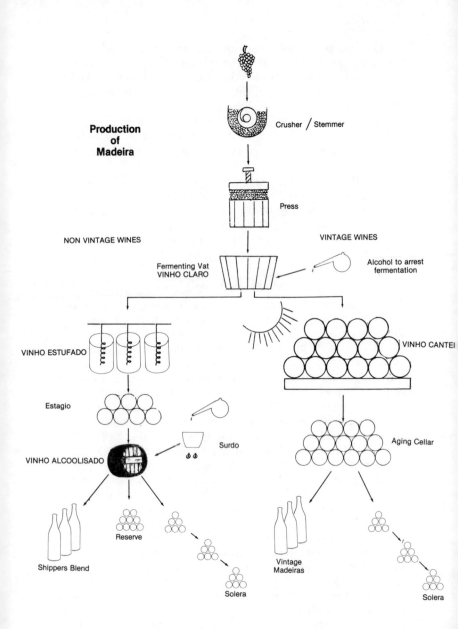

Production of Madeira

Crusher / Stemmer

Press

NON VINTAGE WINES

VINTAGE WINES

Fermenting Vat VINHO CLARO

Alcohol to arrest fermentation

VINHO ESTUFADO

VINHO CANTEI

Estagio

Surdo

Aging Cellar

VINHO ALCOOLISADO

Shippers Blend

Reserve

Solera

Vintage Madeiras

Solera

Baumé; for verdelho, 2-2½° Baumé; for bual, 2½-3½°; for malmsey, 3½° or more—normally, 4-4½° Baumé. (The measure used here, the Baumé scale, indicates specific gravity, or density, in degrees.)

The more common method of sweetening is to ferment the wine dry. Then after the wine has been heated and cooled, a solution of *surdo* is added. *Surdo* is the sweet, fresh must (unfermented grape juice) boiled down to a concentrate, plus alcohol. Wines destined to be sweet are heated in the *estufas* before the *surdo* is added; the *surdo* is not put into the *estufas.* The nonvintage dry, or dryish, wine may be aged apart from the *surdo,* or they may be aged together.

They begin fortifying the dry wine four months after the fermentation and continue from January to March. The fortified wine is referred to as *vinho generoso,* or *vinho alcoolisado.*

The *vinho alcoolisado* is aged in cask for at least three years. Ten years is considered necessary before the wine will have developed into a really good madeira. Some of the wine is aged in casks that vary in size from 548 to 2,000 liters (145 to 520 gallons); most hold 585 to 1,470 liters (155 to 390 gallons). Ovals of Brazilian satinwood are used, also casks of Portuguese or American oak. The 408-liter (108-gallon) pipes are of American oak.

TYPES OF MADEIRA*

There are five basic types of madeira: (1) vintage madeira (bottled in heavier bottles with the name painted on the bottle and a label on the back); (2) *solera* madeira; (3) reserve madeira; (4) the medium quality, or average, madeira; and (5) the shippers' blends such as Rainwater, Southside, etc. — generally used for cooking.

Vintage madeira is made 100 percent from one of the four noble varieties and from a single vintage. Only 5-10 percent of the madeira produced is vintage wine. It is made, on average, five years out of ten. A date on a bottle of madeira is no guarantee that it is a vintage wine; it could be a *solera* madeira.

Solera madeira is a blend of vintages. This type was initiated after phylloxera when there was a serious shortage of wine. It allowed the producers to stretch the available supply and at the same time upgrade the new wines with additions of the fine old vintages. Madeira had previously always been the

*see page 95

81

wine of a single vintage. The *solera* wine carries the date of the year the *solera* was started.

When a new *solera* is established — most are very old — the wine is aged for ten years, after which period 10 percent of it can be bottled. This first bottling is a single-vintage wine. The old wine is then topped up with newer wine, which is at least five years old (all the wine being aged at least five years).

Reserve madeira spends fifteen to twenty, or more, years in cask, mellowing and developing roundness and complexity. This style is bottled from a blend of 80 percent reserve wine, 10 percent *surdo,* and 10 percent of older wine, for bouquet.

The *medium quality madeira,* aged for a minimum of five years, is a blend of 70 percent average wine, 10 percent *surdo,* and 20 percent of older wine aged twenty to thirty years.

The fifth category of wines is the *shippers' blends* such as Rainwater, Southside, and Blandy's Duke of Clarence Malmsey.

Rainwater is an interesting wine, for its name at least. Some say this was a blend of Sercial and Verdelho; others that it was from Sercial grapes grown at high elevations, watered solely by the rain from which it took its name. Undoubtedly there are other than noble grapes in this blend nowadays.

There are other stories regarding the curious name. One says that a Mr. Habisham of Savannah, Georgia, who had ordered some casks of madeira, left them outside when they arrived, like rainwater barrels. Another version, again involving Habisham, says that he developed a system of clarifying the wine which made his madeira the palest in color, so pale that madeira drinkers likened its color — or lack of it — to rainwater.

Then there's the story that some casks of madeira shipped during the rainy season were left sitting on the dock due to a customs delay. The barrels were drenched by the rain during this postponement, and later the wine was found, strangely enough, to have improved under these conditions. Thus it was called Rainwater after its conditioning agent.

The stories are perhaps more interesting than the wine. Rainwater is a medium-dry madeira (usually 2-3° Baumé), light gold in color and never of high quality. It is inexpensive, and often used in cooking.

The *Southside* madeira is sweeter than the Rainwater, but not really sweet. The name is said to come from the origin of the grapes used in its blend. It is supposed to have been at one time a rich blend of wines from vineyards on the south side of the island which produce the better wines. Perhaps, or it may have been named merely to evoke this connotation. We've already mentioned the rather bizarre legend behind the madeira called *Duke of Clarence Malmsey.*

REGULATION*

Madeira is now in a state of change. A code for regulating the wines is in the process of being set up. It will not be the first such code. We know that as early as the 1760s rules were set prohibiting the blending of grapes from the northern side of the island with those from the southern side. And in 1788 the addition of cherry juice to give a nice red color to the wines came to an abrupt halt when all the cherry trees on the island were ordered chopped down to prevent just such adulteration. Madeira wine as we know it today is not red, but ranges from pale gold to mahogany.

Portugal would like to join the Common Market, but EEC (European Economic Community, or Common Market) regulations require that a wine named for a grape variety must be made at least 85 percent from that variety. This will pose a problem for the madeira firms that want to label their non-vintage wines with the names of the noble grapes; this practice, then, will have to be discontinued in the near future.

How would the wines then be named? With fantasy names perhaps, such as Duke of Clarence minus the "Malmsey", or some other evocative description such as has been done with the shipper's blends. Anyone who has seen the myriad of labels that have been made for the various madeiras and markets over the years will have no doubt that the madeira shippers won't have any trouble coming up with names. Winedrinkers, on the other hand, may sometimes be hard put to decipher exactly what they mean.

THE LONGEVITY OF MADEIRA

Madeira is perhaps the world's longest-lived wine. Alec Waugh in *In Praise of Wine* says, "Longevity is the best-known characteristic of Madeira, and a bottle that has been decanted will stay good for half a year." We tasted some pre-phylloxera madeira in 1978—an 1860 Sercial and an 1863 Bual—which showed no signs of old age. In fact they were

*see page 95

quite fine, both having a penetrating nose, great depth, and a long finish.

In Madeira they say the wine should have no less than fifteen to twenty years in cask and that it improves in bottle indefinitely. It is not known to fade with age, except in color. It does lose sweetness in the bottle as it matures. Some have said that it matures only in wood and will last, but not improve, in bottle. This no doubt was said of the lesser wines, those not made by the better methods or with the noble varieties.

H. Warner Allen writes in *A History of Wine* of an impressive tasting of some rare and very old pre-phylloxera madeiras:

> There were thirteen ancestral vintage wines, venerable patriarchs, any one of them worth to the wine-lover a king's ransom . . . the youngest seventy-nine, the oldest a hundred and seventy . . . .
>
> Several of these wines had passed part of their lives in large glass demijohns, wicker-covered bulging jars . . . .
>
> There was Sercial 1860, only withdrawn from demijohn to bottle fifteen months before; the date at which it left the cask was unknown. It was the driest Madeira I ever tasted, quite delightful I thought. Mr. Cossart gave it alpha plus, but pronounced its days as numbered. Terrantez 1862 had spent 43 years in the wood, 31 years in demijohn and 23 years in bottle. It was the Terpsichore of Madeiras with all the elegance of the ageless Muse of Dance, and it tempted me to wonder whether perhaps with the disappearance of the Terrantez vine Madeira might not have lost an exquisite touch of spritely grace with which I had never associated it. The life history of the most famous of all Madeiras, that Methuselah of wine, Cama de Lobos 1789, covered 111 years in the wood, 50 years in demijohn and 9 years in bottle. It challenged and defeated all the legends of the immortal Opimian Falernian, for it was glory on the palate and in the nose—another thirty years and it would certainly not have been reduced to the likeness of rough honey, precious as attar of roses in a blend but quite undrinkable, the condition of Pliny's Opimian after 200 years . . . .
>
> Cama de Lobos 1789, with its majestic presence was embalmed history. Had not its grapes been pressed only a month or so after the fall of the Bastille and just before Louis XVI and his queen were brought by the mob from Versailles to Paris with the guillotine three years ahead? . . .
>
> Possibly its junior by six years, Terrantez 1795, the year of

Napoleon's "whiff of grape-shot," bore up its age with equal sturdiness and even an additional hint of the Terrantez grace after 133 years in the wood. The mere stripling Verdelho 1844 took its place with the others as a perfect example of its type, the triumph over time of the golden mean.*

There is a story told of a barrel of 1792 Bual, presented to ex-Emperor Napoleon when his ship stopped at Funchal on its way to St. Helena. It was thought a fitting choice to ease the rigors of exile on the lonely island. It was then only twenty-three years old, young for madeira, but possessing what was judged a fine potential for aging. But apparently Napoleon had gastric problems, and perhaps someone feared the wine might be injurious to his health in some other way (evidence has been found indicating that he died of poisoning). Five years later, when Napoleon died, the cask was still unbroached. When the merchant in Madeira who had supplied the wine learned of the situation, he managed to get the wine returned. From there it changed hands a few times, being put into demijohns in 1840, and later bottled. André Simon, who tells the story, carried two dozen of these bottles from Madeira to the cellar of the Saintsbury Club in 1933. It must have been quite an experience to taste those historic old vintages.

STORAGE

Bottles of madeira, unlike other wines, can be stored standing up. It seems odd, but the unorthodox position apparently does them no harm (no worry about the wine becoming madeirized!) and the high acidity of the wine might cause the cork to deteriorate if the bottle were left lying on its side.

The wine should not be allowed to get too cold or too warm; 10-degrees to 23-degrees C. (50-degrees to 75-degrees F.) is the ideal temperature range for storing madeira. Sudden changes of temperature are bad for the wine. However, cold is worse for madeira than heat. The latter is rarely a problem —over 50-degrees C. (100-degrees F.) would be too warm. The bottles, of course, should be kept out of the sunlight, as with all wines.

BUYING AND SERVING

There is no need to put the vintage madeira aside to rest after bringing it home from the store. You can even serve it the

*A History of Wine (London: Faber & Faber, 1961).

same evening. If you wish, though, it wouldn't hurt to let it stand for a while—twenty-four hours should suffice—if it has been shaken up. Or perhaps a bit longer if you had a particularly rigorous homeward journey—a straphanging subway ride at rush hour, an especially teeth-jarring train trip, or a brisk jog from the wine shop dodging erratic motorists and heel-nipping dogs.

Sediment is not a problem. The vintage madeiras don't throw much of a deposit, having been aged for a long period in cask where they drop out their sediment. Sometimes the younger wines do have a little sediment, but not enough so that you'd have to decant. Careful pouring should be all that's required. Curiously enough, however, we've noticed that bottles that have been opened for a while do tend to throw a deposit in the bottle, or decanter. Once again, though, simply pouring carefully will assure you a clear glass of wine.

Since the nonvintage wines don't improve in bottle, there is no need to buy stocks of madeira in advance; simply buy as you need it. A bottle will last for months once opened (depending on how fast you drink it, of course). Madeira's resistance to oxidation is very high due to its method of production, the heating in particular. We have tasted old vintage madeiras opened a few months before that seemed to have suffered no ill effects. We were told at one firm in the fall of 1978 that they had just bottled the 1863 Bual from demijohns; before that, it had been in cask fifty years.

The best wines are naturally the vintage madeiras. They are somewhat expensive, perhaps more so than they should be, because of the very limited supply. Many stores mark them up more than other wines, but there are exceptions. Most of the nonvintage madeira, like most sherry, can be rather non-descript, at best a pale shadow of the vintage wines, though we have had some splendid reserve and *solera* madeiras.

Except for vintage madeira, which can be quite fine—some of the marvelous old malmsey in particular—we generally prefer to drink marsala in the same instances; it is a wine that to some degree resembles madeira, in production and in style. We find that marsala *vergine* admirably fills in for madeira sercial. Instead of verdelho with the soup—marsala SOM *secco*. Marsala SOM *dolce* is a fine alternative to bual for our tastes. And in each of these cases the marsala would probably be less expensive.

As for the malmsey, if it is an old vintage malmsey, there is no real substitute except perhaps a vintage port. But old vintage malmsey can be quite an experience and one that really should not be missed.

Madeira has a characteristic penetrating aroma and a subtlety burnt taste. The dry styles are not completely dry; they have an underlying hint of sweetness. And the sweet madeiras are never cloyingly sweet, but have a certain dryness in the background.

Sercial is a pale golden color which deepens with age. The wine is quite dry and has a slightly bitter aftertaste. Sercial makes a good aperitif, served chilled. A good vintage sercial can be enjoyed at cool room temperature.

Sercial may be served also with the meal. It goes well with appetizers of cold shellfish, such as raw oysters or clams. Some have also recommended it with shrimp; perhaps, with certain types of shrimp cocktail such as those with the European-style (mayonnaise and tomato-based) sauce. Sercial can be drunk, too, with soup or consommé.

Verdelho is golden in color and soft on the palate, ranging from dryish to sweet with an underlying dryness. It is the most versatile madeira. The drier style is good to accompany soup or, drunk chilled, as an aperitif. The medium-dry is good with creamed soups. The sweeter verdelho would go with desserts such as light cakes, or with nuts; it is also good for adding to sauces and gravies.

Bual, or *boal,* is amber in color, rich, full-bodied, and sweet. It is best drunk at cool room temperature, with fruit-cake, nuts, or certain cheeses such as the cheddar styles and the blue cheeses. It also goes with some types of fruit, such as pineapple.

Malmsey is mahogany in color, soft, rich, and luscious. It is the finest, rarest, and the most expensive type of madeira (it is also the best-known). Malmsey is a good wine to drink with blue cheeses, nuts, and cakes. In Madeira they recommend it with *bolo de mel,* a dark, rich, honey cake which is a specialty of the island. They also say that an avocado half with a little (about a tablespoon of) malmsey poured into the center makes a nice appetizer. And, of course, it can be enjoyed simply sipped by itself after dinner.

READING THE LABEL

Madeira labels can be rather confusing since they abound in

vague terminology. The terms that have real meaning are listed in the glossary at the end of this chapter. Descriptions such as Rich, Very Full, and Luscious; Pale, Fragrant, Elegant, and Dry; Delicate, Sweet, and Soft; and so forth, can be taken as a guideline of sorts — proprietors' descriptions.

The numerous fantasy and proprietary names are strictly for identification — a tag to remember the wine by.

And, of course, the name of the grape variety (Sercial, Verdelho, Bual, or Malmsey) except on the vintage wines, means no more than that the wine is in the style of that grape — and sometimes not even that.

THE MADEIRA SHIPPERS

Most madeira is made by the Madeira Wine Association*, an organization of Madeira shippers. The Madeira Wine Association was formed in 1925. Blandy's was the first company; Cossart, Gordon and Co. joined about twenty years ago. Today there are twenty-six firms in the organization.

The Association generally buys the grapes for its wines; they sometimes also buy wine if they can't get enough grapes. Some of the directors own vineyards and sell their grapes to the Association. The Madeira Wine Association also bottles wines for other firms, such as Sandeman, Delaforce, and Taylor Fladgate.

The Madeira Wine Association members own over 400 labels and sell wine under most of them in one market or another. The economic situation in the madeira market could not support 400 different wines each separately made. Individual differences, though, will be maintained in the case of a traditional market for a particular style of madeira. So, one producer's Rainwater will be as good, or as mediocre, as another's, differing only perhaps in price.

Among the labels owned by the Madeira Wine Association: Blandy's Madeiras, Lda.; Cossart, Gordon & Co. Ltd.; Leacock & Co. (Wine) Lda.; Luiz Gomes da Conçeicão; Miles Madeiras Lda.; Rutherford and Miles; Power Drury (Wine) Lda.; F.F. Ferraz & Ca. Lda.; Shortridge Lawton & Co.; Tarquinio T. Da Camara Lomelino Lda.; Vinhos Viuva Abudarham and Filhos Lda.; Welsh Brothers (Vinhos) Lda.; Freitas Martins, Caldeira & Ca. Lda.; Gibbs & Co.; Madeira Vitória & Ca. Lda.; Royal Madeira Co. Ltd.; Bianchi's Madeira Lda.; A. Pries Scholtz & Co.; J.B. Spinola Lda.; H.

*The name has since been changed to the Madeira Wine Company.

& C.J. Feist.

Besides the Madeira Wine Association, other producers of madeira wine are Henriques & Henriques; H.M. Borges; Vinhos Barbeitos; Marcelo Gomes & Ca. Lda.; Veiga França & Co. Ltd.; Justino Henriques; Companhia Vinicola; Adegas do Torreão.

It's really not possible to single out and recommend one brand of madeira over another, as there is very little difference among them.

As for the wines of the member firms of the Madeira Wine Association — Blandy's, Leacock, Cossart Gordon, Rutherford and Miles, Welsh Brothers, etc. — there is virtually no difference at all, since most wines of the same type are bottled from the same vat.

MADEIRA WINE COMPANY, LDA. AND THEIR ASSOCIATED COMPANIES

A. Nobrega (Vinhos da Madeira) Lda.
Aguiar, Freitas & Ca. Sucrs., Lda.
Barros, Almeida & Ca. (Madeira) Lda.
Bianchi's Madeira, Lda.
Blandy's Madeiras, Lda.
Casa dos Vinhos Vasconcelos Lda.
Cossart, Gordon & Ca. Lda.
F. F. Ferraz & Ca. Lda.
Freitas Martins, Caldeira & Ca. Lda.
Funchal Wine Company Lda.
J. B. Spinola Lda.
Krown Brothers & Ca. Lda.
Leacock & Co. (Wine) Lda.
Luiz Gomes (Vinhos) Lda.
Madeira Vitôria & Ca. Lda.
Miles Madeiras, Lda.
Power Drury (Wine) Lda.
Royal Madeira & Ca. Lda.
Rutherford & Miles, Lda.
Sociedade Agrîcola da Madeira Lda.
Sociedade dos Vinhos da Madeira Meneres Lda.
Tarquinio T. Camara Lomelino Lda.
Vinhos Donaldson & Ca. Lda.
Vinhos Shortridge Lawton & Ca. Lda.
Vinhos Viuva Abudarham & Fos. Lda.
Welsh Brothers & Ca. Lda.

MADEIRA VINTAGES

A date, by itself, on a bottle of madeira might indicate that it is a vintage wine; then, again, it might be a *solera* date. Sometimes the date is preceeded by the word Solera or Vintage, sometimes not. When it is not, you have to trust your merchant, or the importer — or your luck.

The following vintage charts will hopefully offer some assistance in evaluating madeira, but there are 2 pitfalls: (1) our information was unfortunately incomplete, and (2) *solera* wines are generally started with wines of particularly good vintages. Other vintages were also shipped, other than those listed here; this information basically concerns only those vintages that were highly regarded.

*1789—One of the most highly regarded of all madeira vintages, and especially for the wines of Cama de Lobos.

1792—The Boal especially was highly esteemed.

1795—The Terrantez was much sought after.

1805—A very good year, especially for the wines from Cama de Lobos and São Martinho.

1806—Another very good vintage for the wines of Cama de Lobos and São Martinho.

*1808—The Sercial and Malmsey were especially prized.

1815—Very good Sercial and Boal were produced.

1824—Very good for Boal.

1834—The Boal again fared very well.

1838—The Verdelho was very good.

1839—A good vintage for Malmsey.

1844—The Verdelho and Boal were very good.

*1846—The Terrantez, Boal, Verdelho and Malmsey were considered outstanding.

1851—A good year for Sercial.

1852—Powdery mildew was discovered in the vineyards of Madeira.

1860—The Sercial and Boal did very well.

*1862—The Terrantez and Verdelho were especially fine.

*1865—A very good year for the wines of Cama de Lobos and the Boal.

1870—The Sercial, Boal, Malmsey and Terrantez were highly regarded.

1873—Phylloxera struck the Madeira vineyards.

1893—The Verdelho, Boal and Malmsey were good.

1898—This was the first normal vintage following the phylloxera destruction, and was well regarded.

*1900—The Sercial, Verdelho, Boal and Malmsey were all outstanding.

*1910—An especially good year for Sercial, Verdelho and Boal.

1915—Very good, particularly for Boal.

1920—The Boal was very good.

1926—Another very good vintage for Boal.

* = The most highly regarded vintages.

Checklist of Madeira Vintages

Vintage	Sercial	Verdelho	Boal	Malmsey	Terrantez
1789					
1790				✔	✔
1792			✔		
1794					✔
1795					✔
1803					
1805					
1806					
1808	✔			✔	
1815	✔		✔		
1816	✔				
1822			✔	✔	
1824			✔		
1826					
1830					
1834			✔		
1835	✔				
1836	✔				
1837	✔				
1838		✔			
1839				✔	
1840			✔		
1841				✔	
1842					✔
1844		✔	✔		
1846		✔	✔	✔	✔
1847			✔		
1848			✔		
1849		✔	✔		
1850	✔				
1851	✔		✔	✔	
1853				✔	
1856			✔		
1858		✔			
1860	✔		✔		
1862		✔			✔
1863			✔		
1864	✔		✔		

Checklist of Madeira Vintages (continued)

Vintage	Sercial	Verdelho	Boal	Malmsey	Terrantez
1865			✓		
1866		✓			
1868	✓		✓	✓	
1869			✓		
1870	✓		✓	✓	✓
1871				✓	
1872					
1873					
1874			✓		
1875	✓			✓	
1878			✓		
1880		✓		✓	✓
1882		✓	✓		
1883	✓	✓			
1884			✓		
1885	✓				
1886				✓	
1890	✓			✓	
1892	✓				
1893		✓	✓	✓	
1894			✓		
1895			✓		
1897			✓	✓	
1898					
1900	✓	✓	✓	✓	
1902		✓		✓	
1904				✓	
1905	✓			✓	
1906				✓	
1907		✓		✓	
1908	✓				
1910	✓	✓	✓		
1911			✓		
1913				✓	
1914			✓		
1915			✓	✓	
1916				✓	
1918					
1920			✓	✓	
1926			✓		
1934		✓	✓		
1935			✓		
1940	✓				
1941			✓	✓	
1942				✓	
1944					
1950	✓				
1952		✓		✓	
1954			✓	✓	
1956			✓		
1958			✓		

VINTAGES BY VARIETY

Sercial

1808	1815	1816	1835	1836	1837	1850	1851	1860
1864	1868	1870	1875	1883	1885	1890	1892	1900
1905	1908	1910	1940	1950				

Verdelho

1838	1844	1846	1849	1858	1862	1866	1880	1882
1883	1893	1900	1902	1907	1910	1934	1952	

Boal - Bual

1792	1815	1822	1824	1834	1840	1844	1846	1847
1848	1849	1851	1856	1860	1863	1864	1865	1868
1869	1870	1874	1878	1882	1884	1893	1894	1895
1897	1900	1910	1911	1914	1915	1920	1926	1934
1935	1941	1954	1956	1958				

Malmsey - Malvazia

1790	1808	1822	1839	1841	1846	1851	1853	1868
1870	1871	1875	1880	1886	1890	1893	1897	1900
1902	1904	1905	1906	1907	1913	1915	1916	1920
1941	1942	1952	1954					

Terrantez

1790	1794	1795	1842	1846	1862	1870	1880

Bastardo
1870

Moscatel

1790	1847	1895

MADEIRA GLOSSARY

Boal (boo-AHL). One of the noble grapes of Madeira producing sweet wines. On nonvintage madeira the name Boal only means "in the style of boal madeira" (sweet).

Bual (BOO-ahl). English for Boal.

Cama de Lobos (CAH-mah deh LOH-boshe). A village regarded for its Malmsey grapes and wines.

Câmara de Lobos (cah-MAH-rah deh LOH-boshe). Another name for Cama de Lobos.

Campanârio (cahm-pah-NAH-ree-oh). An area regarded for its vineyards and malmsey wines.

Especial (es-peh-see-AHL). Has little or no meaning.

Estreito de Camâra de Lobos (es-treh-EE-toh deh cah-MAH-rah deh LOH-boshe). An area producing highly regarded sercial wines.

Jardim da Serra (zhar-DEEn dah SEHR-rah). An area highly regarded for its sercial.

Malmsey (MAHLM-zee). One of the noble grapes of Madeira producing the sweetest, richest, and most luscious wines — the best madeiras. On nonvintage madeira, the name Malmsey only means "in the style of malmsey" (richly sweet).

Meiodoce (MEH-yoo DOH-seh). Medium-sweet.

Noble Grape Varieties. There are four grape varieties on Madeira considered noble: Boal, Malmsey, Sercial, and Verdelho.

Rainwater. A rather nondescript blended madeira, off-dry to medium-sweet.

Reserve. A madeira that is aged longer in cask, becoming a rounder and smoother wine.

São Martinho (sow mar-TEEN-yoo). A well-regarded vineyard region.

Seco (SEH-coo). Dry.

Selected. Has little or no meaning.

Sercial (sehr-see-AHL). One of the noble grapes of Madeira producing the lightest and driest wines. On nonvintage madeira, the name Sercial only means "in the style of sercial" (dry).

Solera (soh-LEH-rah). A system of fractional blending used to produce uniformity in the wines from year to year. Theoretically some wine (though minute in quantity) from the year the *solera* was established should be in every bottle. In this system the young wine takes on some of the characteristics of the old vintages.

Southside. Originally referred to the vineyards on the southern coast of Madeira. A proprietary name for a nondescript blended wine that is generally sweeter than Rainwater.

Special. Has little or no meaning.

Superior. Has little or no meaning.

Velhissimo (vel-YEE-see-moh). Very old. Not an indication of quality.

Verdelho (vehr-DEHL-yoo). One of the noble grapes of Madeira producing wines ranging from off-dry to medium-sweet. On nonvintage madeira the name Verdelho only means "in the style of verdelho" (off-dry to medium-sweet).

Vintage. Madeira from a single year. Unlike the non-vintage wines, the vintage madeiras are made from one of the four noble grape varieties. The best madeiras are the vintage wines.

REGULATION UPDATE

Anticipated changes in Portuguese law have recently gone into effect. Regulations set by the EEC on labels of imported wines have also modified the terms now allowed on Madeira wines.

Vintage madeira, besides being required to be 100 percent from the grape and vintage stated on the label, must be aged for no less than twenty years in cask, and two more in bottle.

Solera madeira, unlike solera sherry or marsala, cannot be continuously refreshened; the solera is limited. When madeira is taken from the solera to be bottled, no more than 10 percent of the wine can be drawn off, which is then replaced by wine from a good vintage. This can be done no more than 5 times; the remaining wine can then either be sold as it is, as a solera madeira (with the word "solera" on the label along with the date), or it can be used for blending into other wines. But if it is blended further, it cannot be sold as solera wine.

Reserve madeira is required to be kept for a minimum of five years in cask; special reserve, 10 years; and extra special reserve, fifteen years.

Medium quality madeira must be at least three years old. The terms "selected", "finest" or "choice" are allowed on the label, along with the specification of style, which is described as "dry", "medium dry", "medium rich", and "rich", in place of using the names of the noble varieties — a practice that is being discontinued. Madeira wines carrying the name of one of the noble varieties will in future have to be made from at least 85 percent of the named varietal.

Terraced vineyards along the Douro

Photo compliments of Madeira Wine Association

Harvesters with the typical Madeira baskets

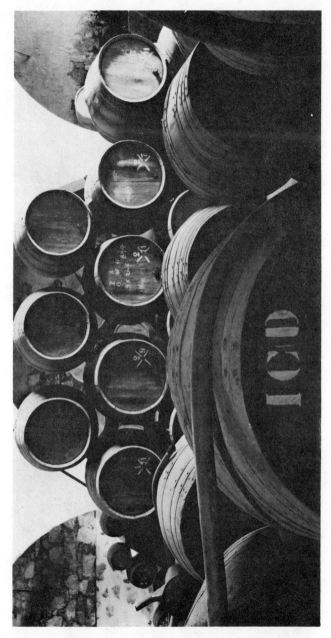

Marsala aging cellar

Sherry grapes being sunned

Photo courtesy of Consejo Regulador Jerez-Xeres-Sherry

Sherry casks stacked in soleras in a modern bodega

Casks in a solera system

Running the Scales

Keo's Cream Sherry Maturing in the sun

III

Marsala

The port of Marsala is on the western tip of Sicily in the
province of Trapani. On three sides Trapani is surrounded by
the Mediterranean. Inside there is another sea — a green sea
of vines rippling in the soft coastal breezes, in some places
extending in all directions as far as the eye can see.

Historians are not sure just when the vine was first cultivated on Sicily, but they agree that the history of viticulture
here is very ancient. Some think that the Elimi, a people of
uncertain origin, may have introduced the vine here. One
theory says that the Elimi were originally from Troy; if so,
they could then have brought the *Vitis vinifera* wine (native to
the Middle East) to Sicily from their homeland. The Elimi
built the cities of Erice, Entella, and Segesta in what is now
the province of Trapani. The ruins of these ancient cities are
today surrounded by vast stretches of vineyards.

Toward the end of the eighth century B.C., Phoenicians
from Carthage in North Africa sailed to the nearby island of
Sicily (less than 150 kilometers/90 miles northeast). They
colonized the western part of the island, giving it the name
Ziz, their word for flower, which may be the origin of the
name Sicily, a land of bright flowers and great natural
beauty.

At about the same time, Greeks from Corinth landed in
eastern Sicily. They settled colonies along the eastern and

southern coasts, naming the island Trinacria, for its triangular shape. If the vine wasn't introduced into Sicily by the earlier Elimi peoples — or even if it was — it was certainly brought by Greek settlers. Viticulture in Sicily has been definitely traced back to the eighth century B.C. and to the Greeks, who planted vineyards there. According to Greek legend, the first vines to grow in Sicily sprang to life near Taormina in the footsteps of the god Dionysus.

In Sicily, then part of Magna Graecia, the vineyards flourished and Sicilian wines represented a major item of trade with other nations. The magnificent ruins of Greek temples, theaters, and monuments at Siracusa, Agrigento, Segesta, Selunite, and many other sites stand as silent reminders of this great age.

The oldest traces of the Carthaginian civilization to be found in Sicily are on the tiny island of Mozia, not far from Marsala. Mozia was destroyed in the fourth century in an attack by Greeks. Refugees fleeing the island founded the city of Lilybaeum in 397 B.C. on Cape Lilibeo (now Cape Boeo) on Sicily proper. This ancient city lies beneath the modern town of Marsala, and its ruined walls are still visible in some places, forming a part of the modern structures built over them.

The Greeks, Carthaginians, and Romans fought over this fertile and strategically placed island, as many other nations would do again in later ages. During the First Punic War between Carthage (or Poemi) and Rome, Lilybaeum, as the most powerful Carthaginian base in Sicily, was in the epicenter of much of the fighting. The town was beseiged by Roman forces but managed to hold out for ten years. In 241 the Roman fleet triumphed over the Carthaginians. With the fall of Lilybaeum the whole island came under Roman rule. Sicily became a Roman province and the city of Lilybaeum the seat of the Roman questor and magistrate.

Under Roman rule, or misrule, Sicily's natural resources were exploited. The vineyards were cut back and wheat fields planted to feed the armies of Rome. Villas, bridges, and aqueducts were built; their ruins today add to the architectural riches that make Sicily an archeological treasurehouse.

During the decline of the Roman Empire, Sicily was invaded by barbarian tribes. In 454 the city of Lilybaeum was sacked by the Vandals under Genseric. Later it was, like the rest of Italy, part of the Ostrogothic kingdom.

In 535 Sicily came under Byzantine rule. Reminders of this period remain in western Sicily in the impressive Byzantine mosaics decorating the Palatine chapel in Palermo and the cathedrals of Monreale and Cefalù.

In the ninth century Saracens invaded Sicily, seizing Panormus (Palermo) in 831 and making it the capital of the Moslem emirate in Sicily. The port of Marsala was burned to the ground by the inhabitants to prevent the Arabs from landing. It was a fine but futile gesture. The Arabs rebuilt the port and named the city Marsah-el-Allah (Port of Allah), later Italianized into its present name. Marsala today still retains an African air.

The Saracens ruled Sicily for 200 years, and western Sicily in particular felt their impact strongly. Arab influence in architecture and decorative arts is still obvious in western Sicily today. It is also evident in the cuisine. *Cùçcussu* or *cùscussu,* a specialty peculiar to the region of Trapani, is simply the north African *couscous* with a Sicilian flair.

The Saracens influenced the cuisine of Sicily in another way, but this one happily no longer has any effect. Their religion forbade alcohol in any form; wine was prohibited.

During the Arab domination, viticulture in Sicily suffered severely; vineyards were abandoned and winemaking nearly became a lost art. As late as the thirteenth century wine had to be imported from the continent.

History records that anyone in Sicily caught drinking wine in public could be condemned to death under the harsh Moslem law. But in the privacy of one's own home, the forbidden pleasures of the beverage inspired poets, such as the Arab Ibu Omar, who wrote:

> Pass around the old golden wine and drink it from morning till night. Drink it to the sound of the lute and to songs worthy of Mabad. Life is not serene if it is not in the shade of sweet Sicily, under a dynasty superior to the imperial dynasty of kings.

The Saracens were finally driven out and Sicily reconquered for Christianity in the eleventh century by the Norman French under the leadership of Count Roger de Hauteville. Sicily, along with Naples, as the Kingdom of the Two Sicilies, was ruled by the Angevin dynasty for over a century. With the return of Christianity and the tradition of wine in the church service, vineyards on Sicily were replanted and Sicilian viticulture revived.

The wine produced, rich and heady from grapes grown under the hot Mediterranean sun, no doubt helped at times to soothe the sorrows of the people who lived on this coveted island, fought over and conquered time and again by foreign rulers. When wars weren't laying waste to the cities and countryside, earthquakes and volcanic eruptions were creating their own destruction. The poet Giovanni Meli of Palermo, in his *Lodi di lu Vinu,* praised wine as the only solace from the sorrows of the world, with a son's devotion calling the wine god "Father" — *"Baccu, ch'è patri miu."*

Sicily became part of the Holy Roman Empire under Frederick II. Then, on the death of the emperor, Sicily came under French domination. This harsh rule came to an abrupt end on Easter Sunday in 1282, with the Sicilian Vespers massacre at Palermo in which virtually every Frenchman on the island was killed, a gory event so dramatically and beautifully depicted in music by Giuseppe Verdi in his opera *I Vespri Siciliani.* The French governors of Sicily were then replaced by the Spanish; until the sixteenth century Sicily was under the crown of Aragon.

Viticulture was not encouraged under the strict Spanish rulers. It was, in fact, actively discouraged. Vineyards were ripped up to be plowed into wheat fields, as they had been under the rule of ancient Rome.

In the days of a smaller population and large tracts of uncultivated land, there was a sort of nomadic viticulture in Sicily. When the vines had completed their growth cycle and become too old to support the small winegrower and his family, rather than rip up the old vines to replant, the farmer would move on to new land and plant a new vineyard.

In 1713, the Treaty of Utrecht awarded Sicily to the Duke of Savoy, then in 1738 it came under Bourbon dominion when Don Carlos of Spain became ruler of the Two Sicilies.

BIRTH OF MARSALA WINE

The history of marsala wine as we know it begins during this period. The wines from Marsala at that time were table wines, high in alcohol, but unfortified.

In 1773 John Woodhouse, a Liverpool merchant, came to Marsala to buy raw materials for his company in England. Drinking the wine of the region during his stay, Woodhouse noted the similarity between the wine of Marsala and those of Madeira and Jerez (sherry), regions with similar climate producing wines that were very popular in eighteenth-century

England. It occured to him that the wine of Marsala could appeal to the same taste.

With the courage of his convictions, Woodhouse took a step that would change his career—and the history of Marsala. He bought supplies of the local wine, and in that same year sent his first shipment, sixty barrels, of marsala wine to England on board the H.M.S. Elizabeth. To stabilize the wine for its rough voyage in the steaming hold of the sailing ship, he strengthened it by adding alcohol to the barrels—1 part alcohol to 50 parts of wine. Woodhouse's venture into the wine trade proved successful and he founded the first cellar for aging wines in Marsala. (In Marsala a "cellar," or *cantina*—*malaseno* in Sicilian dialect—is a high-ceilinged, above-ground building. Underground cellars cannot be dug in Marsala; the sea is just below ground level.) Woodhouse encouraged the farmers to extend their vineyards, promising to buy all their grapes.

In a contract dated March 19, 1800, signed by John Woodhouse and Admiral Horatio Nelson, First Lord of the Admiralty, 500 barrels of marsala wine were to be shipped to Malta for provisioning the British fleet. Nelson's victory at Trafalgar did no harm to the budding interest in marsala wine in England. Lord Nelson was quoted as saying, "Marsala wines are so good that any gentleman may allow them on his table."

In 1806 Benjamin Ingham founded a competing cellar for marsala wines. He was the first to use the *solera* system of fractional blending for maturing the wines. Ingham sent men to Spain to study the *solera* system used there, before setting up his own *solera* in Marsala.

Marsala became a popular wine in Regency and Victorian England, bringing a little Sicilian warmth to that damp, chilly country. By the mid-nineteenth century marsala's popularity rivaled that of madeira and sherry, much as Woodhouse had no doubt anticipated. Marsala was not only being drunk as a sipping wine, as we drink it today, but in the 1850s, according to William Younger in his book, *Gods, Men and Wine,* it was drunk at dinner after the soup course and with the fish.

In 1833, the Englishmen who started the marsala wine industry were joined in competition by a Sicilian businessman, Vincenzo Florio. Rallo, another major marsala house, was established in 1860. Today there are four major producers of Marsala: Florio, Rallo, Pellegrino, and Mirabella; the rest, about fifty in all, are much smaller. In

1929 the firms of Woodhouse, Ingham, and Florio were bought by the S.A.V.I. group. Other good producers of marsala include Alloro, Vito Curatolo, Cudia, Fici, Lombardo, Mineo, and de Vita.

On May 1, 1860, Giuseppe Garibaldi landed at Marsala at the head of his army of *Picciotti* on the start of the Expedition of the Thousand which would drive the Bourbons from Sicily and southern Italy. The great warrior tasted the wines of Marsala during his brief stay in the town, and one type of sweet marsala that he is said to have particularly enjoyed was renamed in his honor, Garibaldi Dolce (GD).

THE MARSALA PRODUCTION ZONE

In the early days of marsala, the wine could be made from grapes or wine produced in any part of Sicily. Now, since the ministerial decree of October 15, 1931, the Marsala zone is limited to specific areas in the provinces of Trapani (Campobello, Castelvetrano, Marsala, Mazara del Vallo, Trani), Palermo (Balestrate, Partinico, San Cipirello, San Giuseppe Iato, Terrasini Favorotta, Trappeto), and Agrigento (Menfi, Sciacca) in the western part of the island. This decree was updated in November of 1950, and today Italian wine law, Denominazione di Origine Controllata (D.O.C.), regulates the production of marsala wine.

In the Marsala growing zone, Catarratto and Inzolia—two of the principal white grapes of Sicily—and Grillo grapes are grown for the wine which will become marsala. The Catarratto variety dominates. Inzolia grapes, producing high sugar levels, account for up to 15 percent of the blend. There are smaller plantings of Grillo. The different varieties used to be planted together indiscriminately in the vineyards. Nowadays they are planted separately.

Some producers have their own vineyards; others buy the grapes or the fresh must to make their wine. Some do a little of both.

The vineyards are planted from the hills of northwestern Sicily to the plains in the south. On the plains of southern Trapani the vineyards extend over tens of thousands of acres. As the popularity of Sicilian wines has increased, the planting of vines has done the same. Today the province of Trapani alone can boast an extent of vineyards equal to that of the whole island of Sicily only twenty-five years ago, and vines are second only to citrus fruit as Sicily's most important agricultural crop in this fertile volcanic earth.

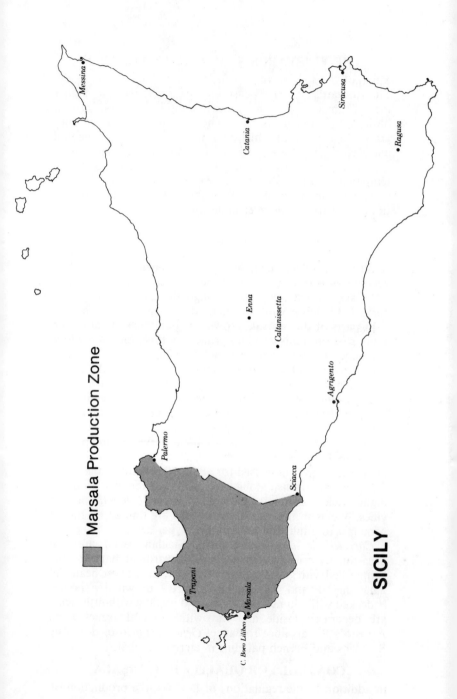

Marsala Production Zone

SICILY

111

THE VINEYARDS, CLIMATE, AND GRAPES

Much of the soil in the vineyards is abundant in iron oxide. The vineyards along the coast, on great shelly reefs not higher than 73 meters (240 feet), are swept by the hot *sirocco* blowing up from the Sahara. The coastal vineyards produce grapes high in sugar which will make wines high in alcohol and well suited to the production of marsala. The climate in the Marsala vineyards, though hot, dry, and sunny, is tempered by the surrounding sea. The balance of climate, soil, and grape varieties in these vineyards favors the production of fortified wine over table wine.

The traditional method of pruning the vines is the *alberello* (little tree) method, which trains the vine shoots very low to the ground to benefit from the reflected heat of the earth, resulting in higher sugar levels. The grapes are allowed to become as ripe as possible. Ninety percent of the Marsala vines are trained this way. Though the quantity of grapes harvested is lower with this method, the quality is higher.

In parts of the Marsala growing region vines are also seen supported on trellises. Vines pruned by this modern *tendone* system are trained on wires attached to high stakes forming a sort of overhead vinebower. This method gives the leaves more exposure to the sun, and increases yields significantly. The *tendone* system is more economical and also lends itself to mechanical harvesting. It is predominantly used, for grapes destined to be made into table wines.

The grapes for marsala are still hand-harvested and pruned either in the *alberello* or the *spalliera* style. In the latter method, which is now used for about 10 percent of the vines, the plants are trained along wires. This method also produces higher yields, as much as double that from *alberello*-pruned vines. Yields in the marsala vineyards are limited by Italian wine law to a maximum of four tons per acre.

Carretti siciliani, the colorful Sicilian carts, are still occasionally seen in the marsala vineyards at harvest time being filled with grapes to carry to the winery. These beautiful hand-carved and hand-painted carts, drawn by ponies bedecked with plumes and tassels and jingling with little bells, are decorated inside and out with colorful scenes from Ariosto's Renaissance romance, *Orlando Furioso,* depicting Saracens and French paladins in eternal combat.

CONTROL FOR QUALITY IN MARSALA

In addition to the regulations of D.O.C., the production of

marsala is watched over by the Consorzio per la Tutela del Vino Marsala. This is a voluntary organization of marsala producers with an interest in protecting and maintaining the quality of marsala wine. The group sets standards which are often higher than those of the D.O.C.; for example, it requires the wines to be aged longer. The Consorzio awards a neck label to wines that meet its standards—a red seal bearing the outline of Sicily.

TYPES OF MARSALA

D.O.C. recognizes four types of marsala:

Marsala fine—dry or sweet, at not less than 17 percent alcohol; also called Italia Particolare, or Italy Particular (IP).

Marsala superiore—dry to sweet, at not less than 18 percent alcohol; includes London Particular (LP), which is somewhat higher in alcohol, Superior Old Marsala (SOM), Garibaldi Dolce (GD), and Old Particular (OP).

Marsala vergine—dry, at not less than 18 percent alcohol; includes the *solera* marsalas. *Vergine,* the highest quality marsala, is produced from a specially selected base wine made from grapes grown in a zone within three miles of the coast which achieves a minimum of 16 percent natural alcohol (as opposed to 12 percent for the others) and is fortified to bring the alcoholic strength up to 18 percent or more.

Marsala speciali—at not less than 18 percent alcohol; includes the flavored marsalas made with a base of *fine* or *superiore* (most likely from the *fine*).

All marsala begins as a dry white wine before it becomes, through a series of changes, the rich, sometimes sweet, amber to walnut brown fortified wine we pour from the bottle. This transformation is achieved through one of two methods—the traditional and the modern.

THE TRADITIONAL METHOD OF PRODUCTION

In the traditional method, the base wine is fortified by the addition of alcohol. If the marsala is to be a *vergine* (dry to extra dry), nothing else is added. For *secco* (dry) marsala, alcohol plus less than 1 percent of *mistella* is added. For *dolce* (sweet) marsala, alcohol and a greater proportion of *mistella* is added to the wine.

In the past, alcohol obtained by distilling the fruit of the *carruba* (carob) tree was often used in marsala. The producers felt that this spirit was preferable to grape brandy, having a pleasant flavor and being less expensive. Today, however, the law states that the alcohol for fortifying marsala can be obtained only from the grape. The producers buy brandy made from wine distilled to 65 proof to fortify the marsala wine.

Mistella, also known as *sifone,* is the sweet juice of freshly crushed grapes—as sweet as sugar (21-22 percent sugar) but with the natural grape flavor—mixed with alcohol which prevents fermentation and retains the natural grape sweetness. The unfermented must is put into small, 604-liter (160-gallon) casks containing about 150 liters (40 gallons) of alcohol. The casks are rolled around to mix the must and alcohol, then left to rest for two to three months so the two components can blend together into a harmonious whole.

THE MODERN METHOD

In the modern method, the base wine is blended with *mosto concentrato* (concentrated must) and *mosto cotto* (cooked must), generally in a proportion of about 100 parts base wine, 6 parts *cotto* and *concentrato,* 6 parts alcohol. D.O.C. sets a minimum of 1 kilo (2.2 pounds) of *cotto* per 102 liters (27 gallons) of marsala for *fine* and *superiore* made by this method.

Mosto cotto, reduced by heating in huge stainless steel vessels to one-third its original volume, becomes dark and thick with a cloyingly sweet molasses-like flavor and a slight bitterness.

This aspect of the "modern" method of marsala production is actually quite an ancient practice, known to the Greeks of the fifth and fourth centuries B.C.

Pliny in his *Natural History* writes of must reduced by cooking:

> *Siraeum,* by some called *hepsema* and in our country *sapa,* is a product of art, not of nature, made by boiling down must to a third of its quantity; must boiled down to only one-half is called *defrutum.*

and again:

> . . . the must itself . . . is boiled down so as to become sweeter in proportion to its strength . . . . In some places they boil the must down into what is called *sapa,* and pour this into their wines to overcome their harshness.

Columella, a Roman writer on agriculture, wrote of adding

defrutum to wine, and even gave a recipe for it.

The modern method, using *cotto* and *concentrato,* has been referred to as the industrial method of making marsala. The traditional method produces a finer wine, but it is also more expensive to make. So, many firms offer both types of marsala.

The modern method became more commonly used in Marsala after *Phylloxera vastatrix* attacked the vineyards of Sicily in the late nineteenth century. This virulent vine louse destroyed the marsala vineyards and seriously threatened the economic future of the town itself. A solution was eventually found in grafting the vines onto resistant rootstock, and today wine is by far the major industry in Marsala (fishing coming in a distant second).

Marsala is produced through a process called *concia,* or curing. This process takes the base wine through its steps of fermentation, filtering, and finally *miscela.* This last step is the blending of the alcohol either with *mistella* or with *cotto* and *concentrato,* and the maturing and blending with *lievito,* or *vecchione,* a reserve of very old marsala.

This *lievito* (literally ''leavening''), as an agent used in the blending of wine, was also known to the ancients. In discussing the addition of very old wines to younger vintages, Pliny described those old wines:

> . . . they have now been reduced to the consistency of honey with a rough flavor, for such in fact is the nature of wines in their old age; and it would not be possible to drink them neat or counteract them with water, as their overripeness predominates even to the point of bitterness but with a very small admixture they serve as a seasoning for improving all other wines.

After the *miscela,* the wine is allowed to knit together. For the *fine,* this takes at least four months; for the *superiore,* a minimum of two years; for the *vergine,* not less than five years.

These are only minimums; many marsalas are given more age, especially those produced by the members of the Consorzio. The SOM Secco and Dolce GD of Rallo, for example, are aged for not less than four years.

No *cotto, concentrato,* or *sifone* is added to the *vergine* (virgin) marsala. This type of marsala is therefore the driest and most natural—and for us, the best of the marsalas.

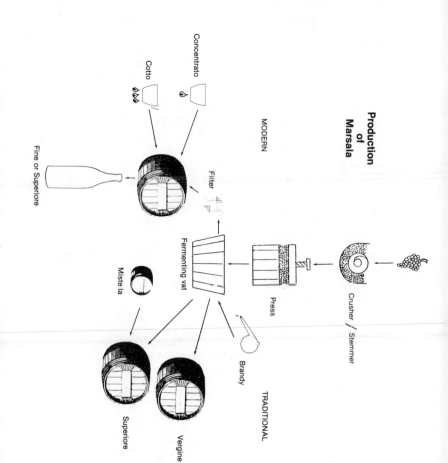

Production of Marsala

MODERN

Concentrato

Cotto

Fine or Superiore

Filter

Fermenting vat

Press

Crusher / Stemmer

Mistella

Brandy

Superiore

Vergine

TRADITIONAL

116

SOLERA

Vergine wines go through a system of fractional blending and maturing based on the Spanish *solera* system brought back by the men sent to Spain by Benjamin Ingham in the nineteenth century. The *solera* in Marsala, however, is not the same as the Spanish *solera* used in Montilla and Jerez today.

In the Marsala *solera,* or *sistema del lievito,* the barrels of wine are normally kept full. The young wine goes through a process of fractional blending, with the transfer *(travaso)* of wine from barrel to barrel, blending the younger wine with older wine, then with barrels of still older wine. This system is sometimes referred to as *vecchione perpetuo.*

No more than 10 percent of the older wine is drawn off for blending; the exact amount depends on the base wine to which it is added, which could be from five to seven years old.

The wines must spend at least five years in the *solera* before bottling, but many are aged for ten years or longer. The Vergine Secco of Fici, for example, is matured in *solera* for at least ten years, as is their Superiore Riserva. Mirabella and Cudia also make *vergine* marsala which is aged for ten or more years in a *solera.* Some houses also age their marsala *superiore* in a *solera*; for example Florio's ACI 1840 and Egadi Superiore Riserva are aged from five to ten years in a *solera.* Marsala *superiore secco* and *dolce,* if they are aged for ten or more years, can be labeled "Riserva." Rallo's SOM Riserva is aged for ten years; their Black Label SOM, Vergine, and Del Nonno Riserva are aged ten years or longer.

Some producers feel that marsala improves in barrel, but only for twenty to thirty years, no longer. After this, the wine is not considered good marsala; it would not be enjoyable drunk straight. This wine becomes *lievito* and is added to the *solera* wine to add mellowness, bouquet, and complexity.

Florio has *solera*s bearing the Florio name from 1840 and 1860; Ingham *solera*s from 1870 and 1834; and Woodhouse *solera*s from 1836 and 1815. Florio marsala from the 1860 *solera,* has been blended with *lievito* from the year 1860. The *lievito* is periodically refreshed with younger wine.

ON AGING MARSALA

Barrel aging a finished marsala for possible development and improvement is apparently not done. When the wine has been matured in the *solera,* it is bottled; there doesn't seem to be any thought of aging marsala in bottle.

Some producers feel that once the wine is in the bottle, it will remain unchanged for as long as a hundred years. The fortification is believed to hold the wine stable. They liken it to vermouth in this respect. Others feel it will change, but not for the better. (An opened bottle drunk over a period of one to two months is considered to show no appreciable alteration and to last unhurt for seven to eight months.)

All the other fortified wines, however, definitely change with bottle age, for better or worse. So, perhaps, it is simply that bottles of marsala have never been laid down to age to see how they would develop. Is it that the Sicilian, having lived for centuries in a world with an unpredictable future, developed the habit of drinking his marsala when he got it and not waiting to see what would happen to it if laid away?

The bottles of the higher categories of marsala sold in Europe are generally cork-finished. This would seem to allow aging, if one were inclined to give it a try. In the United States, one usually sees the screw-cap finish. Rallo uses screw caps on all their marsalas exported to the U.S.A. at the request of their importer.

Although marsala will last in bottle without noticeable alteration for quite a long time, it must undergo some change, if only a very gradual one. This change, in some cases, especially in the lesser grades of wine, will not be for the best, but for the better grades it seems that it could be. Unfortunately, no one we have spoken to has had any experience along these lines.

But it is an intriguing possibility. Why wouldn't the better marsalas—*superiore* and *vergine*—improve in bottle as the better madeiras do? There is actually quite a degree of similarity between these two great fortified wines. The question will remain an open one until somebody gives it a try. And when they do, the reputation of this wine—perhaps the most underrated of the great fortified wines—might improve enormously. Caches of bottles of rare old pre-phylloxera marsala found hidden away from foreign invaders could become hot items at the auction houses, more esteemed than Napoleonic madeiras—mind-boggling.

Marsala exported to European countries is sometimes shipped in *carratone,* or barrels, made of chestnut, a less expensive wood than oak, but the wine is aged in Slavonian oak barrels (except for the *fine,* which gets no wood aging).

The Sicilian producers must go outside their own island for

the wood, or for the barrels, since there is no wood for barrels on the island; virtually all of Sicily's trees were cut down for shipbuilding, which was once a thriving industry there. Many of the ships built were used to transport marsala wines to foreign ports.

Before World War I, the United States was by far the best market for marsala bottled in Italy. It also purchased one-third of the marsala sold in barrel. Marsala was also a very popular wine in England, the market for which it was designed. In his book *The Pleasures of Wine*, Sir Francis Colchester Wemyss writes of his days at the Royal Military College at Sandhurst, where they toasted Queen Victoria each night with glasses of marsala. Today, marsala's best market is Italy, followed by Germany, England, Canada, and the United States.

MARSALA SPECIALI

The *speciali,* or special marsalas, are a new development, dating only from World War I. These wines were designed to sell at lower prices, to the mass market. They have as their base either a *fine* or *superiore,* made with *cotto* and *concentrato,* to which eggs, almond, coffee, or fruit flavors have been added. These flavors are allowed to blend with the marsala base for two to four months before the wine is bottled.

One of the most popular of the marsala *speciali* is egg-flavored marsala — marsala *all'uovo.* Strangely enough, it was invented by a Milanese distiller, Moroni, in 1875. He mixed into 2 liters of marsala 7 eggs creamed in pure alcohol, no doubt inspired by the Sicilian dessert creme, *zabaglione. (Zabaglione,* or *zabaione,* is whipped up from one or two egg yolks, a spoonful of sugar, and about half an eggshell of marsala. This delicious foam is served in a stem glass, cold — or better yet, hot.) Egg-flavored marsala is considered a very healthful drink, in fact it has been recommended as a restorative by Italian doctors.

Another popular marsala *speciale* is the almond-flavored marsala — *alle mandorle.* We find this marsala a good substitute for — and in fact, preferable to — amaretto. It's similar in flavor but lower in alcohol, less sweet — and less expensive.

It should come as no surprise that an almond-flavored marsala would be popular in Sicily, where colorful fruits made of *marzapane* (marzipan) decorate the windows of many a sweet shop. These very sweet almond pastes are evidence once again of the Saracen influence in the island, where they introduced their *martaban* to the enthusiastic response of the inhabitants.

Many other marsala *speciali* are produced, including marsala *al caffè* (coffee), marsala *alle fragole* (strawberry), marsala *al mandarino* (tangerine), and *crema* marsala (creamy in texture and flavored with vanilla). Among our favorite cream marsalas are those of Fici and Alloro. The *speciali* are drunk alone or mixed into desserts.

COOKING WITH MARSALA

A little marsala—*speciali* or *dolce*—mixed into some fine-quality ricotta cheese and garnished with the fruit, nuts, or coffee beans to suit the flavor of the marsala, makes a delicious dessert. Strawberries sprinkled with marsala are also served in Italy.

Marsala *fine* is frequently used in cooking. One company even sells a bottle with a wooden spoon tied to it. The list of recipes made with marsala is extensive, ranging from seafood, vegetable, and meat dishes to desserts. Veal scaloppine is perhaps the best known. Indeed, to many people in the U.S. today, the word "marsala" immediately brings to mind Veal Marsala. For some, sad to say, it is their only experience with marsala wine.

MARSALA—THE WINE

The Marsala wines range in color from pale brown to dark mahogany. Marsala has a penetrating aroma reminiscent of walnuts and raisins, and at times suggesting flowers. It is smooth in texture, sometimes velvety, and somewhat fruity in flavor. It ranges from dry *(vergine)* to very sweet *(dolce* or cream), though even the sweet marsala has a certain dryness to it. The aftertaste on a good marsala is very long and complex.

Marsala secco (dry) is not truly dry; there is a touch of sweetness to it. Marsala *secco,* served lightly chilled—15- to 18-degrees C. (60- to 65-degrees F.), is a fine aperitif, and may accompany the soup course. It also goes with piquant and strong cheeses, as well as with the cheddar types.

Marsala dolce is quite sweet, but with an underlying hint of dryness. It is best served chilled, —13- to 15-degrees C. (55-to 60-degrees F.), and goes well with light cakes. In Sicily they recommend it with *cassata*. It should also go well with another Sicilian specialty, *cannoli* — crunchy pastry tubes with a sweet, creamy filling often flavored with marsala. Marsala *dolce* can also be drunk with the blue or marbled cheeses, especially the queen of marbled cheese — gorgonzola.

Marsala vergine is the driest, and the greatest, of all marsalas. The *vergine* makes a fine aperitif and goes well with nuts, particularly walnuts. In Sicily the *vergine* is sometimes sipped after dinner as well.

We especially like the *vergine* of Rallo, but Florio, Fici and Cudia (a label of Mirabella) also make fine *vergine* marsalas. Giacomo Rallo suggests drinking the *vergine* to accompany gorgonzola, but we prefer to sip it alone without the strong, though marvelous, flavor of the cheese affecting the fine flavor and long, long finish of this wine.

Marsala *vergine* is surely the most underrated of all the fortified wines. Hugh Johnson, in his book *Wine,* says: "The finest Virgin Marsala costs the same, for example, as a second-rate Sherry and is as good a drink, from the point of view of quality, as a first-rate one." We not only agree, but would go one step further and say that marsala *vergine* can be a better drink than a first-rate sherry.

UNFORTIFIED MARSALA

Marsala *vergine* is the purest marsala; nothing is added except alcohol. Dott. Marco de Bartoli has taken this one step further, producing a marsala wine to which nothing is added — not even alcohol.

Dott. de Bartoli, formerly the oenologist at the marsala firm of Cudia, began his own firm, Azienda Agricola Samperi, to make a natural marsala wine in what he felt was the traditional, or original, style of his region.

This wine is not recognized under the marsala DOC regulations; it is not brought up to the official minimum of 18 percent alcohol. It is not labelled marsala, but De Bartoli Vecchio Samperi. The grapes ripen fully under the bright Sicilian sun, achieving a natural alcohol of 16 percent, which produces a full wine, but one more delicate than a (fortified) marsala *vergine*. The De Bartoli doesn't resist as well after the bottle is opened, but it makes a better aperitif for the lower alcohol — and perhaps one that would be drunk up sooner, partly for that very reason.

The De Bartoli Vecchio Samperi is an amber-colored wine

with a penetrating aroma that carries suggestions of nuts and flowers; it is well-balanced, and rich in flavor and glycerine, which give it an impression of sweetness although it is bone dry. It is a wine with class, and style — in fact, one of the best of the marsala wines.

CONSORZIO VOLONTARIO PER LA TUTELA DEL VINO MARSALA

Alloro Giacalone V. & C.
Buffa F.lli
Calamia Salvatore
Curatolo Arini Vito
De Vita F.lli S. & A.
Fici F.lli
Florio & C. S.A.V.I. (includes Ingham and Woodhouse labels)
Frazzitta Agostino & Figli
Genna Diego
Liuzza Giovanni & Figli
Lombardo Marchetti F.
Martinez F.lli
Mineo F.lli
Mirabella S.p.A. (includes Cudia label)
Pellegrino Carlo & C. S.p.A.
Perricone Francesco & Figli
Pipitone Spano' P.
Rallo Diego & Figli
Regina Vincenzo
S.I.V. S.p.A.

SOME MARSALAS WORTHY OF RECOMMENDATION

(** = especially superior quality)
(* = superior quality)

VERGINE
**Rallo 1860
  Cudia Stravecchio
 *De Bartoli Vecchio Samperi (non-DOC)
  De Vita Stravecchio
  Fici Stravecchio
 *Florio
  Mineo Virgin Dry Riserva Reale

SOLERA (Dry)
  *Fici Riserva
  *Florio ACI 1840
  *Florio Riserva Egadi
 **Ingham Riserva Racalia 1870
   Pellegrino Vecchia Riserva 1880
 **Woodhouse Riserva 1815

SECCO SUPERIORE (Superior Dry)
   Alloro
   De Vita SOM
   Fici
   Florio Vecchio Florio SOM
   Martinez
  *Rallo Black Label SOM
   Vito Curatolo Arini Riserva

DOLCE SUPERIORE (Superior Sweet)
   Alloro
   Fici
   Rallo del Nonno
   Rallo Garibaldi Dolce

CREMA ALL 'UOVO
   Alloro Stravecchio
  *Fici

CREMA MANDORLA (Almond Cream)
   Florio
   Cudia

MARSALA GLOSSARY

Caffè (cah-FEH). Coffee-flavored marsala.

Crema (CREH-mah). A very sweet, rich marsala with a vanilla flavor.

Crema all'Uovo (CREH-mah ahl WOH-voh). Cream marsala, very sweet, flavored with egg.

Crema Mandorla (CREH-mah MAHN-dohr-lah). Cream marsala flavored with almonds.

Denominazione di Origine Controllata (deh-noh-mee-naht-ZYOH-neh dee oh-REE-jee-neh cohn-troh-LAH-tah). Regulated under Italian wine law.

Dolce (DOHL-cheh). Sweet.

Fine (FEE-neh). The lowest grade of marsala, dry or sweet. Often used for cooking.

Fragole (FRAH-go-leh). Strawberry-flavored marsala.

GD; Garibaldi Dolce (gah-rih-BAHL-dee DOHL-cheh). A sweet marsala *superiore*.

IP; Italia Particolare (ee-TAH-lyah par-tee-coh-LAH-reh). Sweet or dry marsala *fine*.

Italy Particular. Sweet or dry marsala *fine*.

LP; London Particular. A type of marsala *superiore*.

Mandarino (mahn-dah-REE-noh). Tangerine-flavored marsala.

Mandorla (MAHN-dohr-lah). Almond-flavored marsala.

OP; Old Particular. A type of marsala *superiore*.

Riserva (ree-ZEHR-vah). No legal meaning. However, on wines of the members of the Consorzio this term indicates a marsala that has been aged in barrel for ten years or longer.

Secco (SEC-coh). Dry.

SOM. Superior old marsala.

Solera (soh-LEH-rah). A system of fractional blending and maturing used for the better *superiore* and *vergine* marsalas to produce uniformity.

Speciali (speh-CHAH-lee). The flavored marsalas.

Superior; Superiore (soo-peh-RYOH-reh). A higher classification than marsala *fine,* covering wines higher in alcohol which have been given longer aging. The best *superiore* wines are aged in *solera*. They may be dry or sweet.

Superior Old Marsala. Marsala *superiore*.

Stravecchio (strah-VEHK-kyoh). Very old. This term has no legal meaning.

Vergine (VEHR-jee-neh). The best, driest, most distinctive, and most natural of the marsalas.

IV

Montilla-Moriles

In the sunny province of Andalusía in southern Spain, the area extending from just south of the city of Córdoba to about 100 kilometers (62 miles) north of the Mediterranean port of Malaga is the region of Montilla-Moriles, generally called simply Montilla. The dry, hilly countryside here is planted to olive and almond trees and wide stretches of low-growing vines. Men work the land with donkeys and primitive plows as they have for generations.

The history of wine in this region goes back to ancient times. Some historians believe the vine was introduced here by the Greeks. Ceramic and clay utensils from the eighth century B.C. have been discovered in the Montilla-Moriles region.

In the period from the eleventh to the fifth centuries B.C., Greek traders founded settlements on the Iberian peninsula. The town of Écija, only 30 kilometers (18 miles) from Montilla, was settled by the Greeks. And where the Greeks went, they often planted the vine.

By the third and second centuries B.C., when Spain—or Iberia—was part of the Roman Empire, the wines of this region were well known.

The city of Córdoba, just to the north of Montilla, and the commercial center of the region, was the capitol of Andalusía, the Roman province of Baetica—from Baetis, the

Roman name for the Guadalquivir river. A bridge built by the Romans, Puente Romano, today restored and embellished in Renaissance style, still arches over the Guadalquivir at Córdoba.

The wines of Baetica achieved a certain renown in Rome itself. Wine from Córdoba was served to the Caesars. And they may also have tasted Montilla wine; amphorae bearing the seal of Munda Baetica, the Roman name for Montilla, have been unearthed in Italy. Columella, a Roman writer of Spanish birth, sang the praises of these wines in his *De Re Rustica*.

When the declining Roman Empire was invaded by barbarian tribes, Spain too, a part of the empire, felt the onslaught. Vandals and Visigoths swept into Spain in the fifth century A.D. The Vandals continued on their destructive course all the way to Carthage and beyond. The Visigoths remained, to rule Spain for nearly three centuries.

As they became civilized, we can perhaps assume that they came to appreciate the qualities of the wine of the country, that their kings may even have encouraged viticulture, although no evidence of it has been found.

In the eighth century, Saracen armies from North Africa crossed the Straits of Gibraltar and invaded the Iberian peninsula. The Saracens easily conquered the internally divided Visigothic kingdom. In 711 King Roderic was defeated in the Visigoth's final battle, at Guadalete. This victory marked the beginning of Arab domination in Spain, which would last nearly 800 years. The Arab influence was most strongly felt, and lasted longest, in Andalusía, their Al Andalus.

In 719, the region of Córdoba, which included the villages of Montilla and Moriles, became one of the Arab emirates in Spain under the rule of the Caliphate of Damascus. In 756 Abdu'r-Rahman I became emir of Córdoba, founding a dynasty that would live for two and a half centuries. Under this reign Córdoba was raised to prosperity and fame.

In 929 Abdu'r-Rahman III declared Spain's independence from Damascus, raising Córdoba to a caliphate. Three centuries of peace and prosperity followed. Córdoba in the tenth century was a seat of learning; the University of Córdoba, well known and highly regarded.

The intellectual atmosphere was open and tolerant. And the strict ban on wine laid down in the Koran was not always so strictly followed. Vineyards continued to be cultivated in the region, though to what extent we're not sure. Some were used for the production of table grapes and raisins, but others yielded liquid pleasures.

In this vine-growing region grape juice wasn't the only, or even the most popular, beverage consumed. George Rainbird, in *Sherry and the Wines of Spain,* notes that:

> In Córdoba, it is recorded that an arrested drunk was brought before the Chief Kadi for sentence; but he, wise man, employed a special official who, upon being asked to certify that the accused's breath smelt strongly of wine, would always say that, certainly, the man's breath smelt, but whether of grape-juice or wine it was impossible to tell. Whereupon the judge dismissed the case smartly and saved his soul from the sin of hypocrisy.*

In the literature of the period, Arab writers and poets frequently praised the wine of the region, making special note of the wines of Montilla.

In the eleventh century Al Andalus became fragmented into *taifa* (faction) kingdoms, fighting among themselves, and Christian forces began making deeper inroads into Moorish Spain. With the fall of Córdoba to the Christian armies of the Reconquista (Reconquest) in the thirteenth century, Moors fleeing the city found refuge in the still-flourishing kingdom of Granada, the last Moorish stronghold left in Spain. In 1492 Granada, under the weak boy king Boabdil, finally fell, thus ending the long and often brilliant reign of the Moors in Spain.

Reminders of this era can still be seen in Montilla today in the architecture and decoration of its buildings. The montilla *bodegas,* a number of which are in the city of Córdoba, often have roofs supported by Moorish crenelated arches. Evidence exists that *bodegas,* buildings for the production and storage of wine, had been built during the Moorish occupation. In the town of Montilla itself, with its narrow streets and low buildings, are houses decorated with colorful *azulejos* (glazed pottery tiles), a craft first practiced in Spain by Arab artisans in the twenfth century.

THE WINE TODAY

The wines of Montilla are similar to those from the Sherry region to the south. And the overall quality is higher. But the montilla wines are not nearly so famous as those of Jerez — or

*(London: McGraw-Hill Book Co., 1966).

as the name has been anglicized, Sherry.

Undoubtedly one reason for this is that for a long time the montilla wines were sold under the name of "sherry." Although a council had been formed in 1932 to regulate the wines of Montilla-Moriles and the region was delimited the following year, it wasn't until 1944 that the Spanish Ministry of Agriculture allowed the region to label its wines under the Montilla-Moriles name (for the two major wine towns in the region).

Montilla has no outlet on the sea for shipping its wine directly to foreign ports, which would have spread the reputation of its wines abroad. But wines were shipped to the Sherry ports, and being similar, they were either blended with or simply considered one of the sherry wines.

Since the court case of 1960, montilla is no longer allowed to be labelled sherry—although we have been told, in Montilla, that some montilla wine, like most of that from Huelva (where the wine is also affected by the *flor*), is still shipped to Jerez to be blended into sherry.

THE VINES

The vineyards of Montilla are limited to that region of chalky soil between the Genil and Guadajoz rivers, bordered by the mountain ranges of Cabra and Priego and the Guadalquivir. Montilla is in the northern part; Moriles, in the south. This white soil is called *albero,* the same soil that is known as *albariza* in Jerez.

The best wines come from the Montilla *albero* vineyards in the Sierra de Montilla range south of Montilla, and the Moriles *albero* vineyards in the Moriles Alto (upper Moriles) area.

These vineyards are planted at altitudes of about 1,200 feet, and produce the best fino wines. Olorosos are produced from vines planted on the *ruedos* (plains) around Montilla.

Some 10,000 vineyard owners cultivate the 24,000 hectares (60,000 acres) under vines in Montilla-Moriles. The climate during the growing season is dry and very hot—the long summer here, they say, is the hottest in Spain; the winters are very cold.

The vines, pruned low under the blazing sun to absorb its reflected heat, are mostly Pedro Ximénez. The Pedro Ximénez (PX) grape is thought to be originally from the Rhineland of Germany. It is said that it was brought here in the sixteenth century by a soldier in the Flemish legions, Pero

128

CORDOBA
•

FERNAN-NUNEZ •

• MONTILLA

• AGUILAR

• CABRA

MORILES •

• PUENTE GENIL

• LUCENA

MONTILLA-MORILES

Ximen, for whom it was named. Some speculate that it was the noble Riesling that he brought, others that it was the lowly Elbling. Whatever variety, the PX has adapted well here and produces fine wines.

The Pedro Ximénez grape is known to have been growing in Montilla as early as 1632. On English wine lists of the seventeenth century it appeared under the names of Peter-Sameene and Peter-See-Me.

HARVEST AND FERMENTATION

The harvest in Montilla, reputedly the earliest in Spain, normally starts at the beginning of September. The grapes here need not be laid out on straw mats to dry in the sun, as in Jerez, to concentrate the juice and raise sugar levels. The ripe grapes attain high natural sugars, and the wines achieve 14 to 17 percent alcohol naturally.

The harvested grapes are taken to the press house, where they're put through a crusher-stemmer which removes the stems and breaks the grape skins. The juice that runs off from the crushed grapes is called the ''free-run'' juice. The grapes are then given a preliminary light pressing with modern wine presses and this juice, called the *yema* (yolk), is blended with the free-run. The *mosto,* or must, goes to the fermenting cellars, where a measure of sulphur is added to kill the wild yeast that forms on the grape skins. The *flor* yeast which develops on the fino wine is used for the fermentation.

In the ancient province of Baetica it was the custom to ferment and store the wine in large earthenware jars, called *orcae,* which were shaped like hugh amphorae. Vats in this same unusual shape are still used in Montilla today for fermenting the wine.

These *tinâjas,* as they are known in Spanish, are made of smooth cement or, sometimes, clay. They hold 5,900 to 6,880 liters (1,560 to 1,820 gallons) of must. The equivalent Spanish measure would be 375 to 435 *arrobas* (1 *arroba* = 16 liters). The enormous jars, well over the height of a man, are lined up row upon row in the fermenting sheds; the lip and shoulder curve of the *tinâjas* rise above a wooden floor which allows the winery workers access to the wine.

The *pie de cuba* — a small quantity of must mixed with *flor* yeast taken from the best wine — is put into the bottom of the *tinâja*. When this begins to ferment, *mosto* is added; then more, as each new batch gets caught up in the fermentation, until all the *mosto* is in the *tinájas.* The must ferments for fifteen to thirty days. The first tumultuous fermentation is followed by a slower secondary fermentation.

The *mosto* is left in the *tinájas* until February or March. Then it is cleared with a fining of egg white and *lebrija,* (local clay), to drop out particles in suspension, and moved to cement holding tanks.

CLASSIFICATION

At this point the wine is classified into the two basic categories, fino or oloroso, and put into 586-liter (155-gallon) *butas,* or butts—some larger, some smaller—of American oak.

The grapes actually have already been tentatively classified, by vineyard, even before the harvest. The fino wine is made only from grapes grown in the *albero* vineyards in the Montilla Sierras and the Moriles Alto, but not all grapes from these areas will become fino wine. Some will become oloroso, as will the grapes from the *rueda.*

The grapes from *albero* and *rueda* areas are pressed and vinified separately. For fino montilla, only the free-run juice is used. The finos are lighter wines, with more delicacy and fineness.

At the second classification, made after the fermentation is complete, the finos are tested again and those which are judged not delicate enough are reclassified as olorosos. The olorosos are fuller wines, bigger in body and higher in alcohol.

The sweetness of the grape also helps to determine the type of wine it will become. The grapes are picked at sugar levels to attain 15 to 16 percent alcohol. Normally no alcohol is added to the finos; they are naturally 15½ percent; 2-3 percent alcohol is added to the olorosos. It is very unusual for the wine here to achieve less than 15 percent alcohol, but in such a case alcohol would be added to bring the wine up to the desired level.

A third classification is made by the *capataz,* or cellar-master; this is the classification by nose, further narrowing down the finos. The wine then goes to the *crianza,* or nursery, the first step in its maturing.

The wine in the barrels is sampled by the *capataz* using a *venencia,* or wine thief with an unusual design—a narrow cylindrical cup at the end of a long flexible handle (formerly whalebone and silver, now often plastic and stainless steel).

The *venencia* is plunged down into the partially filled cask, beneath the *flor,* to bring up the sample of wine.

Curiously, in the decoration of a Greek beaker from c. 490 B.C. (pictured in Warner Allen's *A History of Wine),* there is a young man holding what is known in Greek as an *ephebos.* This long-handled cup is of the same design as the *venencia* of Montilla and Sherry. It may actually have been the original *venencia,* its design then copied by the Romans and taken from them by the Spaniards.

Champion *venenciadores,* aiming with precision, can neatly arc the wine from the *venencia* into a *copita,* or wine glass, without spilling a drop.

The wine comes up with bits of *flor* yeast floating in it. The yeast itself has a nutty flavor like that which it imparts to the wine but a bit more pronounced. Any *flor* is filtered out, of course, before the wine is bottled (it tastes a lot better than it looks). The wine is also cold stabilized before shipment.

Wine is cold stabilized by being chilled to a very low temperature. This causes the tartaric acid to crystallize and settle on the bottom of the tank. The wine is then racked off leaving the crystals behind. This practice is quite common today. It is done so that when the wine is chilled by the consumer, it will remain clear and free of crystals.

AGING

The *mosto* from the *crianza* is put into casks with older wine, in a proportion of about 1 part new to 2 parts old.

The casks of oloroso are kept full. The fino casks are left partially empty, about eight-ninths full. In the casks of old fino to which the new fino must is added, the *flor* is already present. There is no *flor* in the oloroso casks.

FLOR

This *flor,* or "flower," is a white yeast which floats on the surface of the wine in the partially empty casks, protecting the wine from oxygen and vinegar bacteria. The *flor* imparts a characteristic nut-like flavor to the wine.

Flor forms on wines from areas scattered throughout Spain as well as in France, where the *fleur* (flower) forms on certain wines in the Jura, such as Château Chalon. This term, flower, may seem an odd one to describe a layer of mold, but when the *flor* is first forming on the wine, it develops in flower-like patches before spreading to join into a complete layer covering the surface of the wine.

The phenomenon of *flor* was known in ancient times. Archestratus described the wine of the Greek island of Lesbos as being overgrown with a white flower.

Pliny writing in the first century A.D. refers to *flos vini,* the wine flower, forming on *orcae* of wine.

> . . . Weak vintages should be kept in jars sunk in the ground, but jars containing strong wines should be exposed to the air . . . . The jars must never be filled quite full . . . .
>
> Flower of wine [*flos vini*] forming is thought to be a good sign if it is white, but a bad sign if it is red, unless it is red wine . . . .

Flor was known in Spain as early as 1616, but its beneficial effects were not appreciated by the winemakers until about 1850. Before that, the butts of wine that developed the mold were thought to have spoiled.

Most of the *flor,* which can become as thick as ¼ of an inch, falls to the bottom of the cask in the extremes of heat in summer and cold in winter. But the *flor* is always present, as at least a thin film floating on the surface of the wine. This is called in Montilla the *"velo de flor,"* the veil of *flor.*

BODEGAS AND THE ENVIRONMENT

The butts of fino are stored in dimly lit, well-ventilated *bodegas* (above-ground aging cellars). The olorosos are kept at warmer temperatures, sometimes outdoors in the sun.

The environment in the *bodega* is very important, with ventilation perhaps the most important factor. The air in the building must be fresh. The best temperature for the *flor* is between 15 and 18 degrees C. (60 to 65 degrees F.). Workers spray water on the earthen floor of the *bodega* in summer to cool it, by evaporation, and to keep up the level of humidity. Woven rope mats hang over the windows to keep out the sun's bright rays.

Pliny also notes, in a rather picturesque manner, the effects of climate and of lunar pull on the wine: "It is laid down that jars must not be opened at mid-winter except on a fine day, and not when a south wind is blowing, or at a full moon."

El Consejo Regulador de la Denominación de Origen, the regulatory board, requires that the young wines of Montilla-Moriles be brought up *(elaborado)* and matured in *bodegas* located in the towns of Montilla, Moriles, Aguilar de la

Solera System

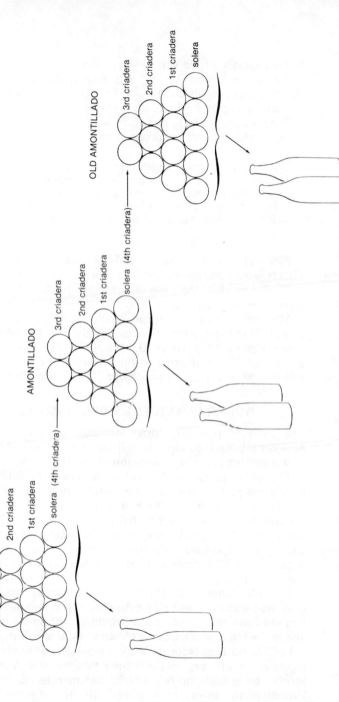

Frontera, Cabra, Córdoba, Lucena, or Puente Genil.

SOLERA

The Montilla wines are matured by the *solera* system of fractional blending, in which new wine becomes educated by the old, taking on its character and complexities. Some say the *solera* system originated in Montilla.

This system is believed to have been invented, or have evolved, in the early 1700s. The oldest *solera* we know of that is still in existence is the 1729 *solera* of Alvear in Montilla, though reputedly there are older ones in Sanlúcar.

Before this, a forerunner of the *solera* system was used in the monasteries in the Rhineland and in the Loire Valley of France, where huge casks of aged wine were refreshed each year with additions of the new wine from the harvest.

The *solera* system came into general use in Spain sometime after the turn of the nineteenth century. The name *"solera"* comes from the Spanish word *suelo,* for floor or ground, here in the sense of foundation. The oldest row of wine barrels at the bottom of the *solera* system is called the *solera.*

In the past the barrels of wine in the *solera* system were stacked one atop the other — the top tiers of *criaderas* above the bottom, *solera,* row. Nowadays it is no longer necessary to stack the barrels this way, since the wine is not moved down from cask to cask by hand, using gravitation, but is pumped from one barrel to another by machine. The casks may even be in different buildings.

But the system of aging and blending remains the same. The wine is drawn off for bottling — not more than 20 to 30 percent — from the *solera* barrels in what was traditionally the bottom row. The wine in the *solera* barrels must then be brought up to the proper level with wine taken from the first *criadera,* the next tier above; the casks are never allowed to become less than half full.

The wine taken from the first *criadera* is then replaced by (younger) wine from the second *criadera,* and that replaced by wine from the third, and so on. The wine from all the barrels in each tier is blended together for uniformity before being transferred to the next lower (older) *criadera.* The top row of barrels is refilled from the *crianza,* where the fresh wine, still referred to as *mosto,* is kept.

The wine taken out to be bottled is often labeled with a *solera* year. This is the year the *solera* was begun, and theoretically there is still some wine in the blend from that vintage, though in minute proportions for a centuries-old *solera*.

While the proportion may be very small, the important thing is not that there is old wine in the blend, but that the new wine has been gradually "educated" each step of the way by the older wine to take on the characteristics of each succeeding *criadera;* when it has been in the *solera* for the time required, it will develop into an extension of the original *solera* wine that it replaced.

In some instances the wine taken from the *solera* casks is not taken out to be bottled; instead it becomes the top *criadera* of a further, more sophisticated, *solera* system of yet older wine.

Fino wines with further age become amontillados. True amontillados are aged finos (false amontillados are blends of lesser wines, which have been sweetened). A montilla firm may have more than one fino *solera* in the *bodega,* the oldest of which is used as a *criadera* in an amontillado *solera*.

There is still a film of *flor* in the barrels of amontillado, but much less than that on the fino wine. Some amontillados are very old, and very complex, and very fine indeed. This perhaps might well have described the cask of amontillado in the tale of the same name by Edgar Allan Poe.

The oloroso montilla is also matured in a *solera* system.

MONTILLA BARS

In the town of Montilla there are a number of wine bars where patrons can order montilla by the glass. The wine may be poured from bottle, or drawn from barrels, marked "Fino," "Amontillado," or "Oloroso." The fino appears to be the most popular type.

To accompany the wine, there are *tapas* (a variety of tasty snacks) — fresh anchovies, mussels, shrimp, skewered meat, and many other tempting delicacies. In one montilla bar we visited, known for its seafood, we tasted some of the best we had eaten in Spain (and Montilla is some distance from the sea) — tiny octopus cooked in oil and garlic served with bread for sopping up the delicious sauce; and the shrimp! — this must have been the specialty of the house. We might have been ankle-deep in shrimp shells as we stood at the bar shucking the tasty critters and tossing their shells onto the most obvious place, in the local manner. Despite the crunch underfoot, the place was clean, apparently well hosed out and freshened up each night in preparation for the next day's hungry crowd.

BUYING AND SERVING

Fino montilla is pale gold in color with a clean aroma suggesting olives — some say they also detect almonds. It is light-bodied, dry, and refreshing. The finos range in alcohol from 15 to 16½ percent.

Fino is at its best served chilled. It makes a fine aperitif and also goes well with *tapas,* such as olives and shellfish, especially clams and oysters.

Good fino montillas:

*Alvear Fino CB
*Alvear Fino Festival
 Fino Bravado (Bodegas Espejo)
 Fino Cañalerma (Bellido y Carrasco SA)
*Fino Pompeyo (J. Cobos)
 Gracia Fino Kiki
 Gran Barquero (Perez Barquero)
 Los Amigos Fino (Perez Barquero)

The finos are best drunk very young — in fact, the younger and fresher they are, the better. The higher alcohol (higher than table wine) doesn't help to preserve their freshness. Finos, like most white wines, lose crispness and character and become dull with age.

For this reason it's a good idea to finish a bottle, once opened, within a few hours, or at the most a few days. Keeping it in the refrigerator will help preserve its freshness longer, and fino, at any rate, is best drunk chilled.

This is not a wine to buy by the case. Buy a bottle or two at a time, as you need them, from a merchant who turns his stock over. Avoid dusty bottles and those with faded or discolored labels (an indication of age). It's worth finding out, in fact, which finos are imported in small quantities and in frequent shipments.

Finos viejos are similar to amontillados. These "old finos" are dry, darker in color, and fuller in body than the simple finos. The finos *viejos* range in alcohol from 17 to 17½ percent. They are best served cool, but not chilled. These fine old wines are good drunk alone or perhaps with nuts.

Good fino *viejo* montillas:

Alvear Finisimo (very fino, about 10 years old)
*Alvear Solera Fundacion Fino (1729 Solera)

Amontillado — literally, in the style of Montilla — is amber in color, dry, and fuller-bodied than fino (true amontillado, that is). It has a nutty aroma and flavor, and more complexity than the fino. Amontillados range in alcohol from 16 to 18 percent. The older amontillados, *amontillados viejos* — aged longer — are over 20 percent.

Amontillados make a good accompaniment to soups, especially consomme. The sweeter amontillados go well with cream soups. Amontillado of either type is good drunk by itself, with nuts or some kinds of cheese — the cheddar types in particular.

Good amontillado montillas:

*Alvear Solera Fundación Amontillado Muy Viejo
*Alvear Amontillado Viejisimo (over 100 years old)
*Alvear Abuelo Diego 1750 Solera Amontillado
 Gracia Amontillado Viejo Montearrut

Palo cortado montilla is a type that is quite rare. In style it is in between an amontillado and an oloroso. It is a dry, pungent montilla, ranging in alcohol from 15 to 18 percent.

Bodega Morena produces a highly regarded Palo Cortado.

Oloroso montilla is mahogany in color. It has an aromatic fragrance and a nutty flavor. On the palate it is full-bodied, dry, and velvety. The olorosos range from 16 to 18 percent in alcohol. Some are lightly sweetened. Oloroso montilla is good drunk with nuts or cheddar-type cheese.

Good oloroso montillas:

*Alvear 1750 Solera
*Spanish Gold Oloroso Mercedes

The *olorosos viejos* are old olorosos, ranging from 19 to 21 percent in alcohol, normally over 20 percent. These wines are fine sipped alone, or perhaps accompanied by nuts.

Good oloroso viejo montillas:

Alvear Oloroso Viejo

Raya montillas are similar to the olorosos but of lesser quality. They range in alcohol from 16 to 18 percent. These wines aren't bottled as rayas, but are used for blending in the less expensive, sweetened, types of montilla.

PX, or *Pedro Ximénez, montilla* is named for the grape variety. These wines are deep, rich brown in color and quite sweet and thick. They reach 20+ percent in alcohol (fortified). The PX montillas are made from sun-dried grapes and have a raisiny flavor. This type of montilla is rich enough to be drunk and enjoyed by itself, but may be accompanied by nuts.

Good Pedro Ximénez montillas:

*Spanish Gold Riserva Especial
*Spanish Gold Extra
 Alvear 1890 Solera
 Alvear 1830 Viejisimo (refreshened, not a *solera* wine)

Cream montillas are quite sweet and smooth, but less thick and raisiny than the PXs. The cream montillas can be drunk with sweet fruit or light cakes.

OVERALL ASSESSMENT

Montilla, though similar to sherry, has some significant differences: montilla is lighter in body and lower in alcohol. It is of higher average quality, and is generally lower in price.

Its being less well known than sherry is undoubtedly a factor in accounting for montilla's lower prices. This, coupled with its higher average quality, makes montilla a better value than sherry. And its lower alcohol makes it — the fino, in particular — a better aperitif, as well as a wine suitable for drinking with food. The production of Montilla-Moriles is less than that of Jerez, and from an area considerably larger. As quantity and quality don't often go together, this might help to account for montilla's higher average quality.

MONTILLA GLOSSARY

Amontillado (ah-mon-tee-YAH-doh). True amontillado is dry. It is a fino which has been aged much longer in the *solera,* becoming fuller in body, darker in color, and higher in alcohol.

Bodega (boh-THEY-gah). A warehouse where wine is aged and stored.

Cream Montilla. A dark, richly sweet, creamy textured montilla.

Criadera (cree-ah-DEH-rah). A scale or tier within a *solera* system, above the bottom *(solera)* tier.

Fino (FEE-noh). The palest and lightest style of montilla with characteristics imparted by the *flor*. Finos are vinified dry.

Flor (flohr). A yeast which forms on certain wines and imparts a unique character to them.

Oloroso (oh-loh-ROH-soh). Olorosos are full-bodied and dark amber to walnut in color. They do not get *flor*. True olorosos are always dry.

Palo Cortado (PAH-loh cohr-TAH-thoh). A rare style of oloroso, finer and more delicate than the regular olorosos.

Solera (soh-LEH-rah). A system of fractional blending to mature and produce uniformity in montilla wines. The young wine is aged with older wine, in fractional amounts, and moved after a period of time into barrels of older, then still older wine, taking on the characteristics of the older wines. The oldest wine in the *solera* is drawn out for bottling and theoretically contains some wine from the date the *solera* was established.

V

Sherry

Sherry wine is produced in an area of Spain between the Guadalquivir and Guadalete rivers on the Atlantic Coast of southern Andalusía. This region is often referred to as the Sherry Triangle; its three points are the towns of Jerez de la Frontera, Puerto de Santa María, and Sanlúcar de Barrameda.

This area, in the province of Cádiz, has a very ancient history. The capital city of the province, from which it takes its name, is thought to be the oldest city in Europe, over 3,000 years old. Some historians believe that Cádiz was founded in the twelfth century B.C. (others say, as early as the fifteenth) by Phoenicians driven out of Canaan by the Israelites; they named their settlement Gádir. This later became the Roman city of Gades, and later still the Spanish Cádiz. The Phoenicians are credited with bringing the grape vine to the Iberian peninsula.

The origin of the town of Jerez is uncertain. Phoenicians, traveling inland from Gádir, established a trading colony at Xera in about 1100 B.C., or perhaps earlier. There is speculation that this may be the present-day Jerez. Some historians think Jerez grew out of the Roman city of ꞏXericium. Roman coins and tablets have been found in the vicinity of Jerez, and a Roman mosaic depicting the vine has been unearthed in the area. But no definite evidence has been found proving that the actual town of Jerez was founded by

Phoenicians or Romans.

By the Roman era the wines of Andalusía—then, the Roman province of Baetica—had achieved a measure of fame. Baetica was listed among the top eighteen wines of the Roman Empire. This could have been the wine of Sherry or Montilla, since both regions were in the province of Baetica. No evidence has been found that amphorae of wine from Xericium itself were exported to Rome. But by the first century A.D., a good proportion of the wine of Baetica was in demand for export.

In 409 A.D., the barbarian Vandals invaded Spain, bringing an end to the Roman civilization there. In the wake of their destruction, they may have left behind the name by which the region came to be known—Wandalusía, the land of the Vandals. They couldn't have left much else for they were soon defeated by another barbarian tribe, the Visigoths, in 414. The Visigoths settled and ruled the region for almost three centuries.

Wandalusía became Al Andalus when the Moors invaded the Iberian peninsula on their conquest of Europe. Jerez was definitely a Moorish city, whether the Moors in fact founded it or took it over. Its name under the Moors was generally transliterated from Arabic as Scheris.

Under Moorish rule the city prospered. The vineyards of the region were not destroyed, but the grapes produced were predominately for eating or making raisins rather than wine—in the beginning, at least. Although the Moslem religion forbade alcohol to its adherents, winemaking was not forbidden. And it has been said that some of the less devout of the Moors were known to enjoy wine at their celebrations. Some Arab poets sang its praises in romantic, and hidden, verse.

On October 9, 1264, the feast day of St. Dionysus Areopagiticus, the Christian army under King Alfonso X entered Jerez and reconquered it for Christianity. It seems rather fitting that it was on the day of St. Dionysus (the name of the Greek god of wine) that the town was recaptured by pro-wine forces. Alfonso established a stronghold at Jerez to command the frontier between Christians and Moslems. In 1380 Jerez was granted the title *"de la Frontera"* in recognition of its important position.

Under Alfonso X, called the Wise, the vineyards were extended and winemaking encouraged. But in 1435 there was a shortage of wine in Jerez, causing the town council to put a prohibition on exports. More vineyards were planted and the region was extended to include previously outlying districts, the *afuera,* which also had the white *albariza* soil typical of the region.

Puerto de Santa María, the second point on the Sherry triangle, is believed to have been founded by Greek military captains, veterans of the Trojan Wars. Puerto is located at the mouth of the Guadalete River, 9 kilometers (5½ miles) southwest of Jerez. The Moors called this port Alcanate. Alfonso the Wise, who captured it in 1260, gave it the Christian name of Santa María de Porto; later, in 1283, redubbing it Gran Puerto de Santa María.

The first known reference to the vineyards of Puerto de Santa María is dated 1288, but vines may have been planted there many years earlier.

Sunlúcar de Barrameda is the most charming of the three major sherry towns. It is a large seaside village 13 kilometers (8 miles) northwest of Jerez. On the beach there are a number of restaurants offering fresh delicacies from the sea to the accompaniment of glasses of cool, dry manzanilla sherry.

By the end of the fifteenth century the fame of the Sanlúcar wines had spread, and they were being exported outside of Spain.

SACK

In the early sixteenth century, sherris-sack began to be regularly imported into England. Sherris-sack was highly praised by Falstaff, a man with a big thirst, in Shakespeare's *King Henry IV:* "If I had a thousand sons, the first humane principle I would teach them should be to forswear thin potations and to addict themselves to sack." Sherris-sack is not believed to have yet reached Britain's shores in Henry IV's time (1367-1413). But by the time the play was written, at the end of the sixteenth century, sack, especially old sack, had already become a popular drink in Merrie Old Elizabethan England.

There are a number of theories offered to explain the use of the word "sack" or "sherris-sack" in reference to sherry. As the most plausible, or most repeated, three theories are worth mentioning. Some writers have suggested "sack" is a corruption, of *sec,* meaning dry. This, though, seems doubtful because the early sherries brought to England are believed to have been sweet wines. The theory that the name comes from the practice of employing a sack in the making of the wine is accepted by some as a reasonable explanation. But straining or filtering the wine through a sack doesn't seem to be a major enough part of the winemaking process to justify its becoming known as "sack" wine. The most plausible explanation seems to be the one advanced by H. Warner Allen in *A History of Wine;* that is, that the name sack comes from the Spanish word *sacar,* meaning to take out or take away—in other words, to export. Jerezanos (the people of Jerez) used the term *saca* for export wines in the phrase *vinos de saca.* This would explain other exported wines—from Málaga, Galicia, the Canaries, and Portugal—also being called sack.

Later it became more common to refer to the wine of Jerez and the rest of the region by its geographical name. In English this came to be written "sherry," as we know it today (it is Xérès in French). The term was used to refer to the wines of Jerez in a text of 1608. And it is specifically stated in Ben Jonson's play *Bartholomew Fair,* written in 1614, that sherry was the name by then used for the wine that was previously called sack.

The sherry shippers say that the name sherry refers to the wines of Jerez and therefore should be reserved for them exclusively, that it should be prohibited for use on wines from other regions (such as South African Cape sherry, Australian sherry, California sherry, etc.). As far as we can judge, the earliest use of the name "sherry" did indeed refer to the wines of Jerez.

But sherry shippers themselves have used names from other areas on their wines. In the fifteenth century, shippers in Puerto de Santa María and Sanlúcar exported a wine produced in Lepe (believed to have been in the region between Seville and Huelva) that they called *vino de Romania,* or Rumneys. Rumneys was the name of a well-regarded sweet wine from an area of southern Greece named Romania by the Romans—quite some distance from Lepe.

One famous sherry firm today sells a brandy in Spain called *Coñac*—pronounced the same as Cognac, which as we know is the name of the region in France producing the most highly regarded brandy in the world. This seems to weaken their case.

CLIMATE AND TERRAIN

The Sherry Triangle covers an area of about 8,000—10,000 hectares (20,000—25,000 acres). It is a dry, sunny, low-lying region; the average altitude of the vineyards is from 100 to 150 meters (300 to 450 feet above sea level). Winter rains, falling mostly from February to mid-May, amount to only about 62 centimeters (25 inches). There is no rain at all from late May until early October. Sherry is bathed in sunshine for 295 days out of the year.

The maturing cellars for sherry must be located in Jerez de la Frontera, Sanlúcar de Barrameda, or Puerto de Santa María. Since 1933, the Sherry Control Board—Consejo Regulador de la Denominación de Origen Jerez-Xérès-Sherry y Manzanilla-Sanlúcar de Barrameda—has regulated the sherry wines.

SOILS

Sherry is known for its snow-white soil, called *albariza,* found in more than 60 percent of the vineyards. Some of this soil is white, but other shades of *albariza* run more to a grayish white. The color depends on the proportion of chalk, ranging from 30 to 80 percent, in combination with sand and clay. The vineyards are in districts called *pagos,* which are determined by their type of soil. There are about forty *pagos* of *albariza* soil in Jerez.

The fino sherries are made from grapes grown in *albariza* soil. Yields are lower on this soil—80 hectoliters/hectare (860 gallons/acre), or over 5 butts of wine per acre. (This, however, is not low; in Burgundy, for example, the normal yield is about 35 hectoliters/hectare (375 gallons/acre). The grape varieties here at Palomino (the major type), Albillo, Perruno, Mantuo Castellano, and Pedro Ximénez grown on the lower slopes of the *albariza pagos.*

Among those considered the best *pagos* are Añina and Balbaína, west of Jerez and north of Puerto; and Carrascal and Macharnudo, north of Jerez. The first two *pagos*, along with Los Tercios, produce the finest finos. Carrascal is regarded for its olorosos; Marcharnudo, adjoining it on the west, for fine amontillados as well as finos.

The Miraflores and Torrebreda *pagos* south of Sanlúcar are considered among the best for manzanilla.

In the area from near Puerto (southwest of Jerez) to beyond Lebrija (northeast of Jerez) the white *albariza* soil is often patched with other, darker, soils.

A second soil type in the sherry vineyards is *barro,* a brownish soil about 30 percent chalk, mixed with iron oxide. *Barro* vineyards are generally found southeast of Jerez in the low-lying areas. These vineyards produce greater yields than those on *albariza* soil, and the wines produced have more body. Two of the better *barro pagos* are El Corchuelo, near Jerez, and Cuárbillos. The same grapes grown in the *albariza* vineyards are grown in the *barro pagos,* plus one other variety, Beba. Over 20 percent of the Sherry vineyards are on *barro* soil.

A third soil type is called *arena.* This is mostly sand, yellowish red in color due to admixtures of iron. This soil type is generally found in *pagos* north and east of Jerez. Vineyards in *arena* soil achieve the highest yields. Monte Alegre is a well-known *arena pago* between Jerez and Cádiz. The grapes grown in the *arena pagos* are Palomino, Mantuos de Pila, and Mollares Negros (could this be the Negra Mole of Madeira?).

GRAPES

Palomino Blanco, or Listan, is by far the most important grape variety in Sherry, producing over 70 percent of the wine. In the different areas the Palomino grape has different names, reflecting the relative insularity of the Sherry villages in the time not so long ago when communication was much more limited. The local name in Puerto is Horgazuela. In Rota and Trebujena, it is called Tempranilla; in Lebrija, Ojo de Liebra; and in Algeciras, Temprana.

Pedro Ximénez, or PX, is the second most important grape for sherry. This variety has been grown in Spain for hundreds of years and is the major variety of Montilla-Moriles. We've been told by a number of people who we believe to be reliable sources, that the sherry producers, in fact, buy some 4 million gallons of Pedro Ximénez each year, most of it from Montilla-Moriles, which they use for sweetening and coloring their wines.

THE VINEYARDS

The first effects of *Phylloxera vastatrix* were discovered in the

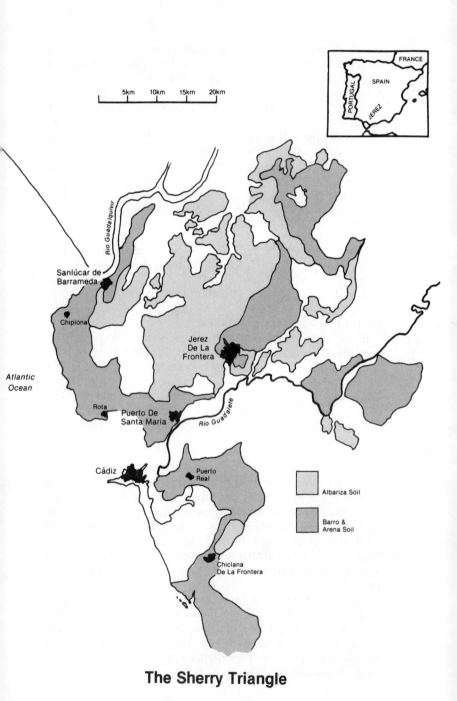

The Sherry Triangle

147

Sherry vineyards in 1898. Despite the sand in the soil of many vineyards, the vines were destroyed in Sherry as almost everywhere else in the winegrowing world. In the end, American rootstocks were found to be the only answer, and the sherry vines were all grafted onto resistant American roots. Before phylloxera, when the European vines were on their own roots, they lived for 70 to 80 years. Now, grafted onto American rootstock, the vines are uprooted and replanted at 25 to 30 years, when their production begins to decline.

The best exposure for the sherry vineyards is considered to be southeast, with the full strength of the sun beating down on the vines, which are protected from the coldest (northerly) winds and frost.

There are 8,100 hectares (20,000 acres) in the production zone; 5,060 hectares (12,500 acres) are in Jerez, the superior zone. (The maturing and exporting zone is Jerez-Sanlúcar-Puerto de Santa María.) Two-thirds of the vineyard area is in the Jerez zone. The rest of the acreage is mostly in Sanlúcar. Puerto has 405 hectares (1,000 acres).

In the superior zone of sherry production, the yield is 80 hectoliters/hectare (860 gallons/acre); for the rest of the area it is somewhat higher — 100 hectoliters/hectare (1,070 gallons/acre). The yields in both of these areas are quite high. The sherry shippers say that for all other wines quantity and quality do not go together, but for sherry it is different. In this case, you may have your high yields and high quality too!

THE HARVEST

The sherry vines are head-pruned; that is, each vine stands alone, like a little bush, and the grape bunches hang from branches that are not trained on wires. The vines flower in early May. By late May or early June, the small bunches of hard little grapes have formed. In about the first week of September the ripe grapes are harvested. The Pedro Ximénez grapes, which attain the highest sugar levels, are the last to be picked.

The vintage begins in Sanlúcar de Barrameda, commencing with a harvest festival, the *Fiesta de la Vendimia,* an old custom revived in 1948. In 1956 the sherry shippers began dedicating the festival each year to another country. Great Britain was the first. In 1970 Canada was so honored; in 1971, and again in 1976, the U.S.A.

SUNNING

After the picking, the grapes are laid out in the sun, traditionally on round mats of *esparto* grass, today more commonly on asbestos, for a period ranging from a few hours (for the finos) to a few days (for the very sweet PX). This reduces the liquid in the grapes, concentrating the juice and making it sweeter. If the grapes are left overnight, they are covered with a second mat, or a polyethylene sheet, to prevent the morning dew from undoing any of the previous day's sunning.

This practice of sunning the harvested grapes has an ancient precedent. Around 700 B.C., the Greek writer Hesiod instructed that grapes be exposed to the sun for ten days and nights and left for five days in the shade before being put into the fermenting vats.

Pliny, in his *Natural History,* says that,

> . . . a wine called in Greek "strained wine," to make which the grapes are dried in the sun for seven days raised seven feet from the ground on hurdles, in an enclosed place where at night they are protected from the damp; on the eighth day they are trodden out, and this process produces a wine of extremely good bouquet and flavour.

The sherry grapes are brought into the press houses at night, when the temperature is cool.

PLASTERING

Before the grapes are pressed, they are sprinkled with *yeso,* or gypsum, about 1 kilo (2 pounds) to each *carretada* (literally, carload) of grapes weighing 690 kilos (1,500 pounds). Plastering is an old tradition in Jerez, and the practice goes back much earlier. Cato recommended plastering with marble dust, as did Columella. Pliny reported that it was the custom in Africa, 2,000 years before his time, to sprinkle gypsum on the grapes before they were fermented.

> The practice in Africa is to soften any roughness with gypsum, and also in some parts of the country with lime. In Greece, on the other hand, they enliven the smoothness of their wines with potter's earth or marble dust.

The ancients and the early sherry winemakers knew that this practice improved their wines but they couldn't have understood just how it did so. The acid in wine normally forms a crust of potassium bitartrate in the barrels (and is made into cream of tartar). It is sometimes seen as little crystals in the bottom of a wine bottle or sparkling on the underside of the cork when a wine has undergone a sudden drop in temperature. The wine of Sherry, like many others produced in hot, sunny climates, is often deficient in acidity. The gypsum helps to retain the tartaric acid in the wine, giving it a better acid balance.

There was a heated controversy over the practice of plastering in Victorian times—when opponents claimed it eliminated potassium bitartrate (cream of tartar) and created potassium sulphate in its place, which they felt was harmful—and perhaps to be feared as an aphrodisiac. The practice is generally prohibited in France as well as many other wine-producing countries. However, proponents claim platering aids in the fermentation process and produces a wine that clarifies more rapidly in the cask, becoming a more brilliant wine.

CRUSH AND FERMENTATION

In the past, the grapes were trodden in a wooden trough, or *lagar,* by *pisadores,* men clad in rolled-up trousers or trunks and leather treading shoes with spiked soles. It's interesting that the treading here was done with those unusual shoes rather than barefoot as in other areas, such as in the Douro for port. Undoubtedly the partially dried grapes were more difficult to crush with bare feet. Nowadays the work is done by mechanical presses.

From the first pressing comes the *mosto de yema,* which is mixed with the free-run juice. This must is used for the finer sherries. The juice pressed out from the final, and heaviest, pressing—called *estrujón*—is used for a thin wine that will be distilled or else used for treating new wine butts to draw out their harsh wood tannins before good wine is put into them. Or it may be made into sherry vinegar.

The fresh must is transferred to the large vats, mostly of cement, where it ferments into wine. The first fermentation begins six to eight hours after the pressing. This is the *fermentacíon tumultuosa,* named for its violent, tumultuous action, which lasts from three days to a week.

The second fermentation, the *lenta* (slow), lasts for two to three months. This fermentation becomes gradually weaker until the wine has fermented dry, when virtually all the grape sugar has been converted into alcohol. At this point the wine will have 12 percent alcohol.

The suspended particles in the wine slowly sink, and the wine falls bright in December or January. The wines are racked off their lees during the period from January to March, and transferred into clean casks. Then they are classified.

FIRST CLASSIFICATION

The first classification is made by sight and, more particularly, by smell. The man making this classification is the *catador* (from *catar,* to smell). The preliminary judging separates the wines into two classes: fino and oloroso. The finos are lighter and more delicate, the olorosos fuller and rather more pungent.

The *catador* marks the casks with the symbol for the category he has assigned to the wine. The highest category is Una Raya (/). These are wines with a clean aroma and good body. Next is Raya y Punto (/.), or in some cellars, Dos Rayas (//). These wines have less body, or are slightly less promising. The next category down is Dos Rayas (//) or Tres Rayas (///), depending on the cellar. These wines have an aroma that is not quite clean, or some other minor defect. The lowest category is Tres Rayas (///) or *mostos de quema,* musts for burning, (#). These are wines that don't have a clean aroma, are too high in acid, or are thin. They are considered unfit for drinking and will be distilled. The sign Ve on a cask means the wine has undergone acetic fermentation and turned into vinegar.

FORTIFICATION

The first class, Una Raya, will be fortified to 15½ percent, and will become fino sherry. The second and third classes will be fortified to 17½-18 percent and will become oloroso. The wines are racked off their lees and fortified, then allowed to rest for one to two weeks.

The date when the wine of Jerez began to be fortified is uncertain. No fortified wines are known to have been made before the twelfth century, and probably not before the fifteenth.

The invention of distillation is credited to the Moors, who had a much more advanced civilization, especially in education and the sciences, than the medieval Europeans. The Moors ruled Spain until the mid-thirteenth century, and the

Spanish could have learned the process from them.

Brandy was well known in Europe by the fourteenth century, and there is evidence that brandy was being made in Jerez by 1580. In the sixteenth century, fortification of wine was well known and encouraged.

By the mid-eighteenth century, the sherry houses were producing a fortified wine that was in strong competition with the fortified wines of Oporto—and both were popular in Great Britain, a country where strength in wine was highly appreciated. Great Britain was to become one of sherry's most important markets.

In Sherry today 13 to 40 litres (3 to 9 gallons) of brandy per butt are added to the wine to bring it up to the proper alcoholic strength. Sherry is believed to need a minimum of 15½ percent alcohol for proper development. In Jerez and Sanlúcar they do not add pure alcohol to the wine, but a mixture half wine and half alcohol, *miteado*. Some houses use *orujo* for the fortifying alcohol; this is a type of marc distilled from the lees, which is kept in stainless-steel tanks.

FLOR

Sherry is a *flor* wine. That is, a layer of *flor* yeast forms on the surface of the (fino) wine in the butts. The *flor*, which looks like a layer of froth or white mold, is the same yeast that is used to ferment the wines.

The *flor* performs a beneficial function, besides imparting its characteristic nutty flavor to the wine. It absorbs oxygen in the butts and protects the wine from vinegar bacteria.

Flor thrives at temperatures between 15-degrees and 21-degrees C. (60-degrees and 70-degrees F.) on wine of not more than 15½ percent alcohol. The sherry butts with a capacity of 580 liters (155 gallons) are never filled up, but are kept only five-sixths full (not more than 490 liters or 130 gallons of wine) for optimum surface volume. The casks are left loosely stoppered to allow air and *flor* yeasts in.

At first the layer of *flor* forms slowly, appearing as patches or islands of white in flower-like shapes, floating on the wine. These gradually spread until a thin film covers the surface of the wine in the casks. In a few weeks this layer grows quite thick—at its thickest about ¾ of an inch.

The *flor* grows, or "rises," in the casks twice a year—in the spring (April or May) when the new shoots are budding in the vineyards, and in the late summer (August or September) when the fruit is becoming ripe on the vines. The *flor* lives for two to three years, then the yeast cells die and fall to the bottom of the barrel. This deposit forms a sort of crust and is referred to as *madre del vino,* the mother of the wine.

It has been said that *flor* is a mystery because some casks develop it and others don't. That is true, but the mystery is exaggerated. The development of the *flor* only on the casks of fino sherry is no mystery; it is well understood in Jerez. The shippers know which vineyards tend to produce wine with the characteristics of fino and which with oloroso. To control this development they make use of alcohol and temperature. They prevent the formation of *flor* in the oloroso by adding more alcohol and by keeping the wine at temperatures above those conducive to the formation of the *flor*. They know that the wood of new butts discourages the *flor* from forming, and that in old butts, which have already had the *flor* in them, it will easily form again. And in the event that the *flor* doesn't develop on the new fino wine, some *flor* yeast will be taken from another cask and added to it.

THE BODEGAS

The height of the *bodegas* and the thickness of their walls provides a good environment for the development of the *flor* and the maturing of the wine. The majority were built at the beginning of the nineteenth century, with thick stone walls and high ceilings. They are dimly lit, and relatively cool even in summer, the temperatures ranging from about 15-degrees to 21-degrees C. (60-degrees to 70-degrees F.).

The *arrumbadores — bodega* workmen — spray the floor periodically with water to lower the temperature and reduce evaporation in the butts. They say the wines in the *bodegas* on the south or southwest side of town develop better, because of the moisture and aeration from the sea breezes which blow in from that direction.

SHERRY BUTTS

The shipping or export butt in Jerez is a *bota* of 30 *arrobas,* or 490 liters (130 gallons). The *bodega* butts — *botas gordas* — are larger, holding 36 *arrobas,* or 586 liters (155 gallons).

Wooden casks have been used in the Sherry district to hold wine since at least the fifteenth century. The first American oak may have come to Europe in the sixteenth century when

153

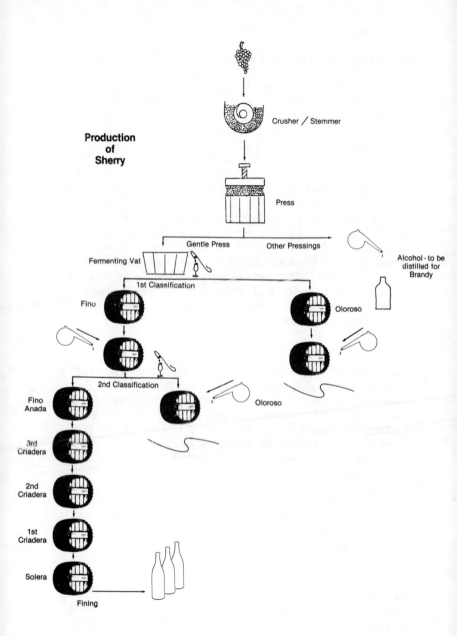

**Production
of
Sherry**

Crusher / Stemmer

Press

Gentle Press   Other Pressings   Alcohol - to be distilled for Brandy

Fermenting Vat

1st Classification

Fino   Oloroso

2nd Classification

Fino Anada   Oloroso

3rd Criadera

2nd Criadera

1st Criadera

Solera

Fining

ships returning from the New World brought wood from the forests along the Mississippi. American white oak from the Appalachian mountains is still the preferred wood for sherry today.

Until 1936 American white oak was used extensively for sherry casks. Then, for financial reasons, the sherry houses began to use more and more of the Spanish oak. Some believe that American white oak is better for the wine because of its finer grain, which prevents too much evaporation, and also because it doesn't impart any undesirable flavors to the wine. Other *bodegas* don't make any distinction between the quality of the American and Spanish oak, but buy the Spanish oak because it is less expensive.

THE VENENCIA

In taking the sample from the cask of sherry for classification, the cellarman uses a *venencia*. The name is believed to derive from *avenencia,* meaning an agreement or bargain, presumably because this dipper is used to bring up the samples from cask during negotiations between buyer and seller.

The *venencia* is the typical wine thief used for sherry and montilla. It is a cup of silver or stainless steel at the end of a long thin handle of whalebone or perhaps plastic. This special shape allows the *venenciador* to reach down below the *flor* in the partially filled casks to bring up the wine.

In Sanlúcar de Barrameda, the typical *venencia* is carved in one piece from a cane of bamboo. The cup at the end of the long handle is formed from the joint in the segment of bamboo which gives it a natural bottom. In Sanlúcar, then, one orders a *"cana"* of manzanilla, rather than a *copa* (cup) or *copita* (the typical sherry glass).

SECOND CLASSIFICATION

The second classification is made some nine months after the harvest, when the casks again are marked by the cellarmaster. The finos are pale and dry, with a distinctive aroma and 15½ to 17 percent alcohol. The olorosos are fuller in body and softer on the palate than the finos, and have a less fine aroma. Those butts of sherry that have only been fortified to 15½ percent but show no tendency to become finos are refortified with more alcohol and are reclassified as olorosos.

The *Finos* are rated: $\bar{\gamma}$ = Fino Palma, with *flor;* / = Raya, fuller-bodied and without *flor;* // = Dos Rayas, coarse; and # = *mostos de quema,* musts for distillation. After the second classification the finos are matured for a period ranging from nine months to three years. These wines are all *añada* — of a single vintage — and are still called *mosto.*

After this period the must goes into the *solera* system.

SOLERA

Sherry is matured by the *solera* system, a method of development intended to produce uniform wines. As we have explained in connection with montilla (page 135-136), it consists of a series of tiers of casks, each tier containing wine of the same type and at the same stage of development. The oldest wine is in the bottom tier, which is called the *solera,* and from which the system takes it name.

There is some evidence, according to Manuel González Gordon, of González Byass, that the first true *solera* was begun, or founded, in Sanlúcar in 1706. The system evolved over a period of many years before it reached its present sophisticated level. The original *soleras* were quite simple — three or four scales of casks stacked one atop the other. When some of the oldest wine was drawn off for shipment, wine from the upper scales was moved down, from the top tier to the next on down to the bottom. Now it is no longer necessary to stack the casks this way, as the wine is moved by pumps. The casks may even be in different buildings.

The fino casks are best stored close to the floor of the *bodega,* where it is cooler. The olorosos can tolerate warmer temperatures; they may even be left outside in the sun.

More stages are needed in the *solera* for the finos than for the olorosos, sometimes eight or more, since the finos vary more from year to year; more scales still are used in the *soleras* of Sanlúcar. In the fino *soleras* the wine takes seven to eight years to mature, from first fermentation to bottling.

Two or three times a year, about 94 to 113 liters (25 to 30 gallons) of wine per barrel is drawn off for bottling from the oldest *solera* casks. It is believed that the best time for taking the wine out is when the *flor* is dormant — in the winter from October to February, or else at the height of summer. This wine is approximately the same age as the wine that will be taken from the *solera* the following year.

ROCIO in Running the Scales

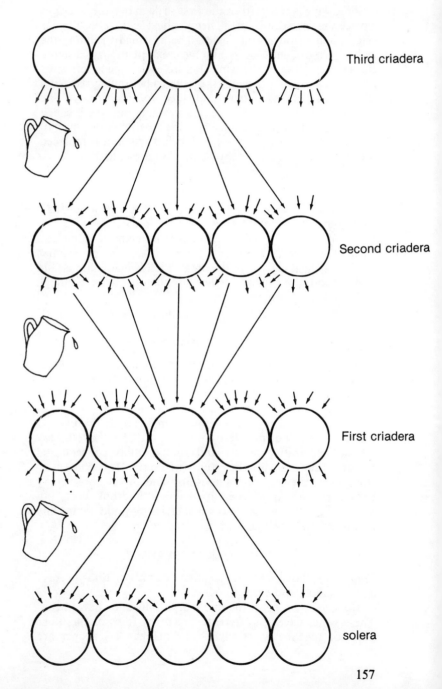

Third criadera

Second criadera

First criadera

solera

157

Some wine is taken from the first scale above the *solera* to replace the wine drawn off. Then the next scale refills the tier below, and so on up the scales. This is called "running the scales" — most unmusical, however, except perhaps for the gurgle and splash of the wine. Before each scale is refreshed with the next younger wine, the wine to be transferred from all the casks in each tier is blended for uniformity. The process of distributing the wine and refilling each tier is called the *rocio;* 98 liters (26 gallons) of wine are distributed over 10 barrels. The wine from the top and last *criadera* is replaced with wine at least one year old, but usually older.

CLARIFICATION

The wine is fined with eggwhites beaten with wine which, as it falls to the bottom of the cask, collects loose particles floating in the wine which would prevent is from being totally clear. Then it is cleared again with *tierra de lebrija,* or Spanish earth, a special clay from the area which is made into a mud and put into the wine to further brighten it — strange though it seems — for bottling.

The alcohol is adjusted again before the wine is bottled.

VINTAGE SHERRY

Some vintage sherry is kept in the *bodegas,* unblended, mostly as a curiosity. At least one shipper, though, has bottled and sold a vintage sherry: Lustau shipped a 1968 Palo Cortado from their vineyards in the Carrascal *pago.*

The very old vintages — and some go back over a century — are undrinkable by themselves. They have a very strong, penetrating aroma and an incredibly concentrated flavor — they are truly the essence of sherry. This concentration makes them seem almost salty, and the alcohol is very high. They are unpleasant in the mouth drunk neat, but added in tiny quantities to other sherries they add complexity and interest, particularly to the bouquet.

THE SHERRY TYPES

Finos are divided into: manzanillas, palmas or finos proper, amontillados, and entre finos.

Manzanilla proper is the fino from Sanlúcar de Barrameda. These wines develop differently from the finos of the other parts of the Sherry Triangle. The manzanillas proper are always finos from Sanlúcar, but the reverse is not true: The finos of Sanlúcar are not all manzanillas. New wine brought from Jerez or Puerto de Santa María to Sanlúcar for maturing can become manzanilla. New wines from Sanlúcar brought up in *bodegas* in Jerez or Puerto de Santa María will not become manzanilla. The environment is the determining factor.

The vineyards in Sanlúcar are harvested one week earlier than those in the other sherry zones, and the grapes are rarely sunned. These grapes have lower sugar and higher acid. The wines are more delicate, have more *flor* character, and are the driest of the sherries. Manzanilla is pale straw-yellow in color and has a faintly bitter aftertaste. It has from 15½ to 16½ percent alcohol, sometimes (though rarely) as much as 17 percent. Manzanilla is the best and most reliable of the fino sherries.

The *finos proper* are rated from one to four palms according to age: Una Palma Υ, Dos Palmas Υ, Tres Palmas Υ, and Cuatro Palmas Υ.

The finos palmas are noted for their penetrating aroma, their delicacy and fineness. They are pale topaz in color, dry and clean. Their flavor hints of olives; some tasters also detect almonds. The finos palmas range in alcohol from 15½ to 17 percent.

The best finos are reputedly those from Puerto de Santa María, which differ from those of Jerez in having a greater and cleaner aroma. Some of the Tio Pepe fino is aged in Jerez and some in Puerto; it is said that the Tio Pepe from Puerto is better.

Garvey is the first firm known to have shipped fino sherry — in 1832. This wine, called San Patricio, was described as having a fine (*fino*) bouquet and a delicate flavor.

Documents show that manzanilla was shipped even earlier. In the old records of the firm Antonio Barbadillo there is an entry stating that 4½ *arrobas* of manzanilla superior were shipped to the Spanish consul in Philadelphia on August 4, 1827. Previously only oloroso and the sweeter styles of sherry had been shipped from the region.

Palma cortada Υ is a fuller-bodied fino that, given age, will become an amontillado. As the fino grows old in cask, it may gain in body and develop depth of bouquet and flavor, becoming a fino amontillado, then an amontillado. Or it may grow stronger in flavor but retain its fino character, becoming the rare *old fino* types: *dos palmas* or *tres palmas.*

Dos Palmas is a fino which, although aged, has not become an amontillado. This very rare fino type is bone dry and intense in flavor — it has been described as the essence of fino.

Tres Palmas, like the Dos Palmas, has not been transformed into an amontillado. This type is like a Dos Palmas, but more so, and is even rarer.

Amontillados are deeper in color than the finos, ranging from tawny gold to golden amber, and fuller in body. They have a clean, pungent, nutty aroma. In flavor they are dry, nut-like, and richer than the finos. The amontillados range in alcohol from 16 to 18 percent, sometimes 20+ percent, if very old.

The best amontillados — in fact, the true amontillados — are aged finos with a minimum of eight years in cask. But much sherry sold as amontillado is unfortunately a bastardized sherry, made from a sweetened blend of lesser-quality wines, perhaps from the entre finos. *Entre fino* is a fino with little merit, lacking the delicacy, distinction, and clean aroma of a fino.

Amontillado was a late-eighteenth-century type of sherry from Montilla. In the last two decades of the eighteenth century, a differentiation began to be made between the finos, manzanillas, amontillados, olorosos, rayas, and palo cortados. The earliest reference found to amontillado is dated 1796.

The *oloroso* classification is broken down into palo cortado, oloroso proper, raya oloroso, and raya.

Palos cortados are wines which have shown no tendency to become finos. They have more bouquet and are clean and crisp, similar to the amontillados, but with more body and color. In these respects they are similar to the olorosos proper.

The casks are rated according to their character, and marked with from one to four palos cortados (cut sticks): Uno Palo Cortado ⊬ , Dos Palos Cortados ≠ , Tres Palos Cortados ≢ , or Cuatro Palos Cortados ≣ according to its character.

Palo cortado is a rare type. Sherry is sometimes sold as palo cortado when actually it is a sweeter version of another type of wine. True palos cortados are always dry.

Dos Cortados sherry is very rare; it is a richly flavored, intense dry wine. The *Tres Cortados* is rarer still; it is older and has achieved more concentration and richness. The rarest

160

of all the dry sherries is the *Cuatro Cortados,* a very old sherry with great concentration of flavor — nearly liqueur-like, but always bone dry.

The *olorosos proper* are darker in color and have more bouquet and body — more stoutness *(gordura)* — than the other sherries. (The name *oloroso* literally means a strong scent.) The olorosos have not been affected by the *flor*, which is killed or prevented from forming by the addition of alcohol, which brings up the alcoholic level of the olorosos to the 18 to 20 percent range, and increases with age to 24 percent. The grapes for oloroso sherry are sunned for up to forty-eight hours, and the casks are often kept in the sun for one to two years, perhaps more.

The olorosos are dry but with a suggestion of sweetness from the rich texture and glycerine of the wine. In color they range from dark golden to deep brown. They are usually darkened with *vino de color.* The olorosos have a nutty aroma and a flavor which can be likened to walnut. They are less pungent than the finos or amontillados. Most olorosos and amontillados sold in the U.S.A. and the U.K. are sweetened wines, probably sweetened rayas.

The *rayas* are coarse wines, generally lacking in character and distinction. The light rayas — rayas finas — are better wines than the simple rayas. The rayas olorosos are of a higher quality than the rayas, but not high enough to be olorosos proper. They are full in body, golden in color, and full-flavored. They have a minimum alcoholic content of 18 percent.

ABOCADOS — THE SWEETENED WINES

Abocado, meaning medium-sweet, is a mixture of dry and sweet wines. The sweet wine in the blend is usually Pedro Ximénez (PX) or Moscatel.

Amoroso is the term for an abocado, made from an oloroso that has been sweetened; it has a smooth, velvety texture.

Cream sherry is a sweetened oloroso, golden mahogany in color.

Pale cream sherry is, as its name suggests, a cream sherry, pale in color; it is lighter in body than the regular cream sherry.

Brown sherry is dark and sweet with a rich intensity.

Old bottled sherry is an oloroso, palo cortado, or

amontillado of fine quality that has been sweetened slightly before bottling. The bottles are stoppered with corks and covered with a wax seal, then laid down to age. With time the wine loses some of its sweetness, and its flavor and character become concentrated and intensified. This type is extremely rare today.

Old East India is a full-bodied, sweetened old oloroso. It takes its name from the original type which was sent on ships to East India and back, crossing the equator twice. Madeira is better known as a wine sent around the world in sailing ships, but it was also done in Spain for sherry, and in Setúbal (Portugal) for the moscatel as well as for a number of other wines.

Pedro Ximénez, named for the grape from which it is made, is the best sweet wine of Sherry. The grapes are picked when very ripe and sun-dried for ten to twenty days on *esparto* mats, covered at night to keep in heat and protect the drying grapes from the morning dew. Then they are pressed. The wine produced is low in alcohol and very high in sugar ($22°$-$25°$ Baumé).

These wines have an extremely dark color. They are thick and velvety and very sweet, with a flavor of raisins. Some of this wine is sold unblended; this is the richly sweet sherry labeled Pedro Ximénez. Some of it is blended with other sherry to add sweetness.

Moscatel wine is not as sweet as Pedro Ximénez, since the Moscatel grapes are given a shorter drying period.

Mistela and *mosto apagado* (quenched must), are made by adding fresh must to a cask containing alcohol (thereby preventing it from fermenting) in proportions of 15 to 18 liters (4 to 4¾ gallons) of alcohol per hectoliter (26½ gallons) of must. This combination of alcohol and grape must is added to the cheaper dry wines for sweetening. The wine produced is lighter in color than that made with sun-dried grapes; they are sweeter than the abocados, but much less so than the Pedro Ximénez. They are about 15 percent in alcohol.

Dulce (sweet) is another name for a blend of fresh grape juice and alcohol used to sweeten the lesser sherries. These wines are light in color and have an alcoholic content of 18 percent.

Vino de color is fresh must mixed with heated must. The heating thickens the must, caramelizes its sugar, and deepens its color. The wine is added to the sweetened type of oloroso.

MANZANILLA & THE WINES OF SANLUCAR DE BARRAMEDA

In Sanlúcar de Barrameda all the different styles of sherry are made, plus a few others: manzanilla fina, olorosa, and pasada. The best known of these is the *manzanilla fina,* the palest, lightest, and driest of all sherries.

Manzanilla doesn't enjoy a great reputation in the world today, not being very well known, but it was obviously known and perhaps much appreciated by the French composer Bizet who referred to it in his opera *Carmen* in 1875. It was manzanilla that the gypsy temptress offered as a lure, along with hints of other pleasures, to the defenseless Don José, promising that if he would join her later at the tavern of Lillas Pastia, she would dance for him the *seguidilla* while they shared glasses of manzanilla—a tempting offer indeed (and one that Don Jose did not pass up).

In Sanlúcar, as in Jerez and Puerto de Santa María, the first classification of the wine takes place after the must is fermented, falls bright, and is racked. This classification sorts out the potential finos and potential olorosos. The finos are further classified as finos and manzanilla finas. The manzanilla finas have more *flor* character than the finos; the *flor* covers the surface of the fina wine throughout the year.

After the first fermentation, the manzanilla will normally be 15 percent in alcohol. If it is less, it will be given a light fortification, bringing it up to 15 to 15½ percent. At that point it may be sent to holding tanks for six months to a year or more, depending on the requirements of the *solera.* Or it may go into the initial stage of the *solera,* spending the first year unblended in the oak barrels in the *añada.* Then it is classified as fino or oloroso and goes on to the particular *solera* from there.

All the wines are fermented dry, and kept dry as they go through the *solera.*

It takes the manzanilla wine at least five years to reach the first *solera* (final row). From there, if it is not bottled, it goes to a further *solera* system. The first finished *solera* becomes the first *criadera* of another, more sophisticated, *solera.*

Given sufficient time, the manzanilla fina develops into an *olorosa* (not to be confused with oloroso); from olorosa it becomes *pasada,* then *amontillada,* or *amontillado.* A regular fino, with age, also becomes an amontillado, but the manzanilla passes through more stages. If the wine is left to iself and not drawn off for bottling, it will pass through all the stages.

From the fina stage through the olorosa stage, the wine is covered with a film of *flor*. In the pasada stage the *flor* begins to die—the wine is passing from olorosa to the next stage, amontillado. It is said that it takes twenty-five years to obtain a truly first-rate pasada.

The pasada is high in alcohol, relative to the other manzanillas—over 16 percent naturally.

There are different *soleras* for the pure Pedro Ximénez (PX), for the Moscatel, and for the *mistela* that is used to sweeten the sweet oloroso and cream sherries. *Mistela blanca "para fina"* is added to make a less austere fino. There is also a *mistela "para oloroso"* for adding to the olorosos.

THE SHERRY SHIPPERS

Today 90 percent of the sherry production is exported; much of it in bottle. But is wasn't always that way. Until 1874 most sherry was sold in bulk—in cask—to English merchants who bottled it under the name of their own firms. The first house to bottle its sherry for export was J. de Fuentes Parrilla, in the years between 1871 and 1873. Other houses adopted the practice not long after and it spread throughout the Sherry region.

Today there are about 60 firms in Jerez, 14 in Puerto, and 21 in Sanlucar. The largest is González Byass, followed by Pedro Domecq.

Bertola's sherries are mediocre sweetened versions of their types. Their cream sherry is highly regarded by some (though not us).

Blasquez produces noted finos and amontillados.

Corney & Barrow, established in 1870, produces a good amontillado.

Croft's Original Pale Cream Sherry is quite good, as is their Palo Cortado. Their other sherries that we've tasted don't come up to the same level, being sweetened versions of their types, and rather mediocre.

Cuvillo makes a highly regarded Palo Cortado.

DeSoto produces an oloroso that is generally well thought of.

Pedro Domecq produces a first-rate fino, La Ina, which is less austere than their competitor, Tio Pepe. Their Rio Viejo Oloroso is also quite good.

Garvey, founded in 1780, produces a fine Fino San Patricio, as well as some other very good sherries.

González Byass, since 1835, produces a number of especially fine sherries, and like most sherry shippers, some that are rather mediocre. Their Tio Pepe ("Uncle Joe") is a first-rate fino, one of the best, if not *the* best of the standard finos. From time to time they release small quantities of Dos Palmas and Tres Palmas — very rare and intense old aged finos. Their Del Duque Muy Viejo is an excellent amontillado. The Oloroso Seco Alfonso and Oloroso Dulce Solera 1847 are both quite good. Some other especially fine, and very rare, sherries that González Byass ships on occasion, in very small amounts, include their Dos Cortados, Tres Cortados and Cuatro Cortados — this last being perhaps the rarest of all the dry sherries. Some other good wines from this firm are the Viña Romano — an old cream sherry, and Matusalém — a very old, sweet oloroso.

Duff Gordon (owned by Osborne) produces quite a good amontillado which they label El Cid. Their vaguely sweet Triangulo Oloroso, sweet Alonso el Sabio Amoroso, and lusciously sweet Old Solera India are also good sherries.

Hartley & Gibson's sherries are sweetened, mediocre versions of their types.

Harvey's Bristol Cream is a good cream sherry; their Bristol Milk isn't bad either. From time to time Harvey's offers old bottled sherries that are considered to be especially fine.

Emilio Lustau, one of the best of the sherry firms, produces a number of fine sherries. Some of their better wines are the Emilio Palo Cortado, Dry Fino, Dry Oloroso, Rare Amontillado, Manzanilla Fina, Fine Rare Fino (an aged fino), and very unusual vintage sherry — Palo Cortado Carrascal, Añáda 1968. Their Rare Palo Cortado, Tonel Emperatríz Eugenia and Pale, Dry Rare Oloroso are also highly regarded.

Osborne, of Puerto de Santa María, established in 1772, produces well-regarded fino, dry oloroso, Moscatel 1870 Solera, and PX 1827 Solera.

Antonio de la Riva, the oldest firm still in existence under the same name in Jerez — since 1776 — produces a Viejisimo 1770, a Manzanilla MZA la Riva, an Oloroso 1830 Solera, and a Tres Palmas (an old fino) all of which are highly regarded by sherry drinkers.

J.M. Rivero, since 1650, produces a good CZ Solera Cream.

The house of **Sandeman** specializes in old olorosos. Their Imperial Corregidor Special Oloroso and Royal Corregidor Finest Oloroso, although sweetened versions of true oloroso, are very fine wines, rich in concentration. El Corregidor is one of Sandeman's finest oloroso vineyards, in the Carrascal district. Royal Esmeralda Finest Amontillado and Royal Ambrosante Finest Palo Cortado are sweetened also, but of fine quality. All of these old-bottled sherries will take some age; in fact, the aging will concentrate their flavors and dry them out a bit. Sandeman's standard sherries tend to be unimpressive, and not improved by the added sweetness.

Terry, founded in 1883, in Puerto de Santa María, produces uneven and generally mediocre sherries. Their best wine, the Camborio Fino, though, can be quite good.

Valdespino's Fino Inocente and Dry Oloroso Solera 1842 are well thought of by sherry drinkers.

Williams & Humbert, founded in 1877, produces a very good, though rare, Dos Cortados — rich and concentrated; we understand that only 24 barrels a year are produced. They also make the well-known Dry Sack sherry. It has been described as a sweetened Palo Cortado; it is not. It is a medium amontillado, somewhat sweetened. This wine has been criticized by some of the other sherry houses for not really being a dry sherry (dry "sack"). But this wine is not mislabelled as fino, unlike some of the sherries purported to be amontillado which are not aged finos at all, but sweetened blends of lesser wines. The Williams & Humbert Pando Fino and Felipón Fino are both fine sherries.

Wisdom & Warter's sherries are, like most, uneven and sweetened for export.

Zoilo Ruiz Mateos produces a highly regarded, very old, Don Zoilo Cream Sherry. Their wines, though, tend to be rather uneven, and expensive.

Antonio Barbadillo, established in Sanlúcar in 1821, produces a first-rate manzanilla, and a good Amontillado Dos Hermanos 1882.

Some other fine manzanillas are the **F. Garcia de Valasco, Infantes Orleans Borbón, La Gaya, La Guita, Marques de Real Tesoro,** and **Solear.**

BUYING AND SERVING SHERRY

In buying sherry, especially the fino, the rule is — the fresher the better. It is wise to buy, at the most, a few bottles at a time, as you need them. And they are best purchased from a store with a good turnover.

Sherry, especially fino sherry, doesn't improve in the bottle. In fact, sherry is at its peak when bottled; it declines from that point on. As a principal in one of the famous sherry houses has said, "The bottle is the wine's coffin."

Sherry should be stored in a cool place with no light. Fino, the most delicate of the sherries, is hurt the most by aging or mistreatment. Sherry should be drunk as soon as possible after the bottle is opened. In his *Notes on a Cellar-book,* George Saintsbury sagely counseled, "When they [sherries] are opened, the finer ones especially, they must be drunk. I have known a bottle of Tio Pepe become appreciably 'withered' between lunch and dinner."

Manzanilla should be served chilled (13-15-degrees C./55-60-degrees F.). It makes a good aperitif. It also goes well with shellfish appetizers, especially oysters, and it would be a fine drink with caviar.

Fino, served chilled (13-15-degrees C./55-60-degrees F.), is a good accompaniment to *tapas*—the Spanish mixed hors d'oeuvres, including tortillas, fresh anchovies, shrimp, Serrano ham, *chorizos*, and especially green olives. There's something in the flavor of the Spanish olive that one finds also in the aroma of fino sherry. Some recommend it as an aperitif, but for us it is too high in alcohol to be served without some tidbit for the stomach's sake.

Amontillado goes well with soups, especially consommé. The slightly sweetened amontillados can accompany cream soups. Amontillados would go well, too, with some types of cheese — for example, cheddar or the cheddar types. Serve amontillado lightly chilled (15-18-degrees C./60-65-degrees F.).

Amontillado has been recommended with roast meat or other entrees. We must disagree. The alcohol in sherry really makes it too strong to drink as a table wine. It is for sipping.

At a special dinner a couple of years ago we originally planned to serve only montilla and sherry, but later decided to offer table wine to those who wanted it during the meal. When the entree was served, almost everyone was asking for the table wine, and only the most dedicated sherry and montilla lovers stayed with those wines—notably with the montilla which has less alcohol than sherry. With the dessert and after the meal, we returned to the sherry and montilla, in the sweet styles.

Oloroso may be drunk with nuts or simply by itself after dinner. The sweetened olorosos go with blue cheese, or with light cakes. Serve lightly chilled (15-18-degrees C./60-65-degrees F.).

The amoroso and cream sherries can be drunk with sweets, such as light cakes. We don't personally recommend it, though. Why drink a sweet sherry when you can drink port? Malmsey madeira and marsala cream also have more to offer. Serve these sweet sherries well chilled (9-13-degrees C./50-55-degrees F.).

In Jerez, and in Spain in general, sherries have a cleaner aroma and taste; the styles are more definite. In England and the United States, sherries are often in-between wines. True amontillados and olorosos are both dry, but these seen in the U.S. and U.K. are often sweetened; even the finos for export are often lightly sweetened.

The sherry producers contend that those markets want a sweeter wine. Maybe. But maybe these buyers never had the opportunity to taste the true types. Perhaps they would prefer them. There could be another reason for sweetening the wine—the producers can use lesser-quality wines in the sweetened types, wines like the rayas and the entre finos. As Gabriel González has said, "Color and sweetness cover a multitude of sins."

SUBSTITUTES FOR SHERRY

We find that in general we prefer the wines of Montilla to those of Sherry, and in place of sherry would substitute a montilla of the same type: fino, amontillado, oloroso, or other. Generally, montilla is lower in alcohol, lower in price, and more consistent in quality.

The only style of sherry that doesn't have an equivalent in montilla is manzanilla. And, actually, manzanilla fina offers the same three advantages as montilla over fino sherry.

If there is one type of sherry that Jerez excels in (at least in the opinion of one of the authors—SW), it is the fino; the best fino sherry is finer than the best montilla fino. We both agree, though, that the montilla finos, on average, are of a higher quality.

An article in the October 1978 issue of *Decanter* magazine described an interesting blind tasting of amontillados: twenty from Jerez, three from Montilla, three from South Africa, and two each from Australia and Cyprus. A panel of wine experts judged the wines, which were served unidentified.

The panel found it often difficult to tell between Montilla and Jerez wines. Some Jerez wines were thought to be South African. [Further] . . . all agreed that in general the Sherries were rather too sweet . . . . The three amontillado-style wines from Montilla must be seriously considered in terms of *value for money* [our emphasis].

There is another type of sherry, though very rare, that is perhaps the pride of Sherry and unequalled in Montilla. This is the old, matured sherry—the very rare Dos Palmas and Tres Palmas, for example, or the extremely rare and yet more intense Dos, Tres, and Cuatro Cortados. So far as we know these types don't exist in Montilla-Moriles; and though Montilla makes some excellent old amontillados and olorosos, we've never tasted one to match the quality of these rare old wines.

OTHER FLOR WINES AND SHERRY TYPES

Sherry is perhaps the most famous of the *flor* wines, but there are a number of other Spanish wines—other than those of Montilla-Moriles—and wines from other countries, that are also affected by the wine flower.

Flor develops on wines from several rather widespread areas. We've heard of *flor* wines from Armenia and Georgia in the Soviet Union, France, Italy, Cyprus, South Africa, and Australia.

SPAIN

Huelva, an Andalusían town northwest of Jerez, produces a *flor* wine. This wine, like that of sherry, is aged in *solera*. But it is rare to see a bottle of the Huelva *flor* wine, since most of it is sent to Jerez and blended into the sherry wines.

In the Estremadura region of south-central Spain, just north of Jerez, a most unusual *flor* wine is produced. This is the red cañamero wine of Montánchez. This is the only red wine we know of to be affected by *flor,* and it would be interesting to know if the *flor* yeast on this wine is red like that described by Pliny. Unfortunately we've never had the opportunity to taste it; it is only available locally.

Tierra del Vino, west of Valladolid in the province of Old Castile in north-central Spain, is the northernmost town in Spain to produce a *flor* wine. This wine is the rueda wine. It, too, is apparently only sold locally.

FRANCE

Without question, the most interesting *flor* wine outside of Spain is Château Chalon, produced in the Jura mountains of eastern France. It has been known for over two centuries. The lords of Arlay, who founded an abbey in the village of Château Chalon, produced a *vin jaune,* "yellow wine," at Château d'Arlay as early as 1774.

This wine might have the distinction of being the first of the modern (since the days of the Roman Empire) vintage wines. No reference to an earlier vintage wine has — to our knowledge — yet been found.

Château Chalon is always the wine of a single year. It attains about 12 percent alcohol naturally; it is not fortified. The wine is stored in 830- to 1,660-liter (220- to 440-gallon) casks which are kept about three-quarters full. This wine is always visitied by the *flor.*

According to local legend, the Savagnin grape used in Château Chalon was brought to the Jura by Benedictine monks from Hungary in about 1000 A.D.

Château Chalon is amber in color with an aroma of walnuts that follows through on the palate. It makes a good aperitif and may be drunk with consommé or cream soup. It is also a good wine to accompany mild cheeses such as emmenthaler ("swiss"), gruyère, or comté. Serve lightly chilled (15 to 18 degrees C./60 to 65 degrees F.).

Château Chalon is sold in a distinctive 20-ounce stubby bottle called a *clavilen.*

This wine continues to improve in bottle for many years. In 1980 we had the opportunity to taste a range of Château Chalon wines including the 1945, 1949, 1952, 1953, and 1955 vintages. We found the older wines to be more flavorful and more complex than the younger ones. Château Chalon is aged in barrel up to 6 years, and needs some bottle age as well to develop its full potential.

ITALY

Flor is said to develop on the *vernaccia di oristano* wine of Sardinia. In the vineyards around the town of Oristano the head-pruned Vernaccia vines are trained close to the ground to absorb its reflected heat. By the time of the harvest, in

September, the grapes have developed high sugar levels; Italian wine law requires vernaccia di oristano to attain at least 15 percent alcohol naturally.

After fermentation the new wine is drawn off into casks that are kept partially filled, where it is aged for at least 2 years. The vernaccia *superiore* is aged longer — 3 years, and has a minimum of 15½ percent alcohol. The vernaccia *riserva* has been aged for 4 years or more, and has an alcohol level of at least 16 percent. The *riserva* reputedly ages very well. Vernaccia di oristano that has been fortified is labelled *liquoroso*. The wine is made in both dry, *secco* — which may actually be off-dry, depending on the producer — and sweet, *dolce*, styles.

Vernaccia di oristano has a golden amber color and a penetrating aroma that suggests nuts and sometimes green olives; it is firm in texture with a clean, lingering finish. It is similar to a montilla.

Perhaps the best producer of vernaccia di oristano is Contini; he makes a fine *riserva*. Silvio Carta (whose wines we haven't tasted) also has a very high reputation. Josta Puddu makes some good wines, particularly the *riservas*. The Cantina Sociale Coop. de la Vernaccia-Oristano makes reliable, if somewhat unexciting, wines under the Sardinian Gold label.

Zedda Piras makes a good *vernaccia di sardegna*, at 16 percent alcohol; which is very similar to vernaccia di oristano.

Since about 1970, the firm of Lungarotti in Umbria has been producing a small amount of a sherry-like fortified wine — *Solleone Dry*. It is made from the same grapes as their white table wine: Trebbiano (70 percent), and Grechetto (30 percent). The wine attains 11-12 percent alcohol naturally, and is fortified to 18 percent with grape alcohol. *Flor* yeast is added, after fermentation to impart its distinctive character to the wine, which is aged in stainless steel or cement tanks. It is the wine of a single vintage, unblended.

Solleone Dry is pale straw in color with an aroma that suggests green olives; it is dry, and firm in texture — more like a montilla than a sherry. Reputedly it will keep for a long time, unlike sherry or montilla.

CYPRUS

Flor develops naturally on certain wines from the island of Cyprus. The Keo sherry is one of these wines. It is aged in a modified *solera* system. The Keo fino lacks the crispness and character of the better Jerez finos, but would make an acceptable substitute for a dry sherry — though a bit pricey (in the U.S.A., at least).

SOUTH AFRICA

Since 1933 the South African sherries have been made with the benefit of *flor*. This *flor* is their own strain, native to the Cape. The Palomino, Pedro Ximénez, and Steen varieties are the three most commonly used grapes in the Cape sherries. The wines are aged by the *solera* system of fractional blending. The Cavendish Cape sherries are very highly regarded.

Of the South African sherries overall, Hugh Johnson in his book *Wine* writes, "There are very few people who can tell the best of the South African sherry from an ordinary Spanish one of the same character." And, at a generally lower price, they offer better value.

AUSTRALIAN SHERRIES

Australian sherries are made in all styles. Some wineries use the *solera* system of fractional blending, others don't. The drier styles are often made with *flor*.

Flor is said to have been introduced into Australia in 1908. The culture is described as being put onto the wine by spatula and then allowed to spread over the entire surface. The wine, generally about 15 percent in alcohol, is held in puncheons or hogsheads under the layer of *flor* for two years or more. After this period, it is drawn off and fortified to 18 percent, then given further oak aging. The amontillados are aged even longer.

Generally the Palomino grape is used for the drier style. Those to be aged under *flor* are often made from the Pedro Ximénez.

Most Australian sherry-style wines are labeled dry, medium-dry, sweet, and so on, which makes it simpler to know before you open the bottle what type of wine you're going to have in your glass than with the more exotic titles — although it must be noted that some labeled "dry" have a touch of sweetness.

The best of the Australian sherries can be quite good. Unfortunately, very little of this wine is seen in the U.S. More, though, is exported to Great Britain, a traditional market for sherry wine.

Most Australian wineries producing fortified wines make sherry wine. And, as with Spanish sherry, some is good, some is bad. Among the more highly regarded:

*All Saint's Light Amontillado
*All Saints' Pale Dry—especially highly regarded.
*Angove's Fino Dry
 Angove's Oloroso Cream *(solera)*
*Berri Mine Host Flor
*Buring's Florita Flor
*Hamilton's Eden Valley Fino
*Hamilton's Private Flor Fino
*Hamilton's Pale Fino
 Hardy's Gold Label Dry *(solera)*
*Hardy's Delphino
 Hardy's Florfino
*Johnston's Pirraminna Pirramimma Flor (very dry)
 Kaiser Stuhl Cream
 Lindeman's Special Cream (aged in a modified *solera*)
*Lindeman's Reserve Fino (aged in a modified *solera*)
 Lindeman's Amorosa Cream (aged in a modified *solera*)
*Lindeman's Reserve Amontillado (aged in a modified *solera*)
*Lindeman's Flor Fino
*McWilliams' Flor Fino
*McWilliams' Dry Friar
 Mildara Chestnut Teal Cream
*Mildara George Dry (bone-dry)
*Mildara Rio Vista Flor Dry
*Mildara Supreme Dry
*Orlando Barossa Fino
*Quelltaler Gransfiesta *(solera)*—considered by many to be Australia's best dry sherry; aged in a *solera* system for seven years.
*Reynella Alicante Flor—one of Australia's most highly regarded dry sherries.
*Reynella Bone-Dry Flor—older and drier than the former.
*Saltram's Alameda Fino Extra Dry
*Woodley's Dry Fino Flor
*Yalumba Galway Fino—normally aged five to six years.
*Yalumba Fino Championship Show—a bone-dry sherry. considered to be one of the country's best.
*Yalumba Chiquita—highly regarded.

* = *flor* sherry

AMERICAN SHERRIES
For the most part, American sherries lack distinction (not unlike, however, the bulk of Spanish sherry). There are three

basic methods used for the production of sherry-style wines: the Spanish method, the baker's method, and the submerged *flor* method. As far as we know, no American sherry is made by the Spanish method.

Baked sherries are more like the wines of Madeira than those of Jerez, and actually could as easily have been named for that other distant region. If is not as famous, however, and this was apparently the determining factor behind this inappropriate choice of name. Baked sherries are fermented, fortified, and then heated to 120 degrees F. for four to six months. We cannot recommend them, regardless of price, as substitutes for real sherry.

In the submerged *flor* method, the new wine which has been fermented with the *flor* yeast, is continuously pumped over the *flor*. Through this mixing action the *flor* character is imparted to the wine more quickly, and less expensively, than when the *flor* simply floats on the surface.

Sherries made by this method are usually not among the higher-quality wines, but can be good value for what they are. **Almaden**'s Flor Fino Sherry is agreeable, pleasant, and very good value at less than half the price of many nondescript Spanish finos.

Generally the best American sherry-type wines are the creams. **Gallo**'s Livingston California Cream Sherry, though lacking the richness of a good Spanish cream, is an exceptionally fine value. **The Christian Brothers**' vintage-dated Meloso Cream Sherry is made mostly from Palomino grapes using the submerged *flor* method. The wine is aged for a period in 189-liter (50-gallon) American oak barrels, then transferred to larger, redwood casks. The 1975, at 20.6 percent alcohol and just under 10 percent residual sugar, is one of the better cream sherries produced in the U.S. **Shenandoah Vineyards** produces an interesting Mission Cream Sherry, from Mission grapes. This sweet, cream sherry type is 18 percent in alcohol. It has a walnut-like aroma and a nutty flavor.

The best American cream sherry that we have tasted is **Angelo Papagni**'s Finest Hour Cream Sherry. In 1971 when his vineyard of White Malaga grapes froze on the vine, concentrating the fruit, Papagni decided to make a California sherry from them. Using the submerged *flor* method, he produced this wine in two styles—a dry and a cream.

The wines were aged in 189-liter (50-gallon) American oak

barrels, which from spring through summer were left outside in the hot sun of California's Madera county. In the fall the barrels were rolled into the winery where they remained until the following spring, when the cycle resumed.

A thousand cases of Angelo Papagni's Finest Hour Dry Sherry — 100 percent from the 1971 vintage — were released in June 1979. The remainder was kept at the winery where it became the base of a modified *solera* for the Dry Sherry that is topped up from time to time with newer vintages — actually more like the early system of blending used in the monastaries than a true *solera*.

Finest Hour Dry Sherry is amber gold in color; it has a richly intense pecan-like aroma with a vague hint of olives in the back. There is some, though not much, residual sugar (less than 1 percent). The wine is well-structured, with good texture and a long, lingering finish.

Finest Hour Cream Sherry, also 1000 cases, was released in June the following year (1980). The remainder was kept to form the basis of the cream sherry aging system. This mahogany-colored wine has 18.7 percent alcohol and 14 percent residual sugar. Its penetrating aroma suggests walnuts and pecans; it is very sweet, but balanced, and smooth in texture.

Both of these wines are cork finished, but it has been our experience that they only age moderately well. The bottles we had in our cellar for two and three years had lost some of their originally expansive aroma.

Angelo Papagni's Finest Hour sherries, both the dry and the sweet, are from our experience easily the finest of the American sherry-style wines.

Most, nearly all, sherry initiations from New York are, at best, mediocre — handicapped by the inferiority of the grapes used, generally the native American varieties.

There is one New York cream sherry, though, that albeit over-priced, is of reasonable quality: **Taylor**'s Empire Cream Sherry. This wine is made from a blend of Concord (a native American labrusca variety) and French-American hybrid grapes. After fortification, the wine is aged for six months in small American oak barrels, then for another fifteen months in 7,570-liter (2,000-gallon) casks.

The "foxy" labrusca character is, though muted, evident on the aroma, which is fairly rich, with a slightly nutty note. The wine is quite sweet, though not cloying, and has a hint of chocolate in the flavor. It lacks the richness of a good Spanish cream sherry, but is balanced and agreeable.

While some acceptable alternatives to Spanish sherry are produced in the U.S., they are generally attractive only because of their low prices. No American fino-style sherry that we know of comes close to the best from Spain. The best Spanish finos, though, are unfortunately as rare as they are fine.

SHERRY GLOSSARY

Amontillado (ah-mon-tee-YAH-thoh). True amontillado is a fino which has been aged much longer in *solera,* becoming fuller in body, darker in color, and higher in alcohol. It is dry. Much amontillado for export is lightly sweetened and often made from lesser wines.

Amoroso (ah-moh-ROH-soh). A sweetened oloroso.

Bodega (boh-THEY-gah). A warehouse where wine is aged and stored.

Brown Sherry. A liqueur-like sherry, dark in color and richly sweet.

Cream Sherry. A dark, richly sweet, creamy-textured sherry.

Criadera (cree-ah-THEH-rah). A scale or tier within a *solera* system, above the bottom *(solera)* tier.

Fino (FEE-noh). The palest and lightest style of sherry with characteristics imparted by the *flor.* Finos are vinified dry, but many finos for export have been slightly sweetened.

Flor (flohr). A type of yeast which forms on certain wines and imparts its particular characteristics to them.

Manzanilla (mahn-zah-NEE-yah). Usually refers to the palest, lightest, driest, and most distinctive of all finos (and of all sherries) — manzanilla fina. Other types of manzanilla, fuller-bodied and darker in color, are also produced.

Old Bottled Sherry. An amontillado, palo cortado, or oloroso of fine quality, slightly sweetened, that is meant to be matured in bottle.

Old East India. A full-bodied, sweetened old oloroso.

Oloroso (oh-loh-ROH-soh). Olorosos are full-bodied and dark golden to deep brown in color. They are not affected by *flor.* True olorosos are always dry. Much of that exported is a sweetened blend of cheaper wines.

Pale Cream. A pale-colored cream sherry.

Palo Cortado (PAH-loh cohr-TAH-thoh). A rare style of oloroso, finer and more delicate than the regular olorosos.

Solera (soh-LEHR-ah). A system of fractional blending used to produce uniformity in sherry wines. The young wine is aged with older wine, in fractional amounts, being moved after a period of time into barrels of older, then still older wine, taking on the characteristics of the older wine. The oldest wine in the *solera* is drawn out for bottling and theoretically contains some wine from the date the *solera* was established.

Appendix A

Comparison of Fortified Wines

Madeira	Marsala	Montilla	Sherry
none	none	none	Manzanilla
none	none	Fino	Fino
Sercial	Vergine	Amontillado	Amontillado
Verdelho	Secco	Oloroso	Oloroso
Boal	Dolce	Cream	Cream
Malmsey	none	none	none
none	Speciali	none	none
none	none	Pedro Ximênez	Pedro Ximênez

Appendix B

Assessment of Quality and Value

Nonvintage

Madeira: Variable in quality.

Marsala: Similar to madeira in character, though less expensive and more even in quality.

Montilla: Similar to sherry, but lower in alcohol, lower in price, and more even in quality.

Sherry: the most uneven, and on average—compared to madeira, marsala, and montilla—the most expensive.

Vintage

Madeira: Consistent and of good quality.

Marsala: None made today; in the past some were bottled.

Montilla: None made.

Sherry: Generally used for blending, rarely offered for sale.

Appendix C

Foods to Complement Fortified Wines

As/With	Wine	Comment
Aperitif	Madeira, sercial	Vintage sercial makes a splendid aperitif
	Marsala, *vergine*	One of our favorite aperitifs
	Montilla, fino	Another especially good aperitif
	Sherry, manzanilla	First-rate
	Sherry, fino	Only if a montilla isn't available (although I do enjoy Tio Pepe—SW)
Hors d'oeuvres or *tapas*	Port, white	Especially with nuts (almonds in particular)
	Madeira, sercial	
	Marsala, *vergine*	
	Montilla, fino	Especially with olives and shellfish
	Sherry, manzanilla	Especially with shellfish, olives, Serrano ham, shrimp
Shellfish appetizer	Madeira, sercial	
	Marsala, *vergine*	
	Montilla, fino	
	Sherry, manzanilla	Our first choice
	Sherry, fino	
caviar	Manzanilla *fina*	A splendid combination
oysters	Manzanilla *fina*	
Soup or consommé	Madeira, verdelho	The drier style
	Marsala, *superiore secco*	
	Montilla, amontillado	
	Sherry, amontillado	
Cheese	Port, tawny	Cheddar, cheddar types
	Port, vintage	Blue, marbled cheeses
	Madeira, verdelho	Cheddar, cheddar types
	Marsala, *superiore secco*	
	Marsala, *superiore dolce*	Marbled cheese, especially gorgonzola
	Montilla, oloroso	Aged gouda
	Sherry, oloroso	

Sweets	Port, ruby	
	Port, tawny	
	Madeira, bual	
	Madeira, malmsey	
	Marsala, *superiore dolce*	
	Montilla, cream	
	Sherry, cream	
After-dinner sipping	Port, vintage	Alone, or with nuts, especially walnuts or almonds
	Port, old tawny	
	Madeira, malmsey	Alone or with nuts
	Marsala, *superiore dolce*	Alone or with nuts
	Montilla, old oloroso	Alone or with nuts
	Montilla, Pedro Ximénez (PX)	Like a liqueur
	Sherry, old oloroso	Alone or with nuts
	Sherry, Pedro Ximénez (PX)	Like a liqueur
Sweet fruit	Port, ruby	
	Port, LBV	
	Madeira, boal	
	Madeira, malmsey	
	Marsala, *dolce*	
	Montilla, cream	
	Montilla, PX	
	Sherry, cream	
	Sherry, PX	

Appendix D

Checklist of Port Shippers and Vintages

Key:

[1]   Sometimes bottled as a single-vineyard: Quinta da Roêda.
[2]   Sometimes shipped as a single-vineyard: Quinta da Corte.
[3]   In lesser years bottled as Guimaraens.
[4]   Their Quinta Malvedos is shipped in lesser years.
[5]   Bottled as Offley Boa Vista.
[6]   In the U.S.A. sold as Taylor Fladgate. In lesser years, the single-vineyard Quinta de Vargellas is often shipped.
[7]   Owns Quinta do Noval.
[8]   Sometimes labelled as Krohn.

Shipper/Vintage	1870	1872	1873	1874	1875	1877	1878
Adams							
Barros Almeida							
Borges							
Burmester				✓			✓
Butler Nephew							
Calem							
Cockburn		✓	✓	✓		✓	✓
Croft[1]		✓	✓			✓	✓
Delaforce[2]		✓		✓		✓	✓
Diez Hermanos							
Dixon							
Dow		✓	✓	✓		✓	✓
Feist							
Ferreira						✓	
Feuerheerd	✓	✓	✓			✓	✓
Fonseca[3]		✓	✓				✓
Gonzalez Byass							
Gould Campbell		✓	✓	✓		✓	✓
Graham[4]		✓	✓	✓		✓	✓
Greens							
Guimaraens							
Hooper							
Hutcheson							
Kingston							
Kopke		✓	✓	✓		✓	✓
Mackenzie		✓		✓		✓	✓
Manoel Porças							
Martinez		✓	✓	✓	✓	✓	✓
Messias							
Millipo							
Morgan		✓	✓	✓		✓	✓
Niepoort							
Offley[5]		✓	✓	✓	✓	✓	✓
Osborne							
Pintos dos Santos							
Quarles Harris							
Quinta do Noval							
Ramos Pintos							
Real Vinicola							
Rebello Valente		✓				✓	✓
Robertson Bros.							
Rocheda							
Royal Oporto							
Sandeman		✓	✓	✓		✓	✓
Smith Woodhouse		✓	✓	✓		✓	✓
Sociedade Constantino							
Southard							
Souza							
Stormouth Tait							
Taylor[6]		✓	✓	✓		✓	✓
Tuke Holdsworth		✓		✓	✓	✓	
VanZeller[7]						✓	✓
Warre		✓	✓			✓	✓
Wiese & Krohn[8]							

182

Key:
[1] Sometimes bottled as a single-vineyard: Quinta da Roêda.
[2] Sometimes shipped as a single-vineyard: Quinta da Corte.
[3] In lesser years bottled as Guimaraens.
[4] Their Quinta Malvedos is shipped in lesser years.
[5] Bottled as Offley Boa Vista.
[6] In the U.S.A. sold as Taylor Fladgate. In lesser years, the single-vineyard Quinta de Vargellas is often shipped.
[7] Owns Quinta do Noval.
[8] Sometimes labelled as Krohn.

Shipper/Vintage	1880	1881	1884	1885	1886	1887
Adams						
Barros Almeida						
Borges						
Burmester						✓
Butler Nephew						
Calem						
Cockburn		✓	✓			✓
Croft[1]		✓	✓	✓		✓
Delaforce[2]		✓	✓			✓
Diez Hermanos						
Dixon			✓			✓
Dow		✓	✓			✓
Feist						
Ferreira						
Feuerheerd		✓	✓			✓
Fonseca[3]		✓	✓			✓
Gonzalez Byass						
Gould Campbell		✓	✓	✓		✓
Graham[4]	✓	✓	✓	✓		✓
Greens						
Guimaraens						
Hooper						
Hutcheson						
Kingston						
Kopke		✓	✓			✓
Mackenzie		✓	✓			✓
Manoel Porças						
Martinez		✓	✓	✓	✓	✓
Messias						
Millipo						
Morgan		✓	✓			✓
Niepoort						
Offley[5]		✓	✓	✓		✓
Osborne						
Pintos dos Santos						
Quarles Harris						
Quinta do Noval						
Ramos Pintos						
Real Vinicola						
Rebello Valente		✓	✓			✓
Robertson Bros.						
Rocheda						
Royal Oporto						
Sandeman	✓	✓	✓			✓
Smith Woodhouse	✓	✓	✓			✓
Sociedade Constantino						
Southard						
Souza						
Stormouth Tait		✓	✓			✓
Taylor[6]	✓	✓	✓			✓
Tuke Holdsworth		✓	✓			✓
VanZeller[7]		✓	✓			✓
Warre		✓	✓			✓
Wiese & Krohn[8]						

Checklist of Port Shippers and Vintages (Continued)

Key:
[1]   Sometimes bottled as a single-vineyard: Quinta da Roêda.
[2]   Sometimes shipped as a single-vineyard: Quinta da Corte.
[3]   In lesser years bottled as Guimaraens.
[4]   Their Quinta Malvedos is shipped in lesser years.
[5]   Bottled as Offley Boa Vista.
[6]   In the U.S.A. sold as Taylor Fladgate. In lesser years, the single-vineyard Quinta de Vargellas is often shipped.
[7]   Owns Quinta do Noval.
[8]   Sometimes labelled as Krohn.

Shipper/Vintage	1888	1890	1892	1894	1896	1897
Adams						
Barros Almeida						
Borges						
Burmester			✔		✔	
Butler Nephew						
Calem						
Cockburn			✔	✔	✔	
Croft[1]			✔	✔	✔	✔
Delaforce[2]			✔	✔	✔	
Diez Hermanos						
Dixon		✔				
Dow		✔	✔		✔	
Feist						
Ferreira				✔	✔	✔
Feuerheerd			✔	✔	✔	
Fonseca[3]		✔			✔	
Gonzalez Byass					✔	
Gould Campbell			✔	✔	✔	
Graham[4]			✔	✔	✔	✔
Greens						
Guimaraens						
Hooper						
Hutcheson						
Kingston						
Kopke			✔	✔	✔	✔
Mackenzie		✔			✔	
Manoel Porças						
Martinez			✔	✔	✔	✔
Messias						
Millipo						
Morgan			✔		✔	
Niepoort						
Offley[5]		✔	✔	✔	✔	✔
Osborne						
Pintos dos Santos						
Quarles Harris						
Quinta do Noval					✔	
Ramos Pintos						
Real Vinicola						
Rebello Valente			✔	✔	✔	✔
Robertson Bros.						
Rocheda						
Royal Oporto						
Sandeman			✔	✔	✔	✔
Smith Woodhouse		✔			✔	✔
Sociedade Constantino						
Southard						
Souza						
Stormouth Tait					✔	
Taylor[6]			✔	✔	✔	
Tuke Holdsworth			✔	✔	✔	
VanZeller[7]			✔	✔	✔	
Warre		✔		✔	✔	
Wiese & Krohn[8]						

Checklist of Port Shippers and Vintages (Continued)

Key:
1   Sometimes bottled as a single-vineyard: Quinta da Roêda.
2   Sometimes shipped as a single-vineyard: Quinta da Corte.
3   In lesser years bottled as Guimaraens.
4   Their Quinta Malvedos is shipped in lesser years.
5   Bottled as Offley Boa Vista.
6   In the U.S.A. sold as Taylor Fladgate. In lesser years, the single-vineyard Quinta de Vargellas is often shipped.
7   Owns Quinta do Noval.
8   Sometimes labelled as Krohn.

Shipper/Vintage	1899	1900	1901	1902	1904	1906
Adams						
Barros Almeida						
Borges						
Burmester		✓			✓	
Butler Nephew						
Calem						
Cockburn		✓			✓	
Croft [1]		✓			✓	
Delaforce [2]		✓			✓	
Diez Hermanos						
Dixon						
Dow	✓				✓	
Feist						
Ferreira		✓			✓	
Feuerheerd		✓			✓	
Fonseca [3]		✓			✓	
Gonzalez Byass		✓			✓	
Gould Campbell		✓			✓	
Graham [4]		✓	✓		✓	
Greens						
Guimaraens						
Hooper						
Hutcheson						
Kingston						
Kopke		✓			✓	
Mackenzie		✓			✓	
Manoel Porças						
Martinez		✓			✓	
Messias						
Millipo						
Morgan		✓			✓	
Niepoort						
Offley [5]		✓		✓	✓	
Osborne						
Pintos dos Santos						
Quarles Harris						
Quinta do Noval		✓			✓	
Ramos Pintos						
Real Vinicola						
Rebello Valente		✓			✓	
Robertson Bros.						
Rocheda						
Royal Oporto						
Sandeman		✓			✓	
Smith Woodhouse		✓			✓	
Sociedade Constantino						
Southard						
Souza						
Stormouth Tait		✓			✓	
Taylor [6]		✓			✓	✓
Tuke Holdsworth		✓			✓	✓
VanZeller [7]					✓	
Warre	✓	✓			✓	
Wiese & Krohn [8]						

185

Key:
[1] Sometimes bottled as a single-vineyard: Quinta da Roêda.
[2] Sometimes shipped as a single-vineyard: Quinta da Corte.
[3] In lesser years bottled as Guimaraens.
[4] Their Quinta Malvedos is shipped in lesser years.
[5] Bottled as Offley Boa Vista.
[6] In the U.S.A. sold as Taylor Fladgate. In lesser years, the single-vineyard Quinta de Vargellas is often shipped.
[7] Owns Quinta do Noval.
[8] Sometimes labelled as Krohn.

Shipper/Vintage	1908	1910	1911	1912	1914	1917
Adams						
Barros Almeida						
Borges					✔	
Burmester		✔		✔		
Butler Nephew						
Calem						
Cockburn		✔		✔		
Croft[1]		✔		✔		✔
Delaforce[2]		✔		✔		✔
Diez Hermanos						
Dixon						
Dow		✔		✔		✔
Feist						
Ferreira	✔			✔		✔
Feuerheerd		✔		✔		✔
Fonseca[3]	✔			✔		
Gonzalez Byass	✔			✔		✔
Gould Campbell	✔			✔		✔
Graham[4]	✔			✔		✔
Greens						
Guimaraens						
Hooper						
Hutcheson						
Kingston						
Kopke		✔		✔		✔
Mackenzie		✔		✔		
Manoel Porças						
Martinez		✔	✔	✔		
Messias						
Millipo						
Morgan		✔		✔		
Niepoort				✔		
Offley[5]		✔	✔	✔		
Osborne						
Pintos dos Santos						
Quarles Harris						
Quinta do Noval		✔		✔		✔
Ramos Pintos						
Real Vinicola						
Rebello Valente		✔	✔	✔		✔
Robertson Bros.						
Rocheda						
Royal Oporto						
Sandeman		✔	✔	✔		✔
Smith Woodhouse		✔		✔		✔
Sociedade Constantino				✔		
Southard						
Souza						
Stormouth Tait		✔		✔		
Taylor[6]	✔			✔		✔
Tuke Holdsworth	✔			✔		✔
VanZeller[7]	✔			✔		✔
Warre	✔			✔		✔
Wiese & Krohn[8]						

Checklist of Port Shippers and Vintages (Continued)

Key:
[1] Sometimes bottled as a single-vineyard: Quinta da Roêda.
[2] Sometimes shipped as a single-vineyard: Quinta da Corte.
[3] In lesser years bottled as Guimaraens.
[4] Their Quinta Malvedos is shipped in lesser years.
[5] Bottled as Offley Boa Vista.
[6] In the U.S.A. sold as Taylor Fladgate. In lesser years, the single-vineyard Quinta de Vargellas is often shipped.
[7] Owns Quinta do Noval.
[8] Sometimes labelled as Krohn.

Shipper/Vintage	1919	1920	1921	1922	1923	1924
Adams						
Barros Almeida						
Borges				✓		✓
Burmester		✓		✓		✓
Butler Nephew				✓		✓
Calem						
Cockburn						✓
Croft[1]		✓		✓		✓
Delaforce[2]	✓	✓				
Diez Hermanos						
Dixon						
Dow	✓	✓				✓
Feist				✓		
Ferreira		✓				✓
Feuerheerd		✓				✓
Fonseca[3]		✓		✓		✓
Gonzalez Byass		✓				
Gould Campbell		✓		✓		✓
Graham[4]		✓				✓
Greens						
Guimaraens						
Hooper					✓	
Hutcheson						
Kingston				✓		✓
Kopke	✓	✓		✓		
Mackenzie	✓	✓		✓		
Manoel Porças						
Martinez	✓			✓		
Messias						
Millipo						
Morgan		✓		✓		✓
Niepoort						
Offley[5]	✓	✓	✓	✓	✓	✓
Osborne						
Pintos dos Santos						
Quarles Harris						
Quinta do Noval	✓	✓			✓	
Ramos Pintos						✓
Real Vinicola						
Rebello Valente		✓	✓	✓		✓
Robertson Bros.						
Rocheda						
Royal Oporto						
Sandeman		✓				✓
Smith Woodhouse		✓				✓
Sociedade Constantino						
Southard				✓		
Souza						
Stormouth Tait		✓		✓		
Taylor[6]		✓		✓		✓
Tuke Holdsworth		✓		✓		✓
VanZeller[7]				✓		✓
Warre		✓		✓		✓
Wiese & Krohn[8]						

Key:
[1] Sometimes bottled as a single-vineyard: Quinta da Roêda.
[2] Sometimes shipped as a single-vineyard: Quinta da Corte.
[3] In lesser years bottled as Guimaraens.
[4] Their Quinta Malvedos is shipped in lesser years.
[5] Bottled as Offley Boa Vista.
[6] In the U.S.A. sold as Taylor Fladgate. In lesser years, the single-vineyard Quinta de Vargellas is often shipped.
[7] Owns Quinta do Noval.
[8] Sometimes labelled as Krohn.

Shipper/Vintage	1925	1926	1927	1929	1930	1931	1933
Adams							
Barros Almeida							
Borges							
Burmester			✓			✓	
Butler Nephew			✓				
Calem							
Cockburn			✓				
Croft[1]			✓				
Delaforce[2]			✓				
Diez Hermanos							
Dixon							
Dow			✓			✓	
Feist							
Ferreira			✓				
Feuerheerd			✓				
Fonseca[3]			✓				
Gonzalez Byass							
Gould Campbell			✓				
Graham[4]		✓	✓				
Greens							
Guimaraens							
Hooper						✓	
Hutcheson							
Kingston			✓				
Kopke		✓	✓				
Mackenzie			✓				
Manoel Porças							
Martinez			✓			✓	
Messias							
Millipo							
Morgan			✓				
Niepoort			✓			✓	
Offley[5]	✓		✓	✓		✓	
Osborne							
Pintos dos Santos							
Quarles Harris			✓				
Quinta do Noval			✓			✓	✓
Ramos Pintos			✓				
Real Vinicola							
Rebello Valente			✓			✓	
Robertson Bros.							
Rocheda							
Royal Oporto							
Sandeman			✓			✓	
Smith Woodhouse			✓				
Sociedade Constantino			✓				
Southard			✓				
Souza							
Stormouth Tait			✓				
Taylor[6]		✓	✓		✓		
Tuke Holdsworth			✓				
VanZeller[7]			✓				
Warre			✓			✓	
Wiese & Krohn[8]			✓				

Key:
1   Sometimes bottled as a single-vineyard: Quinta da Roêda.
2   Sometimes shipped as a single-vineyard: Quinta da Corte.
3   In lesser years bottled as Guimaraens.
4   Their Quinta Malvedos is shipped in lesser years.
5   Bottled as Offley Boa Vista.
6   In the U.S.A. sold as Taylor Fladgate. In lesser years, the single-vineyard Quinta de Vargellas is often shipped.
7   Owns Quinta do Noval.
8   Sometimes labelled as Krohn.

Shipper/Vintage	1934	1935	1937	1938	1939	1940	1941
Adams		✔					
Barros Almeida							
Borges							
Burmester			✔	✔		✔	
Butler Nephew		✔					
Calem			✔				
Cockburn		✔					
Croft[1]		✔					
Delaforce[2]		✔					
Diez Hermanos							
Dixon							
Dow	✔	✔					
Feist							
Ferreira	✔	✔	✔				
Feuerheerd							
Fonseca[3]	✔	✔					
Gonzalez Byass							
Gould Campbell	✔						
Graham[4]			✔			✔	
Greens							
Guimaraens							
Hooper			✔		✔		
Hutcheson							
Kingston							
Kopke		✔					
Mackenzie		✔					
Manoel Porças							
Martinez	✔	✔					
Messias							
Millipo							
Morgan							
Niepoort				✔	✔		
Offley[5]		✔					
Osborne							
Pintos dos Santos							
Quarles Harris	✔						
Quinta do Noval	✔				✔		✔
Ramos Pintos							
Real Vinicola							
Rebello Valente	✔	✔					
Robertson Bros.							
Rocheda							
Royal Oporto	✔						
Sandeman	✔	✔				✔	
Smith Woodhouse		✔					
Sociedade Constantino		✔					✔
Southard							
Souza							
Stormouth Tait							
Taylor[6]		✔		✔			✔
Tuke Holdsworth	✔	✔					
VanZeller[7]		✔					
Warre	✔	✔					
Wiese & Krohn[8]	✔	✔					

Checklist of Port Shippers and Vintages (Continued)

Key:
1. Sometimes bottled as a single-vineyard: Quinta da Roêda.
2. Sometimes shipped as a single-vineyard: Quinta da Corte.
3. In lesser years bottled as Guimaraens.
4. Their Quinta Malvedos is shipped in lesser years.
5. Bottled as Offley Boa Vista.
6. In the U.S.A. sold as Taylor Fladgate. In lesser years, the single-vineyard Quinta de Vargellas is often shipped.
7. Owns Quinta do Noval.
8. Sometimes labelled as Krohn.

Shipper/Vintage	1942	1943	1944	1945	1946	1947
Adams				✔		✔
Barros Almeida		✔		✔		
Borges						
Burmester		✔		✔		
Butler Nephew		✔		✔		✔
Calem						✔
Cockburn						✔
Croft[1]		✔		✔		
Delaforce[2]			✔	✔		✔
Diez Hermanos						
Dixon						
Dow			✔	✔		✔
Feist						
Ferreira				✔		
Feuerheerd	✔	✔	✔	✔		
Fonseca[3]				✔		
Gonzalez Byass	✔			✔		
Gould Campbell	✔					
Graham[4]	✔			✔		
Greens						
Guimaraens						
Hooper		✔				
Hutcheson						
Kingston						
Kopke				✔		
Mackenzie				✔		✔
Manoel Porças						
Martinez				✔		
Messias						
Millipo						
Morgan	✔					
Niepoort	✔			✔		
Offley[5]	✔					
Osborne						
Pintos dos Santos						
Quarles Harris				✔		✔
Quinta do Noval	✔			✔		✔
Ramos Pintos				✔		
Real Vinicola				✔		✔
Rebello Valente	✔			✔		✔
Robertson Bros.	✔			✔		✔
Rocheda						
Royal Oporto				✔		
Sandeman	✔	✔	✔	✔	✔	✔
Smith Woodhouse				✔		✔
Sociedade Constantino				✔		✔
Southard						
Souza						
Stormouth Tait						
Taylor[6]	✔			✔		✔
Tuke Holdsworth		✔		✔		✔
VanZeller[7]						
Warre				✔	✔	✔
Wiese & Krohn[8]						✔

Checklist of Port Shippers and Vintages (Continued)

Key:
[1] Sometimes bottled as a single-vineyard: Quinta da Roêda.
[2] Sometimes shipped as a single-vineyard: Quinta da Corte.
[3] In lesser years bottled as Guimaraens.
[4] Their Quinta Malvedos is shipped in lesser years.
[5] Bottled as Offley Boa Vista.
[6] In the U.S.A. sold as Taylor Fladgate. In lesser years, the single-vineyard Quinta de Vargellas is often shipped.
[7] Owns Quinta do Noval.
[8] Sometimes labelled as Krohn.

Shipper/Vintage	1948	1950	1951	1952	1953	1954
Adams	✔	✔				
Barros Almeida						
Borges						
Burmester		✔				✔
Butler Nephew		✔				
Calem		✔				
Cockburn			✔			
Croft[1]			✔			
Delaforce[2]			✔	✔		
Diez Hermanos						
Dixon						
Dow		✔	✔	✔		✔
Feist						
Ferreira						
Feuerheerd				✔		
Fonseca[3]		✔				
Gonzalez Byass						
Gould Campbell						
Graham[4]		✔	✔			✔
Greens						
Guimaraens						
Hooper						✔
Hutcheson						
Kingston						
Kopke		✔	✔		✔	
Mackenzie		✔	✔		✔	✔
Manoel Porças						
Martinez						
Messias						
Millipo						
Morgan		✔	✔			
Niepoort						
Offley[5]			✔			✔
Osborne						
Pintos dos Santos						
Quarles Harris			✔			
Quinta do Noval		✔	✔			
Ramos Pintos				✔		
Real Vinicola			✔			
Rebello Valente						
Robertson Bros.						
Rocheda						
Royal Oporto						
Sandeman		✔	✔		✔	✔
Smith Woodhouse		✔	✔			
Sociedade Constantino			✔			
Southard						
Souza						
Stormouth Tait						
Taylor[6]		✔				
Tuke Holdsworth			✔			
VanZeller[7]						
Warre		✔	✔		✔	
Wiese & Krohn[8]			✔		✔	

191

Key:
1. Sometimes bottled as a single-vineyard: Quinta da Roêda.
2. Sometimes shipped as a single-vineyard: Quinta da Corte.
3. In lesser years bottled as Guimaraens.
4. Their Quinta Malvedos is shipped in lesser years.
5. Bottled as Offley Boa Vista.
6. In the U.S.A. sold as Taylor Fladgate. In lesser years, the single-vineyard Quinta de Vargellas is often shipped.
7. Owns Quinta do Noval.
8. Sometimes labelled as Krohn.

Shipper/Vintage	1955	1957	1958	1960	1961	1962
Adams	✓			✓		
Barros Almeida						
Borges						
Burmester	✓		✓	✓		
Butler Nephew	✓	✓	✓	✓		
Calem	✓		✓	✓		
Cockburn	✓			✓		
Croft[1]	✓			✓		
Delaforce[2]	✓		✓	✓		
Diez Hermanos						
Dixon						
Dow		✓	✓	✓		
Feist						
Ferreira	✓			✓		
Feuerheerd	✓	✓	✓	✓		
Fonseca[3]	✓	✓		✓		
Gonzalez Byass	✓			✓		
Gould Campbell	✓			✓		
Graham[4]	✓			✓	✓	✓
Greens						
Guimaraens			✓		✓	✓
Hooper			✓	✓		✓
Hutcheson						
Kingston						
Kopke	✓		✓	✓		
Mackenzie	✓	✓	✓	✓		
Manoel Porças				✓		
Martinez	✓		✓	✓		
Messias						
Millipo						
Morgan	✓			✓		
Niepoort	✓			✓		
Offley[5]	✓		✓	✓		✓
Osborne						
Pintos dos Santos	✓	✓	✓	✓		
Quarles Harris	✓		✓	✓		
Quinta do Noval	✓		✓	✓		✓
Ramos Pintos	✓					
Real Vinicola	✓			✓		
Rebello Valente	✓			✓		
Robertson Bros.						
Rocheda						
Royal Oporto			✓	✓		✓
Sandeman	✓	✓	✓	✓		✓
Smith Woodhouse	✓			✓		
Sociedade Constantino			✓			
Southard						
Souza						
Stormouth Tait						
Taylor[6]	✓	✓	✓	✓	✓	
Tuke Holdsworth	✓			✓		
VanZeller[7]						
Warre	✓		✓	✓		
Wiese & Krohn[8]		✓		✓		

Checklist of Port Shippers and Vintages (Continued)

Key:

[1] Sometimes bottled as a single-vineyard: Quinta da Roêda.
[2] Sometimes shipped as a single-vineyard: Quinta da Corte.
[3] In lesser years bottled as Guimaraens.
[4] Their Quinta Malvedos is shipped in lesser years.
[5] Bottled as Offley Boa Vista.
[6] In the U.S.A. sold as Taylor Fladgate. In lesser years, the single-vineyard Quinta de Vargellas is often shipped.
[7] Owns Quinta do Noval.
[8] Sometimes labelled as Krohn.

Shipper/Vintage	1963	1964	1965	1966	1967	1968	1969
Adams	✔			✔			
Barros Almeida							
Borges	✔						
Burmester	✔						
Butler Nephew							
Calem	✔						
Cockburn	✔				✔		
Croft[1]	✔			✔	✔		
Delaforce[2]	✔			✔			
Diez Hermanos							
Dixon							
Dow	✔			✔			
Feist							
Ferreira	✔			✔			
Feuerheerd	✔			✔			
Fonseca[3]	✔			✔			
Gonzalez Byass	✔				✔		
Gould Campbell	✔			✔			
Graham[4]	✔	✔	✔	✔			
Greens							
Guimaraens			✔	✔		✔	
Hooper	✔				✔		
Hutcheson							
Kingston							
Kopke	✔		✔	✔			
Mackenzie	✔			✔			
Manoel Porcas	✔				✔		
Martinez	✔				✔		
Messias							
Millipo							
Morgan	✔			✔			
Niepoort	✔						
Offley[5]	✔			✔	✔		
Osborne							
Pintos dos Santos	✔			✔			
Quarles Harris	✔			✔			
Quinta do Noval	✔			✔			
Ramos Pintos							
Real Vinicola							
Rebello Valente	✔			✔	✔		
Robertson Bros.							
Rocheda							
Royal Oporto	✔				✔		
Sandeman	✔			✔	✔		
Smith Woodhouse	✔			✔			
Sociedade Constantino	✔			✔			
Southard							
Souza							
Stormouth Tait							
Taylor[6]	✔	✔	✔	✔	✔	✔	✔
Tuke Holdsworth	✔			✔			
VanZeller[7]							
Warre	✔			✔			
Wiese & Krohn[8]					✔		

193

Key:
1   Sometimes bottled as a single-vineyard: Quinta da Roêda.
2   Sometimes shipped as a single-vineyard: Quinta da Corte.
3   In lesser years bottled as Guimaraens.
4   Their Quinta Malvedos is shipped in lesser years.
5   Bottled as Offley Boa Vista.
6   In the U.S.A. sold as Taylor Fladgate. In lesser years, the single-vineyard Quinta de Vargellas is often shipped.
7   Owns Quinta do Noval.
8   Sometimes labelled as Krohn.

Shipper/Vintage	1970	1972	1974	1975	1976	1977
Adams						
Barros Almeida	✓			✓		
Borges	✓					
Burmester	✓					
Butler Nephew	✓			✓		
Calem	✓			✓		✓
Cockburn	✓			✓		
Croft[1]	✓			✓		✓
Delaforce[2]	✓	✓	✓	✓		✓
Diez Hermanos	✓			✓		
Dixon						
Dow	✓	✓		✓		✓
Feist	✓					
Ferreira	✓			✓		✓
Feuerheerd	✓					
Fonseca[3]	✓			✓		✓
Gonzalez Byass	✓			✓		
Gould Campbell	✓			✓		✓
Graham[4]	✓			✓		✓
Greens				✓		
Guimaraens						
Hooper						
Hutcheson	✓					
Kingston						
Kopke	✓		✓	✓		✓
Mackenzie	✓					
Manoel Porças	✓			✓		✓
Martinez	✓			✓		
Messias	✓			✓		✓
Millipo	✓					
Morgan	✓					
Niepoort	✓			✓		✓
Offley[5]	✓	✓		✓		✓
Osborne	✓					
Pintos dos Santos	✓		✓	✓		
Quarles Harris	✓			✓		✓
Quinta do Noval	✓	✓		✓		
Ramos Pintos	✓					✓
Real Vinicola	✓					
Rebello Valente	✓			✓		✓
Robertson Bros.						
Rocheda	✓					
Royal Oporto	✓			✓		✓
Sandeman	✓			✓		✓
Smith Woodhouse	✓			✓		✓
Sociedade Constantino						
Southard						
Souza	✓					
Stormouth Tait						
Taylor[6]	✓	✓	✓	✓	✓	✓
Tuke Holdsworth						
VanZeller[7]						
Warre	✓			✓		✓
Wiese & Krohn[8]	✓					

194

Key:
[1]   Sometimes bottled as a single-vineyard: Quinta da Roêda.
[2]   Sometimes shipped as a single-vineyard: Quinta da Corte.
[3]   In lesser years bottled as Guimaraens.
[4]   Their Quinta Malvedos is shipped in lesser years.
[5]   Bottled as Offley Boa Vista.
[6]   In the U.S.A. sold as Taylor Fladgate. In lesser years, the single-vineyard Quinta de Vargellas is often shipped.
[7]   Owns Quinta do Noval.
[8]   Sometimes labelled as Krohn.

Shipper/Vintage	1978	1979	1980
Adams			
Barros Almeida			
Borges			
Burmester			✔
Butler Nephew			
Calem			✔
Cockburn	✔		
Croft[1]	✔		✔
Delaforce[2]	✔	✔	✔
Diez Hermanos			
Dixon			
Dow			✔
Feist			
Ferreira			✔
Feuerheerd			
Fonseca[3]			✔
Gonzalez Byass			
Gould Campbell			✔
Graham[4]			✔
Greens			
Guimaraens			
Hooper			
Hutcheson			
Kingston			
Kopke			
Mackenzie			
Manoel Porcas			
Martinez			
Messias			
Millipo			
Morgan			
Niepoort			✔
Offley[5]			✔
Osborne			
Pintos dos Santos			
Quarles Harris			✔
Quinta do Noval		✔	
Ramos Pintos			
Real Vinicola			
Rebello Valente			✔
Robertson Bros.			
Rocheda			
Royal Oporto			✔
Sandeman			✔
Smith Woodhouse			✔
Sociedade Constantino			
Southard			
Souza			
Stormouth Tait			
Taylor[6]	✔		✔
Tuke Holdsworth			
VanZeller[7]			
Warre			✔
Wiese & Krohn[8]			

Bibliography

Adams, Leon D. *The Wines of America,* 2nd ed. New York: McGraw Hill Book Co., 1978.

Allen, H. Warner. *A History of Wine.* London: Faber & Faber, 1961.

_____. *The Romance of Wine.* New York: Dover Publications, 1971; reprint of E.P. Dutton & Co., 1932.

_____. *Sherry and Port.* London: Constable, 1952.

Amerine, M.A.; H.W. Berg; and W.V. Cruess. *The Technology of Winemaking,* 3rd ed. Westport, Ct.: The AVI Publishing Co., 1972.

Anderson, Burton. *Vino.* Boston: Atlantic-Little, Brown, 1980.

Bespaloff, Alexis. *The Fireside Book of Wine.* New York: Simon & Schuster, 1977.

Bode, Charles G. *Wines of Italy.* New York: Dover Publications, 1974.

Bradford, Sarah. *The Englishman's Wine.* London: Macmillan-St. Martin's Press, 1969.

_____. *The Story of Port.* London: Christie's Wine Publications, 1978.

Broadbent, Michael. *The Great Vintage Wine Book.* New York: Alfred A. Knopf, 1980.

Croft-Cooke, Rupert. *Sherry.* New York: Alfred A. Knopf Inc., 1956.

_____. *Madeira.* London: Putnam, 1961.

Delaforce, John. *The Factory House in Oporto.* London: Christie's Wine Publications, 1979.

Dorozynski, Alexander, and Bell, Bibiane. *The Wine Book.* New York: Golden Press, 1969.

Evans, Len. *Australian Complete Book of Wine,* 2nd imp., rev. ed. Dee Why West, NSW, Australia: Paul Hamlyn Pty., 1977.

Fletcher, Wyndham. *Port.* Convent Garden: Sotheby Parke Bernet, 1978.

Francis, A.D. *The Wine Trade.* New York: Barnes & Noble Import Division of Harper & Row Publications, 1973.

Gold, Alec H., ed. *Wines and Spirits of the World,* 2nd ed. London: Virtue & Co., 1972.

Gordon, Manuel Gonzalez. *Sherry.* London: Cassell, 1972.

de Isasi, Enrique. *Con Una Copa.* Spain: Sherry Institute.

Jeffs, Julien. *The Wines of Europe.* New York: Taplinger Publishing Co., 1970.

197

Johnson, Hugh. *Wine,* rev. ed. New York: Simon & Schuster, 1974.

Layton, T.A. *Wines of Italy.* London: Harper Trade Journal, 1961.

_____. *Wines and Castles of Spain.* London: White Lion Publishers, 1974; reprint of Michael Josephs, 1959.

Lichine, Alexis. *New Encyclopedia of Wines and Spirits.* New York: Alfred A. Knopf, 1974.

Pliny. *Natural History,* rev. ed., vols. 2, 4. Translated by H. Rackham, M.A. London: Loeb Classical Library, 1968.

Postgate, Raymond. *Portuguese Wine.* London: J.M. Dent & Sons, 1969.

Rainbird, George. *Sherry and the Wines of Spain.* London: McGraw-Hill Book Co., 1966.

Ray, Cyril. *The Wines of Italy.* Harmondsworth, England: Penguin Books, 1971.

Read, Jan. *Spain and Portugal.* New York: Monarch, 1977.

Robertson, George. *Port.* London: Faber and Faber, 1978.

Roncarati, Bruno. *Viva Vino: DOC Wines of Italy.* London: Wine and Spirit Publications, 1976.

Root, Waverly. *The Food of Italy.* New York: Atheneum, 1971.

Saintsbury, George. *Notes on a Cellar-Book.* New York: The Macmillan Co., 1933.

Schoonmaker, Frank. *Encyclopedia of Wine,* 6th & 7th eds. New York: Hastings House, 1975 & 1978.

Simon, André. *The History of the Wine Trade in England,* 3 vols. London: The Holland Press, 1964.

Simon, André, ed. *Wines of the World,* 5th rev. ed. New York: McGraw Hill, 1972.

Smith, John Reay. *Discovering Spanish Wines.* London: Robert Hale, 1976.

Taylor, Allan. *What Everybody Wants to Know about Wine.* New York: Alfred A. Knopf, 1934.

Veronelli, Luigi. *Catalogo Bolaffi dei Vini d'Italia n. 4.* Turin: Giulio Bolaffi Editore, 1976.

_____. *The Wines of Italy.* Rome: Canesi Editori.

Wasserman, Sheldon. *The Wines of Italy, A Consumer's Guide.* New York: Stein & Day, 1976.

Waugh, Alec. *In Praise of Wine.* New York: William Morrow & Co., 1959.

Waugh, Harry. *Wine Diary,* vols. 6, 7, and 8. London: Christie's Wine Publications, 1975, 1976 & 1979.

Younger, William. *Gods, Men and Wine.* London: The Wine and Food Society, 1966.

_____. *Christie's Wine Review 1977.* London: Christie's Wine Publications, 1977.

_____. *Disciplinari di Produzione Vini a Denominazione di Origine Controllata,* vol. 2. Conegliano, Italy: Casa Editrice Scarpis, 1971.

_____. *Gonzalez Byass.* Spain: private publication.

_____. *The Great Book of Wine.* New York: Galahad Books, 1970.

_____. *The House of Sandeman,* 3rd ed. Spain: private edition, 1972.

_____. *Sicilia Vitivinicola.* Italy: October, 1973.

_____. *A Tribute to Sherry.* Sherry Institute of Spain.

INDEX

abocado, 161,162
Adams, 41
adega(s), 20, 21
Adegas do Torreão, 89
adulteration, of madeira, 83
    of port, 4, 7, 9
afuera, 143
aging cellar in madeira, 78
    marsala, 109
    port, 27, 29
    sherry, 145, 148, 153
aguardente, 23, 24, 26
albariza, 128, 143, 145, 146
alberello, 112
albero, 128, 131
Albillo, 145
Allen, H. Warner, 1, 73, 84, 132, 144
Alloro, 110, 120, 123
Almaden, 174
almude(s), 28, 31
Alto Corgo, 14, 18
Alvarelhão, 59
Alvear, 135, 137, 138, 139
American native varieties, 10, 60, 70, 71, 73, 175
American oak, 60, 81, 131, 153-155
American port, 58-60
American rootstock, 10, 71, 115, 148
American sherry, 60, 173-176
amontillado(s), 136, 137, 138, 139, 145, 158, 159-160, 161, 162, 163, 164, 165, 166, 167, 168, 169, 172, 176
    accompaniments to, 138, 167
    serving, 138, 167, 168
    viejos, 138
amoroso, 161, 165, 168, 176
añada, 156, 163, 165
Añina, 145

Arab(s), 28, 107, 127, 142
Archestratus, 133
arena, 146
arroba(s), 130, 153, 159
arrumbadores, 153
asbestos, 149
Associação (dos Exportadores do Vinho do Porto), 29-30
Australian port, 60-62
Australian sherry, 144, 169, 172-173
Babosa, 73
Baetica, 125-126, 142
baga, 7, 9
bagaceira, 22, 25-26
bagaço, 26
Baixo Corgo, 10, 14, 16, 18, 23
baked sherry, 174
Balbaína, 145
Barbadillo, Antonio, 159, 166
barcos rabelos, 26-27
Barquero, Perez, 137
barro, 146
Barros, Almeida, 41, 43, 44, 48, 89
Bastardo, 59, 73, 93
BATF, 32, 49
Bearsley, Peter, 4
Beba, 146
beeswings, 10
Bellido y Carrasco, 137
Berkeley Wine Cellars, 60
Bertola, 164
"blackstrap", 8
Blandy, 70, 71, 88, 89
Blandy, Charles, 71
Blasquez, 164
Boal, see Bual
bodega(s), 127, 133-135, 136, 153, 155, 156, 158, 159, 176
    butt, 153
    workmen, 130, 131, 133, 151, 153, 155, 156, 158